# Abraham Lincoln
## Vol. II

*by*

John T. Morse, Jr.

# Abraham Lincoln
## Vol. II
### by JOHN T. MORSE, JR.

ISBN: 978-93-59952-21-5

**Published by**

# DOUBLE 9 BOOKS
2/13-B, Ansari Road
Daryaganj, New Delhi – 110002
info@double9books.com
www.double9books.com
Tel. 011-40042856

# ABOUT THE AUTHOR

John Torrey Morse Jr. (January 9, 1840 – March 28, 1937) was a historian, attorney, and politician in the United States. John Torrey Morse was born on January 9, 1840, in Boston, Massachusetts, to John Torrey Morse Sr. and Lucy Cabot Jackson. After three years of study, he graduated from Harvard College and read law at the office of John Lowell. In 1862, he was admitted to the bar. In 1874, he was elected to the Massachusetts House of Representatives from Boston's Back Bay's 6th Suffolk district. He was sentenced to one year in prison. Morse served on the Harvard Board of Overseers from 1879 until 1891. Harvard conferred on him the honorary degree of Doctor of Literature in 1911. Morse began his legal career by producing many authoritative legal treatises on banking, arbitration, and award, as well as contributing to journals. His legal writing established him as a renowned specialist on the issues. Morse's most major work, a two-volume biography of Alexander Hamilton, was released in 1876. Soon after, in 1880, he left his law practice to pursue literary endeavors. In 1865, Morse married Fanny P. Hovey of Boston. They had two boys, Cabot Jackson Morse and John Torrey Morse III, as well as a daughter, Charlotte. They lived on Boston's Fairfield Street.

# CONTENTS

# CHAPTER I
# EMANCIPATION AND POLITICS

During the spring and summer of 1861 the people of the North presented the appearance of a great political unit. All alleged emphatically that the question was simply of the Union, and upon this issue no Northerner could safely differ from his neighbors. Only a few of the more cross-grained ones among the Abolitionists were contemptuously allowed to publish the selfishness of their morality, and to declare that they were content to see the establishment of a great slave empire, provided they themselves were free from the taint of connection with it. If any others let Southern proclivities lurk in the obscure recesses of their hearts they were too prudent to permit these perilous sentiments to appear except in the masquerade of dismal presagings. So in appearance the Northern men were united, and in fact were very nearly so—for a short time.

This was a fortunate condition, which the President and all shrewd patriots took great pains to maintain. It filled the armies and the Treasury, and postponed many jeopardies. But too close to the surface to be long suppressed lay the demand that those who declared the Union to be the sole issue should explain how it came about that the Union was put in issue at all, why there was any dissatisfaction with it, and why any desire anywhere to be rid of it. All knew the answer to that question; all knew that if the war was due to disunion, disunion in turn was due to slavery. Unless some makeshift peace should be quickly patched up, this basic cause was absolutely sure to force recognition for itself; a long and stern contest must inevitably wear its way down to the bottom question. It was practical wisdom for Mr. Lincoln in his inaugural not to probe deeper than secession; and it was well for multitudes to take arms and contribute money with the earnest asseveration that they were fighting and paying only for the integrity of the country. It was the truth, or rather it was *a* truth; but there was also another and a deeper truth: that he who fought for the integrity of the country, also, by a necessity inherent in the case and far beyond the influence of his volition, fought for the destruction of slavery. Just as soon as this second truth came up and took distinct shape beside the other, angry political divisions sundered the Unionists. Abolition of slavery never displaced Union as a purpose of the war; but the two became mingled, in a duality which could not afterward be resolved into its component parts so that one could be taken and the other could be left. The union of the two issues meant the disunion of the people of the Middle and even of the Northern States.

In the Border States a considerable proportion of the people was both pro-slavery and pro-Union. These men wished to retain their servile laborers under their feet and the shelter of the Union over their heads. At first they did not see that they might as well hope to serve both God and Mammon. Yet for the moment they seemed to hold the balance of power between the contestants; for had all the pro-slavery men in the Border States gone over in a mass to the South early in the war, they might have settled the matter against the North in short order. The task of holding and conciliating this important body, with all its Northern sympathizers, became a controlling purpose of the President, and caused the development of his famous "border-state policy," for which he deserved the highest praise and received unlimited abuse.

The very fact that these men needed, for their comfort, reiterated assurances of a policy not hostile to slavery indicated the jeopardy of their situation. The distinct language of the President alleviated their anxiety so far as the Executive was concerned, but they desired to commit the legislative branch to the same doctrine. Among all those who might have been Secessionists, but were not, no other could vie in respect and affection with the venerable and patriotic John J. Crittenden of Kentucky. This distinguished statesman now became the spokesman for the large body of loyal citizens who felt deeply that the war ought not to impinge in the least upon the great institution of the South. In the extra session of Congress, convened in July, 1861, he offered a resolution pledging Congress to hold in mind: "That this war is not waged upon our part in any spirit of oppression, nor for any purpose of conquest or subjugation, nor with any purpose of overthrowing or interfering with the rights or established institutions of those [the revolted] States; but to defend and maintain the supremacy of the Constitution, and to preserve the Union with all the dignity, equality, and rights of the several States unimpaired." After the example of the Constitution, this resolution was carefully saved from the contamination of a certain offensive word; but every one knew its meaning and its purpose; and with this knowledge all the votes save two in the House of Representatives, and all save five in the Senate, were given for it. [1] "It was," says Mr. Blaine, "a fair reflection of the popular sentiment throughout the North." So Mr. Lincoln's inaugural was ratified.

But events control. The Northern armies ran against slavery immediately. Almost in the very hours when the resolution of Mr. Crittenden was gliding so easily through the House, thousands of slaves at Manassas were doing the work of laborers and servants, and rendering all the whites of the Southern army available for fighting. The handicap was so severe and obvious that it immediately provoked the introduction of a bill freeing slaves belonging to rebels and used for carrying on the war. The Democrats and the men of the Border States generally opposed the measure, with very strong feeling. No matter how plausible the reason, they did not wish slavery to be touched at all. They could not say that this especial bill was wrong, but they felt that it was dangerous. Their protests against it, however, were of no avail, and it became law on August 6. The extreme anti-slavery men somewhat sophistically twisted it into an assistance to the South.

The principle of this legislation had already been published to the country in a very fortunate way by General Butler. In May, 1861, being in command at Fortress Monroe, he had refused, under instructions from Cameron, to return three fugitive slaves to their rebel owner, and he had ingeniously put his refusal on the ground that they were "contraband of war." The phrase instantly became popular. General Butler says that, "as a lawyer, [he] was never very proud of it;" but technical inaccuracy does not hurt the force of an epigram which expresses a sound principle. "Contraband" underlay the Emancipation Proclamation.

Thus the slaves themselves were forcing the issue, regardless of polities and diplomacy. With a perfectly correct instinctive insight into the true meaning of the war, they felt that a Union camp ought to be a place of refuge, and they sought it eagerly and in considerable numbers. Then, however, their logical owners came and reclaimed them, and other commanders were not so apt at retort as General Butler was. Thus it came to pass that each general, being without instructions, carried out his own ideas, and confusion ensued. Democratic commanders returned slaves; Abolitionist commanders refused to do so; many were sadly puzzled what to do. All alike created embarrassing situations for the administration.

General Fremont led off. On August 30, being then in command of the Western Department, he issued an order, in which he declared that he would "assume the administrative powers of the State." Then, on the basis of this bold assumption, he established martial law, and pronounced the slaves of militant or active rebels to be "free men." The mischief of this ill-advised proceeding was aggravated by the "fires of popular enthusiasm which it kindled." The President wrote to Fremont, expressing his fear that the general's action would "alarm our Southern Union friends, and turn them against us; perhaps ruin our rather fair prospect in Kentucky." Very considerately he said: "Allow me, therefore, to ask that you will, as of your own motion, modify that paragraph so as to conform to" the Act of August 6. Fremont replied, in substance, that the President might do this, but that he himself would not! Thereupon Mr. Lincoln, instead of removing the insubordinate and insolent general, behaved in his usual passionless way, and merely issued an order that Fremont's proclamation should be so modified and construed as "to conform with and not to transcend" the law. By this treatment, which should have made Fremont grateful and penitent, he was in fact rendered angry and indignant; for he had a genuine belief in the old proverb about laws being silent in time of war, and he really thought that documents signed in tents by gentlemen wearing shoulder-straps were deserving of more respect, even by the President, than were mere Acts of Congress. This was a mistaken notion, but Fremont never could see that he had been in error, and from this time forth he became a vengeful thorn in the side of Mr. Lincoln.

Several months later, on May 9, 1862, General Hunter proclaimed martial law in Georgia, Florida, and South Carolina, and said: "Slavery and martial law in a free country are altogether incompatible. The persons in these States, heretofore held as slaves, are therefore declared forever free." At once, though not without reluctance, Mr. Lincoln revoked this order, as unauthorized. He further said that, if he had power to "declare the slaves of any State or States free," the propriety of exercising that power was a question which he reserved exclusively to himself. These words he fully made good. The whole country, wild with excitement and teeming with opinions almost co-numerous with its citizens, threatened to bury him beneath an avalanche of advice. But while all talked and wrote madly and endlessly, he quietly held his peace, did what he chose when he chose, and never delegated any portion of his authority over this most important business to any one. He took emancipation for his own special and personal affair; it was a matter about which he had been doing much thinking very earnestly for a long while, and he had no notion of forming now any partnership for managing it.

The trend, however, was not all in one direction. While Butler, Fremont, and Hunter were thus befriending the poor runaways, Buell and Hooker were allowing slave-owners to reclaim fugitives from within their lines; Halleck was ordering that no fugitive slave should be admitted within his lines or camp, and that those already there should be put out; and McClellan was promising to crush "with an iron hand" any attempt at slave insurrection. Amid such confusion, some rule of universal application was sorely needed. But what should it be?

Secretary Cameron twice nearly placed the administration in an embarrassing position by taking very advanced ground upon the negro question. In October, 1861, he issued an order to General Sherman, then at Port Royal, authorizing him to employ negroes in any capacity which he might " deem most beneficial to the service." Mr. Lincoln prudently interlined the words: "This, however, not to mean a general arming of them for military service." A few weeks later, in the Report which the secretary prepared to be sent with the President's message to Congress, he said: "As the labor and service of their slaves constitute the chief property of the rebels, they should share the common fate of war.... It is as clearly a right of the government to arm slaves, when it becomes necessary, as it is to use gunpowder taken from the enemy. Whether it is expedient to do so is purely a military question." He added more to the same purport. He then had his report printed, and sent copies, by mail, to many newspapers throughout the country, with permission to publish it so soon as the telegraph should report the reading before Congress. At the eleventh hour a copy was handed to Mr. Lincoln, to accompany his message; and then, for the first time, he saw these radical passages. Instantly he directed that all the postmasters, to whose offices the printed copies had been sent on their way to the newspaper editors, should be ordered at once to return these copies to the secretary. He then ordered the secretary to make a change, equivalent to an omission, of this inflammatory paragraph. After this emasculation the paragraph only stated that "slaves who were abandoned by their owners on the advance of our troops" should not be returned to the enemy.

When the Thirty-seventh Congress came together for the regular session, December 2, 1861, anti-slavery sentiment had made a visible advance. President Lincoln, in his message, advised recognizing the independence of the negro states of Hayti and Liberia. He declared that he had been anxious that the "inevitable conflict should not degenerate into a violent and remorseless revolutionary struggle," and that he had, therefore, "thought it proper to keep the integrity of the Union prominent as the primary object of the contest on our part." Referring to his enforcement of the law of August 6, he said: "The Union must be preserved, and hence all indispensable means must be employed." The shadow which pro-slavery men saw cast by these words was very slightly, if at all, lightened by an admission which accompanied it,—that "we should not be in haste to determine that radical and extreme measures, which may reach the loyal as well as the disloyal, are indispensable." Further he said that already, by the operation of the Act of August 6, numbers of persons had been liberated, had become dependent on the United States, and must be provided for. He anticipated that some of the States might pass similar laws for their own benefit; in which case he recommended Congress to "provide for accepting such persons from such States, according to some mode of valuation, in lieu, *pro tanto*, of direct taxes, or upon some other plan to be agreed on." He desired that these negroes, being "at once deemed free," should be colonized in some "climate congenial to them," and he wished an appropriation for acquiring territory for this purpose. Thus he indicated with sufficient clearness the three cardinal points of his own theory for emancipation: voluntary action of the individual slave States by the exercise of their own sovereign power; compensation of owners; and colonization. Congress soon showed that it meant to strike a pace much more rapid than that set by the President; and the friends of slavery perceived an atmosphere which made them so uneasy that they thought it would be well to have the Crittenden resolution substantially reaffirmed. They made the effort, and they failed, the vote standing 65 yeas to 71 nays. All which this symptom indicated as to the temper of members was borne out during the session by positive and aggressive legislation. Only a fortnight had passed, when Henry Wilson, senator from Massachusetts, introduced a bill to emancipate the slaves in the District of Columbia, and to pay a moderate compensation to owners. The measure, rightly construed as the entering point of the anti-slavery wedge, gave rise to bitter debates in both houses. The senators and representatives from the slave States manifested intense feeling, and were aided with much spirit by the Democrats of the free States. But resistance was useless; the bill passed the Senate by a vote of 29 to 14, and the House by 92 to 38. On April 16 the President signed it, and returned it with a message, in which he said: "If there be matters within and about this Act which might have taken a course or shape more satisfactory to my judgment, I do not attempt to specify them. I am gratified that the two principles of compensation and colonization are both recognized and practically applied in the Act." It was one of the coincidences of history that by his signature he now made law that proposition which, as a member of the House of Representatives in 1849, he had embodied in a bill which then hardly excited passing notice as it went on its quick way to oblivion.

The confused condition concerning the harboring and rendition of fugitive slaves by military commanders, already mentioned, was also promptly taken in hand. Various bills and amendments offered in the Senate and in the House were substantially identical in the main purpose of making the recovery of a slave from within the Union lines practically little better than impossible. The shape which the measure ultimately took was the enactment of an additional article of war, whereby all officers in the military service of the United States were "prohibited from using any portion of the forces under their respective commands for the purpose of returning fugitives from service or labor;" any officer who should violate the article was to be dismissed from the service. Again the men from the Border States, rallying their few Democratic allies from the North to their assistance, made vehement opposition, and again they were overwhelmed beneath an irresistible majority: 83 to 42 in the House, 29 to 9 in the Senate. The President signed the bill on March 13, 1862, and thereafter "nigger hunting" was a dangerous sport in the Union camps.

On March 24, Mr. Arnold [2] of Illinois introduced a bill ambitiously purporting "to render freedom national and slavery sectional." It prohibited slavery wherever Congress could do so, that is to say, in all Territories, present and future, in all forts, arsenals, dockyards, etc., in all vessels on the high seas and on all national highways beyond the territory and jurisdiction of the several States. Both by its title and by its substance it went to the uttermost edge of the Constitution and, in the matter of Territories, perhaps beyond that edge. Mr. Arnold himself supported it with the bold avowal that slavery was in deadly hostility to the national government, and therefore must be destroyed. Upon a measure so significant and so defended, debate waxed hot, so that one gentleman proposed that the bill should be sent back to the committee with instructions not to report it back "until the cold weather." The irritation and alarm of the Border States rendered modification necessary unless tact and caution were to be wholly thrown to the winds. Ultimately, therefore, the offensive title was exchanged for the simple one of "An Act to secure freedom to all persons within the Territories of the United States," and the bill, curtailed to accord with this expression, became law by approval of the President on June 19.

A measure likely in its operation to affect a much greater number of persons than any other of those laws which have been mentioned was introduced by Senator Trumbull of Illinois. This was "for the confiscation of the property of rebels, and giving freedom to the persons they hold in slavery." It made the slaves of all who had taken up arms against the United States "forever thereafter free." It came up for debate on February 25, and its mover defended it as "destroying to a great extent the source and origin of the rebellion, and the only thing which had ever seriously threatened the peace of the Union." The men of the Border States, appalled at so general a manumission, declared that it would produce intolerable conditions in their States, leading either to reënslavement or extermination. So strenuous an anti-slavery man as Senator Hale also suggested that the measure was unconstitutional. Similar discussion upon similar propositions went forward contemporaneously in the House. For once, in both bodies, the Democrats won in many skirmishes. Ultimately, as the outcome of many amendments, substitutes, recommitments, and conferences, a bill was patched up, which passed by 27 to 12 in the Senate and 82 to 42 in the House, and was approved by the President July 17. It was a very comprehensive measure; so much so, that Mr. Blaine has said of it: "Even if the war had ended without a formal and effective system of emancipation, it is believed that this statute would have so operated as to render the slave system practically valueless."

The possibility of enlisting negroes as soldiers received early consideration. Black troops had fought in the Revolution; why, then, should not black men now fight in a war of which they themselves were the ultimate provocation? The idea pleased the utilitarian side of the Northern mind and shocked no Northern prejudice. In fact, as early as the spring of 1862 General Hunter, in the Department of the South, organized a negro regiment. In July, 1862, pending consideration of a bill concerning calling forth the militia, reported by the Senate Committee on Military Affairs, amendments were moved declaring that "there should be no exemption from military service on account of color," permitting the enlistment of "persons of African descent," and making "forever thereafter free" each person so enlisted, his mother, his wife, and his children. No other measure so aroused the indignation of the border-state men. Loyalty to the Union could not change their opinion of the negro. To put arms into the hands of slaves, or ex-slaves, was a terrible proposition to men who had too often vividly conceived the dread picture of slave insurrection. To set black men about the business of killing white men, to engage the inferior race to destroy the superior race, seemed a blasphemy against Nature. A few also of the Northerners warmly sympathized with this feeling. Black men shooting down white men was a spectacle which some who were friends of the black men could not contemplate without a certain shudder. Also many persons believed that the white soldiers of the North would feel degraded by having regiments of ex-slaves placed beside them in camp and in battle. Doubts were expressed as to whether negroes would fight, whether they would not be a useless charge, and even a source of peril to those who should depend upon them. Language could go no farther in vehemence of protest and denunciation than the words of some of the slave-state men in the House and Senate. Besides this, Garrett Davis of Kentucky made a very effective argument when he said: "There is not a rebel in all Secessia whose heart will not leap when he hears that the Senate of the United States is originating such a policy. It will strengthen his hopes of success by an ultimate union of all the slave States to fight such a policy to the death." It was, however, entirely evident that, in the present temper of that part of the country which was represented in Congress, there was not much use in opposing any anti-slavery measure by any kind of argument whatever; even though the special proposition might be distasteful to many Republicans, yet at last, when pressed to the issue, they all faithfully voted Yea. In this case the measure, finally so far modified as to relate only to slaves of rebel owners, was passed and was signed by the President on July 17. Nevertheless, although it thus became law, the certainty that, by taking action under it, he would alienate great numbers of loyalists in the Border States induced him to go very slowly. At first actual authority to enlist negroes was only extorted from the administration with much effort. On August 25 obstinate importunity elicited an order permitting General Saxton, at Hilton Head, to raise 5,000 black troops; but this was somewhat strangely accompanied, according to Mr. Wilson, with the suggestive remark, that it "must never see daylight, because it was so much in advance of public sentiment." After the process had been on trial for a year, however, Mr. Lincoln said that there was apparent "no loss by it in our foreign relations, none in our home popular sentiment, none in our white military force,—no loss by it anyhow or anywhere." On the other hand, it had brought a reinforcement of 130,000 soldiers, seamen, and laborers. "And now," he said, "let any Union man who complains of this measure test himself by writing down in one line that he is for subduing the rebellion by force of arms, and in the next that he is for taking these 130,000 men from the Union side, and placing them where they would be best for the measure he condemns." Yet so ineradicable was the race prejudice that it was not until the spring of 1864, after all efforts for action by Congress had failed, that the attorney-general declared black soldiers to be entitled to the same pay as white soldiers. Regarding a soldier merely as a marketable commodity, doubtless the white was worth more money; yet life was about the same to each, and it was hard to see why one should be expected to sell his life for fewer dollars than satisfied the other.

Besides these measures, Congress gave evidence of its sentiments by passing an act for appointing diplomatic representatives to Hayti and Liberia; also further evidence by passing certain legislation against the slave trade.

The recital of all these doings of the legislators sufficiently indicates the hostility of Congress towards slavery. In fact, a large majority both in the Senate and in the House had moved out against it upon nearly every practicable line to the extremity of the constitutional tether. Neither arguments, nor the entreaties of the border-state men, nor any considerations of policy, had exercised the slightest restraining influence. It is observable that this legislation did not embody that policy which Mr. Lincoln had suggested, and to which he had become strongly attached. On the contrary, Congress had done everything to irritate, where the President wished to do everything to conciliate; Congress made that compulsory which the President hoped to make voluntary. Mr. Lincoln remained in 1862, as he had been in 1858, tolerant towards the Southern men who by inheritance, tradition, and the necessity of the situation, constituted a slaveholding community. To treat slave-ownership as a crime, punishable by confiscation and ruin, seemed to him unreasonable and merciless. Neither does he seem ever to have accepted the opinion of many Abolitionists, that the negro was the equal of the white man in natural endowment. There is no reason to suppose that he did not still hold, as he had done in the days of the Douglas debates, that it was undesirable, if not impossible, that the two races should endeavor to abide together in freedom as a unified community. In the inevitable hostility and competition he clearly saw that the black man was likely to fare badly. It was by such feelings that he was led straight to the plan of compensation of owners and colonization of freedmen, and to the hope that a system of gradual emancipation, embodying these principles, might be voluntarily undertaken by the Border States under the present stress. If the executive and the legislative departments should combine upon the policy of encouraging and aiding such steps as any Border State could be induced to take in this direction, the President believed that he could much more easily extend loyalty and allegiance among the people of those States,—a matter which he valued far more highly than other persons were inclined to do. Such were his views and such his wishes. To discuss their practicability and soundness would only be to wander in the unprofitable vagueness of hypothesis, for in spite of all his efforts they were never tested by trial. It must be admitted that general opinion, both at that day and ever since, has regarded them as visionary; compensation seemed too costly, colonization probably was really impossible.

After the President had suggested his views in his message he waited patiently to see what action Congress would take concerning them. Three months elapsed and Congress took no such action. On the contrary, Congress practically repudiated them. Not only this, it was industriously putting into the shape of laws many other ideas, which were likely to prove so many embarrassments and obstructions to that policy which the President had very thoughtfully and with deep conviction marked out for himself. He determined, therefore, to present it once more, before it should be rendered forever hopeless. On March 6, 1862, he sent to Congress a special message, recommending the adoption of a joint resolution: "That the United States ought to cooperate with any State which may adopt gradual abolishment of slavery, giving to such State pecuniary aid, to be used by such State in its discretion, to compensate for the inconvenience, both public and private, produced by such change of system." The first paragraph in the message stated briefly the inducements to the North: "The Federal government would find its highest interest in such a measure, as one of the most efficient means of self-preservation. The leaders of the existing insurrection entertain the hope that this government will ultimately be forced to acknowledge the independence of some part of the disaffected region, and that all the slave States north of such part will then say: 'The Union for which we have struggled being already gone, we now choose to go with the Southern section.' To deprive them of this hope substantially ends the rebellion; and the initiation of Emancipation completely deprives them of it as to all the States initiating it. The point is that ... the more northern [States] shall, by such initiation, make it certain to the more southern that in no event will the former ever join the latter in their proposed Confederacy. I say 'initiation,' because in my judgment gradual and not sudden emancipation is better for all. In the mere financial or pecuniary view, any member of Congress, with the census tables and Treasury reports before him, can readily see for himself how very soon the current expenditures of this war would purchase, at fair valuation, all the slaves in any named State."

The second paragraph hinted at that which it would have been poor tact to state plainly,—the reasons which would press the Border States to accept the opportunity extended to them. "If resistance continues, the war must also continue; and it is impossible to foresee all the incidents which may attend, and all the ruin which may follow it. Such as may seem indispensable, or may obviously promise great efficiency toward ending the struggle, must and will come. The proposition now made, though an offer only, I hope it may be esteemed no offense to ask whether the pecuniary consideration tendered would not be of more value to the States and private persons concerned than are the institution and property in it, in the present aspect of affairs." The suggestion, between the lines, to the border slave-owners could not be misunderstood: that they would do better to sell their slaves now than to be deprived of them later. The President's proposition was not cordially received. Pro-slavery men regarded it as an underhand movement against the institution. Mr. Crittenden expressed confidence in the President personally, but feared that the resolution "would stir up an emancipation party" in the loyal slave States. Thus the truth was made plain that emancipation, by any process, was not desired. In a debate upon a cognate measure, another Kentuckian said that there was "no division of sentiment on this question of emancipation, whether it is to be brought about by force, by fraud, or by purchase of slaves out of the public treasury." Democrats from Northern States, natural allies of the border-state men, protested vehemently against taxing their constituents to buy slave property in other States. Many Republicans also joined the

Democracy against Mr. Lincoln, and spoke even with anger and insult. Thaddeus Stevens, the fierce and formidable leader of the Radicals, gave his voice against "the most diluted milk-and-water gruel proposition that had ever been given to the American nation." Hickman of Pennsylvania, until 1860 a Democrat, but now a Republican, with the characteristic vehemence of a proselyte said: "Neither the message nor the resolution is manly and open. They are both covert and insidious. They do not become the dignity of the President of the United States. The message is not such a document as a full-grown, independent man should publish to the nation at such a time as the present, when positions should be freely and fully defined." In the Senate, Mr. Powell of Kentucky translated the second paragraph into blunt words. He said that it held a threat of ultimate coercion, if the cooperative plan should fail; and he regarded "the whole thing" as "a pill of arsenic, sugar-coated."

But, though so many insisted upon uttering their fleers in debate, yet, when it came to voting, they could not well discredit their President by voting down the resolution on the sole ground that it was foolish and ineffectual. So, after it had been abused sufficiently, it was passed by about the usual party majority: 89 to 34 in the House; 32 to 10 in the Senate. Thus Congress somewhat sneeringly handed back to the President his bantling, with free leave to do what he could with it.

Not discouraged by such grudging and unsympathetic permission, Mr. Lincoln at once set about his experiment. He told Lovejoy and Arnold, strenuous Abolitionists, but none the less his near friends, that they would live to see the end of slavery, if only the Border States would cooperate in his project. On March 10, 1862, he gathered some of the border-state members and tried to win them over to his views. They listened coldly; but he was not dismayed by their demeanor, and on July 12 he again convened them, and this time laid before them a written statement. This paper betrays by its earnestness of argument and its almost beseeching tone that he wrote it from his heart. The reasons which he urged were as follows:—

"Believing that you of the Border States hold more power for good than any other equal number of members, I felt it a duty which I cannot justifiably waive to make this appeal to you.

"I intend no reproach or complaint when I assure you that, in my opinion, if you all had voted for the resolution in the gradual emancipation message of last March, the war would now be substantially ended.

"And the plan therein proposed is yet one of the most potent and swift means of ending it. Let the States which are in rebellion see definitely and certainly that in no event will the States you represent ever join their proposed Confederacy, and they cannot much longer maintain the contest. But you cannot divest them of their hope to ultimately have you with them as long as you show a determination to perpetuate the institution within your own States; beat them at election as you have overwhelmingly done, and, nothing daunted, they still claim you as their own. You and I know what the lever of their power is. Break that lever before their faces, and they can shake you no more forever. Most of you have treated me with kindness and consideration; and I trust you will not now think I improperly touch what is exclusively your own, when, for the sake of the whole country, I ask: can you, for your States, do better than to take the course I urge? Discarding punctilio and maxims adapted to more manageable times, and looking only to the unprecedentedly stern facts of our case, can you do better in any possible event? You prefer that the constitutional relation of the States to the nation shall be practically restored without disturbance of the institution; and if this were done, my whole duty in this respect under the Constitution and my oath of office would be performed. But it is not done, and we are trying to accomplish it by war.

"The incidents of the war cannot be avoided. If the war continues long, as it must if the object be not sooner attained, the institution in your States will be extinguished by mere friction and abrasion, — by the mere incidents of the war. It will be gone, and you will have nothing valuable in lieu of it. Much of its value is gone already. How much better for you and your people to take the step which at once shortens the war, and secures substantial compensation for that which is sure to be wholly lost in any other event. How much better to thus save the money which else we sink forever in the war. How much better to do it while we can, lest the war erelong render us pecuniarily unable to do it. How much better for you, as seller, and the nation, as buyer, to sell out and buy out that without which the war never could have been, than to sink both the thing to be sold and the price of it in cutting one another's throats. I do not speak of emancipation at once, but of a decision at once to emancipate gradually."

He closed with an ardent appeal to his hearers, as "patriots and statesmen," to consider his proposition, invoking them thereto as they "would perpetuate popular government for the best people in the world."

Thirty gentlemen listened to this paper and took two days to consider it. Then twenty of them signed a response which was, in substance, their repudiation of the President's scheme. They told him that hitherto they had been loyal "under the most discouraging circumstances and in face of measures most distasteful to them and injurious to the interests they represented, and in the hearing of doctrines, avowed by those who claimed to be his friends, most abhorrent to themselves and their constituents." They objected that the measure involved "interference with what exclusively belonged to the States;" that perhaps it was unconstitutional; that it would involve an "immense outlay," beyond what the finances could bear; that it was "the annunciation of a sentiment" rather than a "tangible proposition;" they added that the sole purpose of the war must be "restoring the Constitution to its legitimate authority." Seven others of the President's auditors said politely, but very vaguely, that they would "ask the people of the Border States calmly, deliberately, and fairly to consider his recommendations." Maynard, of the House, and Henderson, of the Senate, alone expressed their personal approval.

Even this did not drive all hope out of Mr. Lincoln's heart. His proclamation, rescinding that order of General Hunter which purported to free slaves in certain States, was issued on May 19. In it he said that the resolution, which had been passed at his request, "now stands an authentic, definite, and solemn proposal of the nation to the States and people most interested in the subject-matter. To the people of these States I now earnestly appeal. I do not argue; I beseech you to make the arguments for yourselves. You cannot, if you would, be blind to the signs of the times. I beg of you a calm and enlarged consideration of them, ranging, if it may be, far above personal and partisan politics. This proposal makes common cause for a common object, casting no reproaches upon any. It acts not the Pharisee. The change it contemplates would come gently as the dews from Heaven, not rending or wrecking anything. Will you not embrace it? So much good has not been done by one effort in all past time as in the providence of God it is now your high privilege to do. May the vast future not have to lament that you have neglected it!"

This eloquent and beautiful appeal sounds deeply moving in the ears of those who read it in these days, so remote from the passions and prejudices of a generation ago; but it stirred little responsive feeling and no responsive action in 1862. In fact, the scheme was not practicable.

It may be—it probably must be—believed that compensated emancipation and colonization could never have been carried out even if Northern Republicans had been willing to pay the price and Southern slave-owners had been willing to accept it, and if both had then cordially united in the task of deporting the troublesome negro from the country. The vast project was undoubtedly visionary; it was to be criticised, weighed, and considered largely as a business enterprise, and as such it must be condemned. But Mr. Lincoln, who had no capacity for business, was never able to get at this point of view, and regarded his favorite plan strictly in political and humanitarian lights. Yet even thus the general opinion has been that the unfortunate negroes, finding themselves amid the hard facts which must inevitably have attended colonization, would have heartily regretted the lost condition of servitude. Historically the merits of the experiment, which the Southern Unionists declined to have put to the test of trial, are of no consequence; it is only as the scheme throws light upon the magnanimity of Mr. Lincoln's temperament and upon certain limitations of his intellect, that the subject is interesting. That he should rid himself of personal vindictiveness and should cherish an honest and intense desire to see the question, which had severed the country, disposed of by a process which would make possible a sincere and cordial reunion, may be only moderately surprising; but it is most surprising to note the depth and earnestness of his faith that this condition could really be reached, and that it could be reached by the road which he had marked out. This confidence indicated an opinion of human nature much higher than human nature has yet appeared entitled to. It also anticipated on the part of the Southerners an appreciation of the facts of the case which few among them were sufficiently clear-minded to furnish. It is curious to observe that Lincoln saw the present situation and foresaw the coming situation with perfect clearness, at the same time that he was entirely unable to see the uselessness of his panacea; whereas, on the other hand, those who rejected his impracticable plan remained entirely blind to those things which he saw. It seems an odd combination of traits that he always recognized and accepted a fact, and yet was capable of being wholly impractical.

In connection with these efforts in behalf of the slaveholders, which show at least a singular goodness of heart towards persons who had done everything to excite even a sense of personal hatred, it may not be seriously out of place to quote a paragraph which does not, indeed, bear upon slavery, but which does illustrate the remarkable temper which Mr. Lincoln maintained towards the seceding communities. In December, 1861, in his annual message to this Congress, whose searching anti-slavery measures have just been discussed, he said:—

"There are three vacancies on the bench of the Supreme Court.... I have so far forborne making nominations to fill these vacancies for reasons which I will now state. Two of the outgoing judges resided within the States now overrun by revolt; so that if successors were appointed in the same localities, they could not now serve upon their circuits; and many of the most competent men there probably would not take the personal hazard of accepting to serve, even here, upon the Supreme Bench. I have been unwilling to throw all the appointments northward, thus disabling myself from doing justice to the South on the return of peace; although I

may remark that to transfer to the North one which has heretofore been in the South would not, with reference to territory and population, be unjust."
[3]  To comment upon behavior and motives so extraordinary is, perhaps, as needless as it is tempting.

> [1] Also in the House Thaddeus Stevens and Lovejoy, and in the Senate Sumner, did not vote.

> [2] Lincoln's intimate personal and political friend, and afterward his biographer.

> [3] Annual Message to Congress, December, 1861.

# CHAPTER II
## THE SECOND ACT OF THE MCCLELLAN DRAMA

It is time now to return to the theatre of war in Virginia, where, it will be remembered, we left the Confederate forces in the act of rapidly withdrawing southward from the line of intrenchments which they had so long held at Manassas. This unexpected backward movement upon their part deprived the Urbana route, which McClellan had hitherto so strenuously advocated, of its chief strategic advantages, and therefore reopened the old question which had been discussed between him and Mr. Lincoln. To the civilian mind a movement after the retreating enemy along the direct line to Richmond, now more than ever before, seemed the natural scheme. But to this McClellan still remained unalterably opposed. In the letter of February 3 he had said: "The worst coming to the worst, we can take Fort Monroe as a base and operate with complete security, although with less celerity and brilliancy of results, up the Peninsula." This route, low as he had then placed it in order of desirability, he now adopted as the best resource, or rather as the only measure; and his judgment was ratified upon March 13 by unanimous approval on the part of his four corps commanders. They however made their approval dependent upon conditions, among which were: that, before beginning the advance along this line, the new rebel ram Merrimac (or Virginia), just finished at Norfolk on the James River, should be neutralized, and that a naval auxiliary force should silence, or be ready to aid in silencing, the rebel batteries on the York River. In fact, and very unfortunately, the former of these conditions was not fulfilled until the time of its usefulness for this specific purpose was over, and the latter condition was entirely neglected. It was also distinctly stipulated that "the force to be left to cover Washington shall be such as to give an entire feeling of security for its safety from menace." Keyes, Heintzelman and McDowell conceived "that, with the forts on the right bank of the Potomac fully garrisoned, and those on the left bank occupied, a covering force, in front of the Virginia line, of 25,000 men would suffice." Sumner said: "A total of 40,000 for the defense of the city would suffice." [4] On the same day Stanton informed McClellan that the President "made no objection" to this plan, but directed that a sufficient force should be left to hold Manassas Junction and to make Washington "entirely secure." The closing sentence was: "At all events, move ... at once in pursuit of the enemy by some route." Thus at last two important facts were established: that the route up the Peninsula should be tried; and that the patience of the administration was exhausted.

Though the enemy upon his retreat was burning bridges and destroying railroads behind him, and making his possible return towards Washington a slow, difficult process, which he obviously had no mind to undertake, still this security of the capital rested as weightily as ever upon Lincoln's mind. His reiteration and insistence concerning it made perfectly plain that he was still nervous and disquieted about it, though now certainly with much less reason than heretofore. But with or against reason, it was easy to see that he was far from resting in the tranquillity of conviction that Washington could never be so safe as when the army of Virginia was far away upon the Peninsula. Nevertheless, after the condition in its foregoing shape had been so strenuously imposed by Mr. Lincoln and tacitly accepted by McClellan, the matter was left as if definitely settled; and the President never demanded [5] from the general any distinct statement concerning the numerical or specific allotment of the available forces between the two purposes. The neglect was disastrous in its consequences; and must also be pronounced both blameworthy and inexplicable, for the necessity of a plain understanding on the subject was obvious.

The facts seem to be briefly these: in his letter of February 3, McClellan estimated the force necessary to be taken with him for his campaign at 110,000 to 140,000 men, and said: "I hope to use the latter number by bringing fresh troops into Washington." On April 1 he reported [6] the forces left behind him as follows: —

| | | |
|---|---|---|
| At Warrenton, there is to be | 7,780 | men |
| At Manassas, there is to be | 10,859 | men |
| In the Valley of the Shenandoah | 35,467 | men |
| On the Lower Potomac | 1,350 | men |
| | | |
| In all | 55,456 | men |

He adds: "There will thus be left for the garrisons, and the front of Washington, under General Wadsworth, 18,000 men, exclusive of the batteries under instruction." New levies, nearly 4,000 strong, were also expected. He considered all these men as properly available "for the defense of the national capital and its approaches." The President, the politicians, and some military men were of opinion that only the 18,000 ought to be considered available for the capital. It was a question whether it was proper to count the corps of Banks in the Shenandoah Valley. McClellan's theory was that the rebels, by the circumstances attendant upon their present retreating movement, had conclusively annulled any chance of their own return by way of Manassas. Banks greatly outnumbered Stonewall Jackson, who had only about 15,000 men, or less, in the Shenandoah Valley. Also Washington was now entirely surrounded by satisfactory fortifications. McClellan, therefore, was entirely confident that he left everything in good shape behind him. In fact, it was put into even better shape than he had designed; for on March 31 the President took from him Blenker's division of 10,000 men in order to strengthen Fremont, who was in the mountain region westward of the Shenandoah Valley. "I did so," wrote Mr. Lincoln, "with great pain.... If you could know the full pressure of the case, I am confident that you would justify it." It was unfortunate that the President could not stand against this "pressure," which was not military, but political. Fremont could do, and did, nothing at all, and to reinforce him was sheer absurdity. [7] Against it McClellan protested almost indignantly, but was "partially relieved by the President's positive and emphatic assurance" that no more troops "should in any event be taken from" him, or "in any way detached from [his] command."

Orders had been issued on February 27, to Mr. Tucker, assistant secretary of war, to prepare means of transporting down the Potomac, troops, munitions, artillery, horses, wagons, food, and all the vast paraphernalia of a large army. He showed a masterly vigor in this difficult task, and by March 17 the embarkation began. On April 2 McClellan arrived at Fortress Monroe. On the very next day he was disturbed by the revocation of the orders which had left him in command of that place and had allowed him to "draw from the troops under General Wool a division of about 10,000 men, which was to be assigned to the First Corps." Another and a serious disappointment also occurred at once; he found that the navy could not be utilized for assisting in an attack on Yorktown, or for running by it so as to land forces in rear of it. He must therefore depend wholly upon his army to force a way up the Peninsula. This he had stated to be an unsatisfactory alternative, because it involved delay at Yorktown. Nevertheless, having no choice, he began his advance on April 4. He had with him only 58,000 men; but more were on the way, and McDowell's corps was to be brought forward to join him as rapidly as transportation would permit. His total nominal force was smaller than the minimum which, on February 3, he had named as necessary; yet it was a fine body of troops, and he had lately said to them: "The army of the Potomac is now a real army, magnificent in material, admirable in discipline, excellently equipped and armed. Your commanders are all that I could wish."

In two days he was before the fortifications which the rebels had erected at Yorktown, and which stretched thence across the Peninsula to the James River. He estimated the force behind these intrenchments, commanded by General Magruder, at 15,000 to 20,000 men, easily to be reinforced; in fact, it was much less. Thereupon, he set about elaborate preparations for a siege of that city, according to the most thorough and approved system of military science. He was afterward severely blamed for not endeavoring to force his way through some point in the rebel lines by a series of assaults. [8] This was what Mr. Lincoln wished him to do, and very nearly ordered him to do; for on April 6 he sent this telegram: "You now have over 100,000 troops with you.... I think you better break the enemy's line from Yorktown to Warwick River at once." An entry in McClellan's "Own Story," under date of April 8, comments upon this message and illustrates the unfortunate feeling of the writer towards his official superior: "I have raised an awful row about McDowell's corps. The President very coolly telegraphed me yesterday that he thought I had better break the enemy's lines at once! I was much tempted to reply that he had better come and do it himself." Thus is made evident the lamentable relationship between the President, who could place no confidence in the enterprise and judgment of the military commander, and the general, who had only sneers for the President's incapacity to comprehend warfare. It so happened, however, that the professional man's sarcasm was grossly out of place, and the civilian's proposal was shrewdly right, as events soon plainly proved. In fact what Mr. Lincoln urged was precisely what General Johnston anticipated and feared would be done, because he knew well that if it were done it would be of fatal effect against the Confederates. But, on the other hand, even after the clear proof had gone against him, McClellan was abundantly supplied with excuses, and the vexation of the whole affair was made the greater by the fact that these excuses really seemed to be good. His excuses always were both so numerous and so satisfactory, that many reasonably minded persons knew not whether they had a right to feel so angry towards him as they certainly could not help doing. The present instance was directly in point. General Keyes reported to him that no part of the enemy's line could "be taken by assault without an enormous waste of life;" and General Barnard, chief engineer of the army, thought it uncertain whether they could be carried at all. Loss of life and uncertainty of result were two things so abhorred by McClellan in warfare, that he now failed to give due weight to the consideration that the design of the Confederates in interposing an obstacle at this point was solely to delay him as much as possible, whereas much of the merit of his own plan of campaign lay in rapid execution at the outset. The result was, of course, that he did not break any line, nor try to, but instead thereof "presented plausible reasons" out of his inexhaustible reservoir of such commodities. It was unfortunate that the naval coöperation, which McClellan had expected, [9] could not be had at this juncture; for by it the Yorktown problem would have been easily solved without either line-breaking or reason-giving.

Precisely at this point came into operation the fatal effect of the lack of understanding between the President and the general as to the division of the forces. In the plan of campaign, it had been designed to throw the corps of McDowell into the rear of Yorktown by such route as should seem expedient at the time of its arrival, probably landing it at Gloucester and moving it round by West Point. This would have made Magruder's position untenable at once, long before the natural end of the siege. But at the very moment when McClellan's left, in its advance, first came into actual collision with the enemy, he received news that the President had ordered McDowell to retain his division before Washington—"the most infamous thing that history has recorded," he afterward wrote. [10] Yet the explanation of this surprising news was so simple that surprise was unjustifiable. On April 2, immediately after McClellan's departure, the President inquired as to what had been done for the security of Washington. General Wadsworth, commanding the defenses of the city, gave an alarming response: 19,000 or 20,000 entirely green troops, and a woeful insufficiency of artillery. He said that while it was "very improbable" that the enemy would attack Washington, nevertheless the "numerical strength and the character" of his forces rendered them "entirely inadequate to and unfit for their important duty." Generals Hitchcock and Thomas corroborated this by reporting that the order to leave the city "entirely secure" had "not been fully complied with." Mr. Lincoln was horror-struck. He had a right to be indignant, for those who ought to know assured him that his reiterated and most emphatic command had been disobeyed, and that what he chiefly cared to make safe had not been made safe. He promptly determined to retain McDowell, and the order was issued on April 4. Thereby he seriously attenuated, if he did not quite annihilate, the prospect of success for McClellan's campaign. It seems incredible and unexplainable that amid this condition of things, on April 3, an order was issued from the office of the secretary of war, to stop recruiting throughout the country!

This series of diminutions, says McClellan, had "removed nearly 60,000 men from my command, and reduced my force by more than one third.... The blow was most discouraging. It frustrated all my plans for impending operations. It fell when I was too deeply committed to withdraw.... It was a fatal error."

Error or not, it was precisely what McClellan ought to have foreseen as likely to occur. He had not foreseen it, however, and nothing mitigated the disappointment. Unquestionably the act was of supreme gravity. Was Mr. Lincoln right or wrong in doing it? The question has been answered many times both Yea and Nay, and each side has been maintained with intense acrimony and perfect good faith. It is not likely that it will ever be possible to say either that the Yeas have it, or that the Nays have it. [11] For while it is certain that what actually *did* happen coincided very accurately with McClellan's expectations; on the other hand, it can never be known what *might have* happened if Lincoln had not held McDowell, and if, therefore, facts had not been what they were.

So far as Mr. Lincoln is concerned, the question, what military judgment was correct,—that is, whether the capital really was, or was not, absolutely secure,—is of secondary consequence. The valuation which he set on that safety was undeniably correct; it certainly was of more importance than McClellan's success. If he had made a mistake in letting McClellan go without a more distinct understanding, at least that mistake was behind him. Before him was the issue whether he should rest satisfied with the deliberate judgment given by McClellan, or whether, at considerable cost to the cause, he should make the assurance greater out of deference to other advice. He chose the latter course. In so doing, if he was not vacillating, he was at least incurring the evils of vacillation. It would have been well if he could have found some quarter in which permanently to repose his implicit faith, so that one consistent plan could have been carried out without interference. Either he had placed too much confidence in McClellan in the past, or he was placing too little in him now. If he could not accept McClellan's opinion as to the safety of Washington, in preference to that of Wadsworth, Thomas, and Hitchcock, then he should have removed McClellan, and replaced him with some one in whom he had sufficient confidence to make smooth coöperation a possibility. The present condition of things was illogical and dangerous. Matters had been allowed to reach a very advanced stage upon the theory that McClellan's judgment was trustworthy; then suddenly the stress became more severe, and it seemed that in the bottom of his mind the President did not thus implicitly respect the general's wisdom. Yet he did not displace him, but only opened his ears to other counsels; whereupon the buzz of contradictory, excited, and alarming suggestions which came to him were more than enough to unsettle any human judgment. General Webb speaks well and with authority to this matter: "The dilemma lay here,— whose plans and advice should he follow, where it was necessary for him to approve and decide?... Should he lean implicitly on the general actually in command of the armies, placed there by virtue of his presumed fitness for the position, or upon other selected advisers? We are bold to say that it was doubt and hesitation upon this point that occasioned many of the blunders of the campaign. Instead of one mind, there were many minds influencing the management of military affairs." A familiar culinary proverb was receiving costly illustration.

But, setting the dispute aside, an important fact remains: shorn as he was, McClellan was still strong enough to meet and to defeat his opponents. If he had been one of the great generals of the world he would have been in Richmond before May Day; but he was at his old trick of exaggerating the hostile forces and the difficulties in his way. On April 7 he thought that Johnston and the whole Confederate army were at Yorktown; whereas Johnston's advance division arrived there on the 10th; the other divisions came several days later, and Johnston himself arrived only on the 14th.

On April 9 Mr. Lincoln presented his own view of the situation in this letter to the general:—

"Your dispatches complaining that you are not properly sustained, while they do not offend me, do pain me very much.

... "After you left I ascertained that less than 20,000 unorganized men, without a single field battery, were all you designed to be left for the defense of Washington and Manassas Junction, and part of this even was to go to General Hooker's old position. General Banks's corps, once designed for Manassas Junction, was diverted and tied up on the line of Winchester and Strasburg, and could not leave it without again exposing the upper Potomac and the Baltimore and Ohio Railroad. This presented, or would present, when McDowell and Sumner should be gone, a great temptation to the enemy to turn back from the Rappahannock and sack Washington. My implicit order that Washington should, by the judgment of all the commanders of army corps, be left entirely secure, had been neglected. It was precisely this that drove me to detain McDowell.

"I do not forget that I was satisfied with your arrangement to leave Banks at Manassas Junction; but when that arrangement was broken up, and nothing was substituted for it, of course I was constrained to substitute something for it myself. And allow me to ask, do you really think I should permit the line from Richmond, via Manassas Junction, to this city, to be entirely open, except what resistance could be presented by less than 20,000 unorganized troops? This is a question which the country will not allow me to evade.

"There is a curious mystery about the number of troops now with you. When I telegraphed you on the 6th, saying you had over a hundred thousand with you, I had just obtained from the secretary of war a statement taken, as he said, from your own returns, making 108,000 then with you and en route to you. You now say you will have but 85,000 when all en route to you shall have reached you. How can the discrepancy of 23,000 be accounted for?

"As to General Wool's command, [12] I understand it is doing for you precisely what a like number of your own would have to do if that command was away.

"I suppose the whole force which has gone forward for you is with you by this time. And if so, I think it is the precise time for you to strike a blow. By delay the enemy will relatively gain upon you,—that is, he will gain faster by fortifications and reinforcements than you can by reinforcements alone. And once more let me tell you, it is indispensable to you that you strike a blow. I am powerless to help this. You will do me the justice to remember I always insisted that going down the bay in search of a field, instead of fighting at or near Manassas, was only shifting, and not surmounting, a difficulty; that we would find the same enemy, and the same or equal intrenchments, at either place. The country will not fail to note, is now noting, that the present hesitation to move upon an intrenched enemy is but the story of Manassas repeated.

"I beg to assure you that I have never written you or spoken to you in greater kindness of feeling than now, nor with a fuller purpose to sustain you, so far as, in my most anxious judgment, I consistently can. But you must act."

McClellan, in consternation and almost despair at the repeated pruning of his force, now begged for at least a part of McDowell's corps, which, he said on April 10, was "indispensable;" "the fate of our cause depends upon it." Accordingly Franklin's division was sent to him; and then, after all this palaver, he kept it a fortnight on shipboard, until Yorktown was evacuated!

On May 1 the President, tortured by the political gadflies in Washington, and suffering painfully from the weariness of hope so long deferred, telegraphed: "Is anything to be done?" A pitiful time of it Mr. Lincoln was having, and it called for a patient fortitude surpassing imagination. Yet one little bit of fruit was at this moment ripe for the plucking! After about four weeks of wearisome labor the general had brought matters to that condition which was so grateful to his cautious soul. At the beginning of May he had reduced success to a certainty, so that he expected to open fire on May 5, and to make short work of the rebel stronghold. But it so happened that another soldier also had at the same time finished his task. General Magruder had delayed the Union army to the latest possible hour, he had saved a whole valuable month; and now, quite cheerfully and triumphantly, in the night betwixt May 3 and May 4, he quietly slipped away. As it had happened at Manassas, so now again the Federals marched unopposed into deserted intrenchments; and a second time the enemy had so managed it that their retreat seemed rather to cast a slur upon Union strategy than to bring prestige to the Union arms.

McClellan at once continued his advance, with more or less fighting, the rebels steadily drawing back without offering battle on a large scale, though there was a sharp engagement at Williamsburg. He had not even the smaller number of men which he had originally named as his requirement, and he continued pertinaciously to demand liberal reinforcements. The President, grievously harassed by these importunate appeals, declared to McClellan that he was forwarding every man that he could, while to friends nearer at hand he complained that sending troops to McClellan was like shoveling fleas across a barnyard; most of them didn't get there! At last he made up his mind to send the remainder of McDowell's corps; not because he had changed his mind about covering Washington, but because the situation had become such that he expected to arrange this matter by other resources.

The fight at Williamsburg took place on May 5. McClellan pushed after the retiring enemy, too slowly, as his detractors said, yet by roads which really were made almost impassable by heavy rains. Two days later, May 7, Franklin's force disembarked and occupied West Point. This advance up the Peninsula now produced one important result which had been predicted by McClellan in his letter of February 3. On May 8 news came that the Confederates were evacuating Norfolk, and two days later a Union force marched into the place. The rebels lost many heavy guns, besides all the advantages of the navy yard with its workshops and stores; moreover, their awe-inspiring ram, the Merrimac, alias the Virginia, was obliged to leave this comfortable nestling-place, whence she had long watched and closed the entrance to the James River. Her commander, Tatnall, would have taken her up that stream, but the pilots declared it not possible to float her over the shoals. She was therefore abandoned and set on fire; and early in the morning of May 11 she blew up, leaving the southern water-way to Richmond open to the Union fleet. [13] It was a point of immense possible advantage. Later McClellan intimated that, if he had been left free to act upon his own judgment, he would probably have availed himself of this route; and some writers, with predilections in his favor, have assumed that he was prevented from doing so by certain orders, soon to be mentioned, which directed him to keep the northerly route for the purpose of effecting a junction with McDowell. But this notion seems incorrect; for though he doubtless had the James River route under consideration, yet dates are against the theory that he wished to adopt it when at last it lay open. On the contrary, he continued his advance precisely as before. On May 16 his leading columns reached White House; headquarters were established there, and steps were immediately taken to utilize it as a depot and base of supplies. The York River route was thus made the definitive choice. Also the advance divisions were immediately pushed out along the York River and Richmond Railroad, which they repaired as they went. On May 20 Casey's division actually crossed the Chickahominy at Bottom's Bridge, and the next day a large part of the army was in position upon the north bank of that stream. Obviously these operations, each and all, ruled out the James River route, at least as a part of the present plan. Yet it was not until they were well under way, viz., on May 18, that the intelligence reached McClellan, on the strength of which he and others afterward assumed that he had been deprived of the power to select the James River route. What this intelligence was and how it came to pass must now be narrated.

By this time, the advance along the Peninsula had so completely "relieved the front of Washington from pressure," that Mr. Lincoln and his advisers, reassured as to the safety of that city, now saw their way clear to make McDowell's corps, strengthened to a force of 41,000 men, contribute actively to McClellan's assistance. They could not, indeed, bring themselves to move it by water, as McClellan desired; but the President ordered McDowell to move down from Fredericksburg, where he now lay, towards McClellan's right wing, which McClellan was ordered to extend to the north of Richmond in order to meet him. But, in the words of the Comte de Paris, "an absurd restriction revealed the old mistrusts and fears." For McDowell was strictly ordered not to uncover the capital; also, with a decisive emphasis indicative of an uneasy suspicion, McClellan was forbidden to dispose of McDowell's force in contravention of this still primary purpose. Whether McDowell was under McClellan's control, or retained an independent command, was left curiously vague, until McClellan forced a distinct understanding.

Although McClellan, writing to Lincoln, condemned rather sharply the method selected for giving to him the aid so long implored, yet he felt that, even as it came to him, he could make it serve his turn. Though he grumbled at the President's unmilitary ways, he afterward admitted that the "cheering news" made him "confident" of being "sufficiently strong to overpower the large army confronting" him. There was no doubt of it. He immediately extended his right wing; May 24, he drove the Confederates out of Mechanicsville; May 26, General Porter took position at Hanover Junction only fifteen miles from McDowell's head of column, which had advanced eight miles out of Fredericksburg. The situation was not unpromising; but unfortunately that little interval of fifteen miles was never to be closed up.

May 24, Mr. Lincoln wrote to McClellan, and after suggesting sundry advisable movements, he said: "McDowell and Shields [14] both say they can, and positively will, move Monday morning." Monday was the 26th. In point of fact, McDowell, feeling time to be of great value, urged the President to let him move on the morning of Sunday, the 25th; but Mr. Lincoln positively refused; the battle of Bull Run had been fought on a Sunday, and he dreaded the omen. [15] This feeling which he had about days was often illustrated, and probably the reader has observed that he seemed to like dates already marked by prestige or good luck; thus he had convened Congress for July 4, and had ordered the general advance of the armies for February 22; it was an indication of the curious thread of superstition which ran through his strange nature, —a remnant of his youth and the mysterious influence of the wilderness. But worse than a superstitious postponement arrived before nightfall on Saturday. A dispatch from Lincoln to McClellan, dated at four o'clock that afternoon, said: "In consequence of General Banks's critical position, I have been compelled to suspend General McDowell's movements to join you. The enemy are making a desperate push upon Harper's Ferry, and we are trying to throw General Fremont's force and part of General McDowell's in their rear." The brief words conveyed momentous intelligence. It is necessary to admit that Mr. Lincoln was making his one grand blunder, for which there is not even the scant salvation of possible doubt. All that can be said in palliation is, that he was governed, or at least strongly impelled, by the urgent advice of the secretary of war, whose hasty telegrams to the governors of several States show that he was terror-stricken and had lost his head. Mr. Blaine truly says that McDowell, thus suddenly dispatched by Mr. Lincoln upon a "fruitless chase," "was doing precisely what the President of the Confederate States would have ordered, had he been able to issue the orders of the President of the United States." There is no way to mitigate the painful truth of this statement, made by a civilian, but amply sustained by the military authorities on both sides. [16]

The condition was this. The retention of McDowell's corps before Washington published the anxiety of the administration. The Confederate advantage lay in keeping that anxiety alive and continuing to neutralize that large body of troops. Strategists far less able than the Southern generals could not have missed so obvious a point, neither could they have missed the equally obvious means at their disposal for achieving these purposes. At the upper end of the valley of the Shenandoah Stonewall Jackson had an army, raised by recent accretions to nearly or quite 15,000 men. The Northern generals erelong learned to prognosticate Jackson's movements by the simple rule that at the time when he was least expected, and at the place where he was least wanted, he was sure to turn up. [17] The suddenness and speed with which he could move a body of troops seemed marvelous to ordinary men. His business now was to make a vigorous dashing foray down the valley. To the westward, Fremont lay in the mountains, with an army which checked no enemy and for the existence of which in that place no reasonable explanation could be given. In front was Banks, with a force lately reduced to about 5,000 men. May 14, Banks prudently fell back and took position in Strasburg. [18] Suddenly, on May 23, Jackson appeared at Front Royal; on the next day he attacked Banks at Winchester, and of course defeated him; on the 25th Banks made a rapid retreat to the Potomac, and Jackson made an equally rapid pursuit to Halltown, within two miles of Harper's Ferry. The news of this startling foray threw the civilians of Washington into a genuine panic, by which Mr. Lincoln was, at least for a few hours, not altogether unaffected. [19] Yet, though startled and alarmed, he showed the excellent quality of promptitude in decision and action; and truly it was hard fortune that his decision and his action were both for the worst. He at once ordered McDowell to move 20,000 troops into the Shenandoah Valley, and instructed Fremont also to move his force rapidly into the valley, with the design that the two should thus catch Jackson in what Mr. Lincoln described as a "trap." [20] McDowell was dismayed at such an order. He saw, what every man having any military knowledge at once recognized with entire certainty, and what every military writer has since corroborated, that the movement of Jackson had no value except as a diversion, that it threatened no serious danger, and that to call off McDowell's corps from marching to join McClellan in order to send it against Jackson was to do exactly that thing which the Confederates desired to have done, though they could hardly have been sanguine enough to expect it. It was swallowing a bait so plain that it might almost be said to be labeled. For a general to come under the suspicion of not seeing through such a ruse was humiliating. In vain McDowell explained, protested, and entreated with the utmost vehemence and insistence. When Mr. Lincoln had made up his mind, no man could change it, and here, as ill fortune would have it, he had made it up. So, with a heavy heart, the reluctant McDowell set forth on his foolish errand, and Fremont likewise came upon his,—though it is true that he was better employed thus than in doing nothing,—and Jackson, highly pleased, and calculating his time to a nicety, on May 31 slipped rapidly between the two Union generals,—the closing jaws of Mr. Lincoln's "trap,"—and left them to close upon nothing. [21] Then he led his pursuers a fruitless chase towards the head of the valley, continuing to neutralize a force many times larger than his own, and which could and ought to have been at this very time doing fatal work against the Confederacy. Presumably he had saved Richmond, and therewith also, not impossibly, the chief army of the

South. The chagrin of the Union commanders, who had in vain explained the situation with entire accuracy, taxes the imagination.

There is no use in denying a truth which can be proved. The blunder of Mr. Lincoln is not only undeniable, but it is inexcusable. Possibly for a few hours he feared that Washington was threatened. He telegraphed to McClellan May 25, at two o'clock P.M., that he thought the movement down the valley a "general and concerted one," inconsistent with "the purpose of a very desperate defense of Richmond;" and added, "I think the time is near when you must either attack Richmond, or give up the job and come to the defense of Washington." How reasonable this view was at the moment is of little consequence, for within a few hours afterward the character of Jackson's enterprise as a mere foray became too palpable to be mistaken. Nevertheless, after the President was relieved from such fear for the capital as he might excusably have felt for a very brief period, his cool judgment seemed for once in his life, perhaps for the only time, to be disturbed. The truth is that Mr. Lincoln was a sure and safe, almost an infallible thinker, when he had time given him; but he was not always a quick thinker, and on this occasion he was driven to think quickly. In consequence he not only erred in repudiating the opinions of the best military advisers, but even upon the basis of his own views he made a mistake. The very fact that he was so energetic in the endeavor to "trap" Jackson in retreat indicates his understanding of the truth that Jackson had so small a force that his prompt retreat was a necessity. This being so, he was in the distinct and simple position of making a choice between two alternatives, viz.: either to endeavor to catch Jackson, and for this object to withhold what was needed by and had been promised to McClellan for his campaign against Richmond; or, leaving Jackson to escape with impunity, to pursue with steadiness that plan which it was Jackson's important and perfectly understood errand to interrupt. It is almost incredible that he chose wrong. The statement of the dilemma involved the decision. Yet he took the little purpose and let the great one go. Nor even thus did he gain this lesser purpose. He had been warned by McDowell that Jackson could not be caught, and he was not. Yet even had this been otherwise, the Northerners would have got little more than the shell while losing the kernel. Probably Richmond, and possibly the Southern army, fell out of the President's hand while he tried without success to close it upon Jackson and 15,000 men.

The result of this civilian strategy was that McClellan, with his projects shattered, was left with his right wing and rear dangerously exposed. Jackson remained for a while a mysterious *bête noire*, about whose force, whereabouts, and intentions many disturbing rumors flew abroad; at last, on June 26, he settled these doubts in his usual sharp and conclusive way by assailing the exposed right wing and threatening the rear of the Union army, thus achieving "the brilliant conclusion of the operations which [he] had so successfully conducted in the Valley of Virginia."

Simultaneously with the slipping of Jackson betwixt his two pursuers on May 31, General Johnston made an attack upon the two corps [22] which lay south of the Chickahominy, in position about Seven Pines and Fair Oaks. Battle was waged during two days. Each side claimed a victory; the Southerners because they had inflicted the heavier loss, the Northerners because ultimately they held their original lines and foiled Johnston's design of defeating and destroying the Northern army in detail. The result of this battle ought to have proved to McClellan two facts: that neither in discipline nor in any other respect were the Southern troops more formidable than his own; also that the Southerners were clearly not able to overwhelm him with such superior numbers as he had supposed; for in two days they had not been able to overwhelm much less than half of his army. These considerations should have encouraged him to energetic measures. But no encouragement could counteract the discouragement inflicted by the loss of McDowell's powerful corps and the consequent wrecking of his latest plan. Nearly to the end of June he lay immovable. "June 14, midnight. All quiet in every direction," — thus he telegraphed to Stanton in words intended to be reassuring, but in fact infinitely vexatious. Was he, then, set at the head of this great and costly host of the nation's best, to rest satisfied with preserving an eternal quietude, — like a chief of police in a disorderly quarter? Still he was indefatigable in declaring himself outnumbered, and in demanding more troops; in return he got assurances, with only the slight fulfillment of McCall's division. Every two or three days he cheeringly announced to the administration that he was on the verge of advancing, but he never passed over the verge. Throughout a season in which blundering seemed to become epidemic, no blunder was greater than his quiescence at this time. [23] As if to emphasize it, about the middle of June General Stuart, with a body of Confederate cavalry, actually rode all around the Union army, making the complete circuit and crossing its line of communication with White House without interruption. The foray achieved little, but it wore the aspect of a signal and unavenged insult.

In Washington the only powerful backing upon which McClellan could still rely was that of the President, and he was surely wearing away the patience of his only friend by the irritating attrition of promises ever reiterated and never redeemed. No man ever kept his own counsel more closely than did Mr. Lincoln, and the indications of his innermost sentiments concerning McClellan at this time are rare. But perhaps a little ray is let in, as through a cranny, by a dispatch which he sent to the general on June 2: "With these continuous rains I am very anxious about the Chickahominy,— so close in your rear, and crossing your line of communication. Please look to it." This curt prompting on so obvious a point was a plain insinuation against McClellan's military competence, and suggests that ceaseless harassment had at last got the better of Lincoln's usually imperturbable self-possession; for it lacked little of being an insult, and Mr. Lincoln, in all his life, never insulted any man. As a spot upon a white cloth sets off the general whiteness, so this dispatch illustrates Lincoln's unweariable patience and long-suffering without parallel. McClellan, never trammeled by respect, retorted sharply: "As the Chickahominy has been almost the only obstacle in my way for several days, your excellency may rest assured that it has not been overlooked." When finally the general became active, it was under the spur of General Jackson, not of President Lincoln. Jackson compelled him to decide and act; and the result was his famous southward movement to the James River. Some, adopting his own nomenclature, have called this a change of base; some, less euphemistically, speak of it as a retreat. According to General Webb, it may be called either the one or the other with equal propriety, for it partook of the features of each. [24] It is no part of the biographer of Lincoln to narrate the suffering and the gallantry of the troops through those seven days of continuous fighting and marching, during which they made their painful way, in the face of an attacking army, through the dismal swamps of an unwholesome region, amid the fierce and humid heats of the Southern summer. On July 1 they closed the dread experience by a brilliant victory in the desperate, prolonged, and bloody battle of Malvern Hill.

In the course of this march a letter was sent by McClellan to Stanton which has become famous. The vindictive lunge, visibly aimed at the secretary, was really designed, piercing this lesser functionary, to reach the President. Even though written amid the strain and stress of the most critical and anxious moment of the terrible "Seven Days," the words were unpardonable. The letter is too long to be given in full, but the closing sentences were:—

"I know that a few thousand more men would have changed this battle [25] from a defeat to a victory. As it is, the government must not and cannot hold me responsible for the result. I feel too earnestly to-night. I have seen too many dead and wounded comrades to feel otherwise than that the government has not sustained this army. If you do not do so now, the game is lost. If I save this army now, I tell you plainly that I owe no thanks to you or to any other persons in Washington. You have done your best to sacrifice this army." [26] It was safe to write thus to Mr. Lincoln, whose marvelous magnanimity was never soiled by a single act of revenge; but the man who addressed such language to Stanton secured a merciless and unscrupulous enemy forever.

Though, at the close of this appalling week, the troops at last were conquerors on the banks of the James, they were in a position not permanently tenable, and before they could rest they had to fall back another march to Harrison's Landing. The rear guard reached this haven on the night of July 3, and the army, thus at last safely placed and in direct communication with the fleet and the transports, was able to recuperate, [27] while those in authority considered of the future. Certain facts were established: first, concerning the army,— that before it met the baptism of heavy fighting it had been brought into a splendid condition of drill and efficiency, and that by that baptism, so severe and so long continued, it had come as near as volunteers could come to the excellence of veterans and regulars; also that it was at least a match for its opponents; and, finally, strange to say, it was very slightly demoralized, would soon again be in condition for an advance, and felt full confidence and strong affection for its commander. Brilliant and enthusiastic tributes have been paid to these men for their endurance amid disease and wounds and battle; but not one word too much has been said. It is only cruel to think of the hideous price which they had paid, and by which they had bought only the capacity to endure further perils and hardship. Second, concerning McClellan; it was to be admitted that his predictions as to points of strategy had been fulfilled; that he had managed his retreat, or "change of base," with skill, and had shown some qualities of high generalship; but it was also evident that he was of a temperament so unenterprising and apprehensive as to make him entirely useless in an offensive campaign. Yet the burden of conducting a successful offense lay upon the North. Must Mr. Lincoln, then, finally accept the opinion of those who had long since concluded that McClellan was not the man for the place?

A collateral question was: What should be done next? McClellan, tenacious and stubborn, was for persisting in the movement against Lee's army and Richmond. He admitted no other thought than that, having paused to gather reinforcements and to refresh his army, he should assume the offensive, approaching the city by the south and southwest from the James River base. Holding this purpose, he was impolitic in sending very dolorous dispatches on July 4 and 7, intimating doubts as to his power to maintain successfully even the defensive. Two or three days later, however, he assumed a better tone; and on July 11 and 12 he reported "all in fine spirits," and urged that his army should be "promptly reinforced and thrown again upon Richmond. If we have a little more than half a chance, we can take it." He continued throughout the month to press these views by arguments which, though overruled at the time, have since been more favorably regarded. Whether or not they were correct is an item in the long legacy of questions left by the war to be disputed over by posterity; in time, one side or the other may desist from the discussion in weariness, but, from the nature of the case, neither can be vanquished.

Whether McClellan was right or wrong, his prestige, fresh as it still remained with his devoted troops, was utterly gone at Washington, where the political host was almost a unit against him. The Committee on the Conduct of the War had long been bitterly denouncing him; and he had so abused the secretary of war that even the duplicity of Mr. Stanton was unequal to the strain of maintaining an appearance of good understanding. New military influences also fell into the same scale. General Pope, the latest "favorite," now enjoying his few weeks of authority, endeavored to make it clear to Mr. Lincoln that to bring McClellan back from the Peninsula was the only safe and intelligent course. Further, on July 11, President Lincoln appointed General Halleck general-in-chief. It may be said, in passing, that the appointment turned out to be a very bad mistake; for Halleck was as dull a man as ever made use of grand opportunities only to prove his own incompetence. Now, however, he came well recommended before Lincoln, and amid novel responsibilities the merit of any man could only be known by trial. Halleck did not arrive in Washington till near the end of the month, then he seemed for a while in doubt, or to be upon both sides of the question as to whether the army should be advanced or withdrawn; but ultimately, in the contemptuous language of Mr. Swinton, he "added his strident voice in favor of the withdrawal of the army from the Peninsula." This settled the matter; for the President had decided to place himself under the guidance of his new military mentor; and, moreover, his endurance was worn out.

In the way of loyalty the President certainly owed nothing further to the general. All such obligations he had exhaustively discharged. In spite of the covert malicious suggestions and the direct injurious charges which tortured the air of the White House and vexed his judgment, he had sustained McClellan with a constancy which deserved warm gratitude. This the general never gave, because he could never forgive Mr. Lincoln for refusing to subordinate his own views to those of such a military expert as himself. This point, it is true, Lincoln never reached; but subject only to this independence of opinion and action, so long as he retained McClellan in command, he fulfilled toward him every requirement of honor and generosity. The movement across the Peninsula, whatever construction might possibly be put upon it, seemed in Washington a retreat, and was for the President a disappointment weighty enough to have broken the spirit of a smaller man. Yet Lincoln, instead of sacrificing McClellan as a scapegoat, sent to him on July 1 and 2 telegrams bidding him do his best in the emergency and save his army, in which case the people would rally and repair all losses; "we still have strength enough in the country and will bring it out," he said,—words full of cheering resolution unshaded by a suspicion of reproach, words which should have come like wine to the weary. The next day, July 3, he sent a dispatch which even McClellan, in his formal report, described as "kind:" "I am satisfied that yourself, officers, and men have done the best you could. All accounts say better fighting was never done. Ten thousand thanks for it." But when it came to judgment and action the President could not alleviate duty with kindness. To get information uncolored by passage through the minds of others, he went down to Harrison's Landing on July 7, observed all that he could see, and talked matters over. Prior to this visit it is supposed that he had leaned towards McClellan's views, and had inclined to renew the advance. Nor is it clearly apparent that he learned anything during this trip which induced him to change his mind. Rather it seems probable that he maintained his original opinion until General Halleck had declared against it, and that then he yielded to General Halleck as he had before yielded to General McClellan, though certainly with much less reluctance. At the same time the question was not considered wholly by itself, but was almost necessarily complicated with the question of deposing McClellan from the command. For the inconsistency of discrediting McClellan's military judgment and retaining him at the head of the army was obvious.

Thus at last it came about that McClellan's plan lost its only remaining friend, and on August 3 came the definite order for the removal of the army across the Peninsula to Acquia Creek. The campaign against Richmond was abandoned. McClellan could not express his indignation at a policy "almost fatal to our cause;" but his strenuous remonstrances had no effect; his influence had passed forever. The movement of the army was successfully completed, the rear guard arriving at Yorktown on August 20. Thus the first great Peninsula campaign came to its end in disappointment and almost in disaster, amid heart-burnings and criminations. It was, says General Webb, "a lamentable failure,—nothing less." There was little hope for the future unless some master hand could control the discordant officials who filled the land with the din of their quarreling. The burden lay upon the President. Fortunately his good sense, his even judgment, his unexcitable temperament had saved him from the appearance or the reality of partisanship and from any entangling or compromising personal commitments.

In many ways and for many reasons, this story of the Peninsula has been both difficult and painful to write. To reach the truth and sound conclusions in the many quarrels which it has provoked is never easy, and upon some points seems impossible; and neither the truth nor the conclusions are often agreeable. Opinion and sympathy have gradually but surely tended in condemnation of McClellan and in favor of Lincoln. The evidence is conclusive that McClellan was vain, disrespectful, and hopelessly blind to those non-military but very serious considerations which should have been allowed to modify the purely scientific strategy of the campaign. Also, though his military training was excellent, it was his misfortune to be placed amid exigencies for which neither his moral nor his mental qualities were adapted. Lincoln, on the other hand, displayed traits of character not only in themselves rare and admirable, but so fitted to the requirements of the times that many persons have been tempted to conceive him to have been divinely led. But against this view, though without derogating from the merits which induce it, is to be set the fact that he made mistakes hardly consistent with the theory of inspiration by Omniscience. He interfered in military matters; and, being absolutely ignorant of military science, while the problems before him were many and extremely perplexing, he blundered, and on at least one occasion blundered very badly. After he has been given the benefit of all the doubt which can be suggested concerning the questions which he disposed of, the preponderance of expert authority shows a residuum of substantial certainty against him. It is true that many civilian writers have given their judgments in favor of the President's strategy, with a tranquil assurance at least equal to that shown by the military critics. But it seems hardly reasonable to suppose that Mr. Lincoln became by mere instinct, and instantly, a master in the complex science of war, and it is also highly improbable that in the military criticism of this especial campaign, the civilians are generally right and the military men are generally wrong. On the whole it is pleasanter as well as more intelligent to throw out this foolish notion of miraculous knowledge suddenly illuminating Mr. Lincoln with a thorough mastery of the art of war. It is better not to believe that he became at once endowed with acquirements which he had never had an opportunity to attain, and rather to be content with holding him as a simple human being like the rest of us, and so to credit our common humanity with the inspiring excellence of the moral qualities displayed by him in those months of indescribable trial.

How much of expectation had been staked upon that army of the Potomac! All the Northern people for nearly a year kept their eyes fastened with aching intensity upon it; good fortunes which befell elsewhere hardly interrupted for a moment the absorption in it. The feeling was well illustrated by the committee of Congress, which said that in the history of this army was to be found all that was necessary for framing a report on the Conduct of the War; and truly added that this army had been "the object of special care to every department of the government." It occurred to many who heard this language, that matters would have gone better with the army if the political and civil departments had been less lavish of care and attention. None the less the fact remained that the interest and anticipation of the whole loyal part of the nation were concentrated in the Virginia campaign. Correspondingly cruel was the disappointment at its ultimate miscarriage. Probably, as a single trial, it was the most severe that Mr. Lincoln ever suffered. Hope then went through the painful process of being pruned by failure, and it was never tortured by another equal mutilation. Moreover, the vastness of the task, the awful cost of success, were now, for the first time, appreciated. The responsibility of a ruler under so appalling a destiny now descended with a weight that could never become greater upon the shoulders of that lonely man in the White House. A solitary man, indeed, he was, in a solitude impressive and painful to contemplate. Having none of those unofficial counselors, those favorites, those privy confidants and friends, from whom men in chief authority are so apt to seek relief, Mr. Lincoln secretively held his most important thoughts in his own mind, wrought out his conclusions by the toil of his own brain, carried his entire burden wholly upon his own shoulders, and in every part and way met the full responsibility of his office in and by himself alone. It does not appear that he ever sought to be sustained or comforted or encouraged amid disaster, that he ever endeavored to shift upon others even the most trifling fragment of the load which rested upon himself; and certainly he never desired that any one should ever be a sharer in any ill repute attendant upon a real or supposed mistake. Silent as to matters of deep import, self-sustained, facing alone all grave duties, solving alone all difficult problems, and enduring alone all consequences, he appears a man so isolated from his fellow men amid such tests and trials, that one is filled with a sense of awe, almost beyond sympathy, in the contemplation.

> [4] This language was too vague to make known to us now
> what Sumner's demand was; for one of the questions bitterly
> in dispute soon became: what forces were properly to be
> regarded as available "for the defense of the city."

[5] McClellan says that he offered to General Hitchcock, "who at that time held staff relations with his excellency, the President, and the secretary of war," to submit a list of troops, to be left for the defense of Washington, with their positions; but Hitchcock replied that McClellan's judgment was sufficient in the matter. McClellan's *Report*, 683. VOL. II.

[6] By letter to the adjutant-general, wherein he requested the transmission of the information to the secretary of war. *Report of Comm. on Conduct of the War*, ii. pt. i. 13. The addition in the *Report* is erroneous, being given as 54,456 instead of 55,456.

[7] See Comte de Paris, *Civil War in America*, i. 626, 627.

[8] See discussion by Swinton, *Army of Potomac*, 108 *et seq*.

[9] Perhaps he was not justified in counting upon it with such apparent assurance as he had done. Webb, *The Peninsula*, 37-42.

[10] General Webb says that this question is "the leading point of dispute in the campaign and may never be satisfactorily set at rest." But he also says: "To allow the general to remain in command, and then cut off the very arm with which he was about to strike, we hold to have been inexcusable and unmilitary to the last degree." Swinton condemns the withholding McDowell (*Army of the Potomac*, 104), adding, with fine magnanimity, that it is not necessary to impute any "really unworthy motive" to Mr. Lincoln!

[11] It seems to me that military opinion, so far as I can get at it, inclines to hold that the government, having let McClellan go to the Peninsula with the expectation of McDowell's corps, ought to have sent it to him, and not to have repaired its own oversight at his cost. But this does not fully meet the position that, oversight or no oversight, Peninsula-success or Peninsula-defeat, blame here or blame there, when the President had reason to doubt the safety of the capital, he was resolved, and rightly resolved, to put that safety beyond *possibility of question*, by any means or at any cost. The truth is that to the end of time one man will think one

way, and another man will think another way, concerning this unendable dispute.

[12] General Wool was in command at Fortress Monroe. It had been originally arranged that General McClellan should draw 10,000 men from him. But this was afterward countermanded. The paragraph in the President's letter has reference to this.

[13] A slight obstruction by a battery at Drury's Bluff must have been abandoned instantly upon the approach of a land force.

[14] Whose command had been added to McDowell's.

[15] Colonel Franklin Haven, who was on General McDowell's staff at the time, is my authority for this statement. He well remembers the reason given by Mr. Lincoln, and the extreme annoyance which the general and his officers felt at the delay.

[16] "The expediency of the junction of this [McD.'s] large corps with the principal army was manifest," says General Johnston. *Narr. 131.*

[17] Jackson used to say: "Mystery, mystery, is the secret of success."

[18] The Comte de Paris is very severe, even to sarcasm, in his comments on the President's orders to Banks (*Civil War in America*, ii. 35, 36, and see 44); and Swinton, referring to the disposition of the armies, which was well known to have been made by Mr. Lincoln's personal orders, says: "One hardly wishes to inquire by whose crude and fatuous inspiration these things were done." *Army of Potomac*, 123. Later critics have not repeated such strong language, but have not taken different views of the facts.

[19] Observe the tone of his two dispatches of May 25 to McClellan. McClellan's *Report*, 100, 101.

[20] The Comte de Paris prefers to call it a "chimerical project." *Civil War in America*, ii. 45. Swinton speaks of "the skill of the Confederates and the folly of those who controlled the operations of the Union armies." *Army of Potomac*, 122.

[21] Yet, if Fremont had not blundered, the result might have been different. Comte de Paris, *Civil War in America*, ii. 47.

[22] The Third, under Heintzelman, and the Fourth, under Keyes.

[23] Even his admirer, Swinton, says that any possible course would have been better than inaction. *Army of Potomac*, 140, 141.

[24] *The Peninsula*, 188. Swinton seems to regard it in the same light. *Army of Potomac*, 147.

[25] Gaines's Mill, contested with superb courage and constancy by the Fifth Corps, under Porter, against very heavy odds.

[26] McClellan's *Report*, 131, 132. See, also, his own comments on this extraordinary dispatch; *Own Story*, 452. He anticipated, not without reason, that he would be promptly removed. The Comte de Paris says that the two closing sentences were suppressed by the War Department, when the documents had to be laid before the Committee on the Conduct of the War. *Civil War in America*, ii. 112. Another dispatch, hardly less disrespectful, was sent on June 25. See McClellan's *Report*, 121.

[27] For a vivid description of the condition to which heat, marching, fighting, and the unwholesome climate had reduced the men, see statement of Comte de Paris, an eyewitness. *Civil War in America*, ii. 130.

# CHAPTER III
# THE THIRD AND CLOSING ACT OF
# THE MCCLELLAN DRAMA

As it seems probable that Mr. Lincoln did not conclusively determine against the plan of McClellan for renewing the advance upon Richmond by way of Petersburg, until after General Halleck had thus decided, so it is certain that afterward he allowed to Halleck a control almost wholly free from interference on his own part. Did he, perchance, feel that a lesson had been taught him, and did he think that those critics had not been wholly wrong who had said that he had intermeddled ignorantly and hurtfully in military matters? Be this as it might, it was in accordance with the national character to turn the back sharply upon failure and disappointment, and to make a wholly fresh start; and it was in accordance with Lincoln's character to fall in with the popular feeling. Yet if a fresh start was intrinsically advisable, or if it was made necessary by circumstances, it was made in unfortunate company. One does not think without chagrin that Grant, Sherman, Sheridan lurked undiscovered among the officers at the West, while Halleck and Pope were pulled forth to the light and set in the high places. Halleck was hopelessly incompetent, and Pope was fit only for subordinate command; and by any valuation which could reasonably be put upon McClellan, it was absurd to turn him out in order to bring either of these men in. But it was the experimental period. No man's qualities could be known except by testing them; and these two men came before Lincoln with records sufficiently good to entitle them to trial. The successes at the West had naturally produced good opinions of the officers who had achieved them, and among these officers John Pope had been as conspicuous as any other. For this reason he was now, towards the close of June, 1862, selected to command the "Army of Virginia," formed by uniting the corps of Fremont, McDowell, and Banks. [28] Fremont resigned, in a pet at having an officer who was his junior in the service placed over his head; but he was no loss, since his impetuous temperament did not fit him for the duties of a corps commander. He was succeeded by General Sigel. The fusing of these independent commands, whose separate existence had been a wasteful and jeopardizing error, was an excellent measure.

General Pope remained in Washington a few weeks, in constant consultation with the administration. How he impressed Lincoln one would gladly know, but cannot. He had unlimited self-confidence, and he gave it to be understood at once that he was a fighting man; but it showed an astounding lack of tact upon his part that, in notifying the troops of this, his distinguishing characteristic, he also intimated that it would behoove them to turn over a new leaf now that he had come all the way from the West in order to teach Eastern men how to win victories! The manifesto which he issued has become famous by its folly; it was arrogant, bombastic, little short of insulting to the soldiers of his command, and laid down principles contrary to the established rules of war. Yet it had good qualities, too; for it was designed to be stimulating; it certainly meant fighting; and fortunately, though Pope was not a great general, he was by no means devoid of military knowledge and instincts, and he would not really have committed quite such blunders as he marked out for himself in his rhetorical enthusiasm. On the whole, however, the manifesto did harm; neither officers nor soldiers were inclined to receive kindly a man who came presumably on trial with the purpose of replacing McClellan, whom they loved with deep loyalty; therefore they ridiculed part of his address and took offense at the rest of it. Mr. Lincoln could hardly have been encouraged; but he gave no sign.

On July 29 Pope left Washington and joined his army, near Culpepper. He had not quite 45,000 men, and was watched by Jackson, who lay near Gordonsville with a scant half of that number. On August 9 Banks was pushed forward to Cedar Mountain, where he encountered Jackson and attacked him. In "a hard-fought battle, fierce, obstinate, sanguinary," the Federals were worsted; and such consolation as the people got from the gallantry of the troops was more than offset by the fact, which became obvious so soon as the whole story was known, that our generals ought to have avoided the engagement and were outgeneraled both in the bringing it on and in the conducting it.

Greatly as Jackson was outnumbered by Pope, he could hope for no reinforcements from Lee so long as McClellan, at Harrison's Landing, threatened Richmond. But when gratifying indications showed the purpose to withdraw the Northern army from the Peninsula the Southern general ventured, August 13, to dispatch General Longstreet northward with a strong force. Soon afterward he himself followed and took command. Then for two or three days ensued a sharp matching of wits betwixt the two generals. By one of those audacious plans which Lee could dare to make when he had such a lieutenant as Jackson to carry it out, Jackson was sent upon a rapid march by the northward, around the army of Pope, to cut its communications. He did it brilliantly; but in doing it he necessarily offered to Pope such an opportunity for fighting the Southern forces in detail as is rarely given by a good general to an adversary whom he fears. Pope would fain have availed himself of the chance, and in the effort to do so he hurried his troops hither and thither, mingled wise moves with foolish ones, confused his subordinates, fatigued his men, and finally accomplished nothing. Jackson retired safely from his dangerous position, rejoined the rest of the Southern army, and then the united force had as its immediate purpose to fight Pope before he could receive reinforcements from McClellan's army, now rapidly coming forward by way of Washington. *E converso*, Pope's course should have been to retire a day's march across Bull Run and await the additional troops who could at once join him there. Unfortunately, however, he still felt the sting of the ridicule which his ill-starred manifesto had called forth, and was further irritated by the unsatisfactory record of the past few days, and therefore was in no temper to fall back. So he did not, but stayed and fought what is known as the second battle of Bull Run. In the conflict his worn-out men showed such constancy that the slaughter on both sides was great. Again, however, the bravery of the rank and file was the only feature which the country could contemplate without indignation. The army was beaten; and retired during the evening of August 30 to a safe position at Centreville, whither it should have been taken without loss two days earlier. [29] Thus was fulfilled, with only a trifling inaccuracy in point of time, the prediction made by McClellan on August 10, that "Pope will be badly thrashed within ten days." [30]

In all this manoeuvring and fighting the commanding general had shown some capacity, but very much less than was indispensable in a commander who had to meet the generals of the South. Forthwith, also, there broke out a series of demoralizing quarrels among the principal officers as to what orders had been given and received, and whether or not they had been understood or misunderstood, obeyed or disobeyed. Also the enemies of General McClellan tried to lay upon him the whole responsibility for the disaster, on the ground that he had been dilatory, first, in moving his army from Harrison's Landing, and afterward, in sending his troops forward to join Pope; whereas, they said, if he had acted promptly, the Northern army would have been too strong to have been defeated, regardless of any incompetence in the handling of it. Concerning the former charge, it may be said that dispatches had flown to and fro between Halleck and McClellan like bullets between implacable duelists; Halleck ordered the army to be transported, and McClellan retorted that he was given no transports; it is a dispute which cannot be discussed here. Concerning the other charge, it was also true that the same two generals had been for some days exchanging telegrams, but had been entirely unable to understand each other. Whose fault it was cannot easily be determined. The English language was giving our generals almost as much trouble as were the Southerners at this time; so that in a few short weeks material for endless discussion was furnished by the orders, telegrams, and replies which were bandied between Pope and Porter, McClellan and Halleck. A large part of the history of the period consists of the critical analysis and construing of these documents. What did each in fact mean? What did the writer intend it to mean? What did the recipient understand it to 'mean? Did the writer make his meaning sufficiently clear? Was the recipient justified in his interpretation? Historians have discussed these problems as theologians have discussed puzzling texts of the New Testament, with not less acerbity and with no more conclusive results. Unquestionably the capacity to write two or three dozen consecutive words so as to constitute a plain, straightforward sentence would have been for the moment a valuable adjunct to military learning.

The news of the defeat brought dismay, but not quite a panic, to the authorities in Washington. In fact, there was no immediate danger for the capital. The army from the Peninsula was by this time distributed at various points in the immediate neighborhood; and a force could be promptly brought together which would so outnumber the Confederate army as to be invincible. Yet the situation demanded immediate and vigorous action. Some hand must seize the helm at once, and Pope's hand would not do; so much at least was entirely certain. He had been given his own way, without interference on the part of President or secretary, and he had been beaten; he was discredited before the country and the army; nothing useful could now be done with him. Halleck was utterly demoralized, and was actually reduced to telegraphing to McClellan: "I beg of you to assist me, in this crisis, with your ability and experience." It was the moment for a master to take control, and the President met the occasion. There was only one thing to be done, and circumstances were such that not only must that thing be done by him, but also it must be done by him in direct opposition to the strenuous insistence of all his official and most of his self-constituted advisers. It was necessary to reinstate McClellan.

It was a little humiliating to be driven to this step. McClellan had lately been kept at Alexandria with no duty save daily to disintegrate his own army by sending off to Washington and to the camp of his own probable successor division after division of the troops whom he had so long commanded. Greatly mortified, he had begged at least to be "permitted to go to the scene of battle." But he was ignored, as if he were no longer of any consequence whatsoever. In plain truth it was made perfectly obvious to him and to all the world that if General Pope could win a victory the administration had done with General McClellan. Mr. Lincoln described the process as a "snubbing." Naturally those who were known to be the chief promoters of this "snubbing," and to have been highly gratified by it, now looked ruefully on the evident necessity of suddenly cutting it short, and requesting the snubbed individual to assume the role of their rescuer. McClellan's more prominent enemies could not and would not agree to this. Three members of the cabinet even went so far as formally to put in writing their protest against restoring him to the command of any army at all; while Stanton actually tried to frighten the President by a petty threat of personal consequences. But this was foolish. The crisis was of the kind which induced Mr. Lincoln to exercise power, decisively. On this occasion his impersonal, unimpassioned temperament left his judgment free to work with evenness and clearness amid the whirl of momentous events and the clash of angry tongues. No one could say that he had been a partisan either for or against McClellan, and his wise reticence in the past gave him in the present the privilege of untrammeled action. So he settled the matter at once by ordering that McClellan should have command within the defenses of Washington.

By this act the President gave extreme offense to the numerous and strenuous band with whom hatred of the Democratic general had become a sort of religion; and upon this occasion even Messrs. Nicolay and Hay seem more inclined to apologize for their idol than to defend him. In point of fact, nothing can be more misplaced than either apology or defense, except criticism. Mr. Lincoln could have done no wiser thing. He was simply setting in charge of the immediate business the man who could do that especial business best. It was not a question of a battle or a campaign, neither of which was for the moment imminent; but it was a question of reorganizing masses of disorganized troops and getting them into shape for battles and campaigns in the future. Only the intensity of hatred could make any man blind to McClellan's capacity for such work; and what he might be for other work was a matter of no consequence just now. Lincoln simply applied to the instant need the most effective help, without looking far afield to study remote consequences. Two remarks, said to have been made by him at this time, indicate his accurate appreciation of the occasion and the man: "There is no one in the army who can man these fortifications and lick these troops of ours into shape half so well as he can." "We must use the tools we have; if he cannot fight himself, he excels in making others ready to fight."

On September 1 Halleck verbally instructed McClellan to take command of the defenses of Washington, defining this to mean strictly "the works and their garrisons." McClellan says that later on the same day he had an interview with the President, in which the President said that he had "always been a friend" of the general, and asked as a favor that the general would request his personal friends among the principal officers of the army to give to General Pope a more sincere and hearty support than they were supposed to be actually rendering. [31] On the morning of September 2, McClellan says, "The President informed me that Colonel Keelton had returned from the front; that our affairs were in a bad condition; that the army was in full retreat upon the defenses of Washington, the roads filled with stragglers, etc. He instructed me to take steps at once to stop and collect the stragglers; place the works in a proper state of defense, and go out to meet and take command of the army, when it approached the vicinity of the works, then to place the troops in the best position, —committing everything to my hands." By this evidence, Mr. Lincoln intrusted the fate of the country and with it his own reputation absolutely to the keeping of McClellan.

McClellan was in his element in fusing into unity the disjointed fragments of armies which lay about in Virginia like scattered ruins. His bitterest tractors have never denied him the gift of organization, and admit that he did excellent service just now for a few days. But circumstances soon extended his field of action, and gave detraction fresh opportunities. General Lee, in a bold and enterprising mood, perhaps attributable to the encouraging inefficiency of his Northern opponents, moved up the banks of the Potomac and threatened an irruption into Maryland and even Pennsylvania. It was absolutely necessary to watch and, at the right moment, to fight him. For this purpose McClellan was ordered to move along the north bank of the river, but under strict injunctions at first to go slowly and cautiously and not to uncover Washington. For General Halleck had not fully recovered his nerve, and was still much disquieted, especially concerning the capital. Thus the armies drew slowly near each other, McClellan creeping forward, as he had been bidden, while Lee, with his usual energy, seemed able to do with a thousand men more than any Northern general could do with thrice as many, and ran with exasperating impunity those audacious risks which, where they cannot be attributed to ignorance on the part of a commander, indicate contempt for his opponent. This feeling, if he had it, must have received agreeable corroboration from the clumsy way in which the Federals just at this time lost Harper's Ferry, with General Miles's garrison. The Southern troops, who had been detailed against it, rapidly rejoined General Lee's army; and again the people saw that the South had outmarched and outgeneraled the North.

With all his troops together, Lee was now ready to fight at the convenience or the pleasure of McClellan, who seemed chivalrously to have deferred his attack until his opponent should be prepared for it! The armies were in presence of each other near where the Antietam empties into the Potomac, and here, September 17, the bloody conflict took place.

The battle of Antietam has usually been called a Northern victory. Both the right and the left wings of the Northern army succeeded in seizing advanced positions and in holding them at the end of the fight; and Lee retreated to the southward, though it is true that before doing so he lingered a day and gave to his enemy a chance, which was not used, to renew the battle. His position was obviously untenable in the face of an outnumbering host. But though upon the strength of these facts a victory could be claimed with logical propriety, yet the President and the country were, and had a right to be, indignant at the very unsatisfactory proportion of the result to the means. Shortly before the battle McClellan's troops, upon the return to them of the commander whom they idolized, had given him a soul-stirring reception, proving the spirit and confidence with which they would fight under his orders; and they went into the fight in the best possible temper and condition. On the day of the battle the Northern troops outnumbered the Southerners by nearly two to one; in fact, the Southern generals, in their reports, insisted that they had been simply overwhelmed by enormous odds against which it was a marvel of gallantry for their men to stand at all. The plain truth was that in the first place, by backwardness in bringing on the battle, McClellan had left Lee to effect a concentration of forces which ought never to have been permitted. Next, the battle itself had not been especially well handled, though perhaps this was due rather to the lack of his personal attention during its progress than to errors in his plan. Finally, his failure, with so large an army, of which a part at least was entirely fresh, to pursue and perhaps even to destroy the reduced and worn-out Confederate force seemed inexplicable and was inexcusable.

The South could never be conquered in this way. It had happened, on September 12, that President Lincoln heard news apparently indicating the withdrawal of Lee across the Potomac. He had at once sent it forward to McClellan, adding: "Do not let him get off without being hurt." Three days later, he telegraphed: "Destroy the rebel army if possible." But McClellan had been too self-restrained in his obedience. He had, indeed, hurt Lee, but he had been very careful not to hurt him too much; and as for destroying the rebel army, he seemed unwilling to enter so lightly on so stupendous an enterprise. The administration and the country expected, and perfectly fairly expected, to see a hot pursuit of General Lee. They were disappointed; they saw no such thing, but only saw McClellan holding his army as quiescent as if there was nothing more to be done, and declaring that it was in no condition to move!

It was intolerably provoking, unintelligible, and ridiculous that a ragged, ill-shod, overworked, under-fed, and beaten body of Southerners should be able to retreat faster than a great, fresh, well-fed, well-equipped, and victorious body of Northerners could follow. Jackson said that the Northern armies were, kept in too good condition; and declared that he could whip any army which marched with herds of cattle behind it. But the North preferred, and justly, to attribute the inefficiency of their troops to the unfortunate temperament of the commander. Mr. Lincoln looked at the unsatisfactory spectacle and held his hand as long as he could, dreading perhaps again to seem too forward in assuming control of military affairs. Patience, however, could not endure forever, nor common sense be always subservient to technical science. Accordingly, on October 6, he ordered McClellan to cross the Potomac, and either to "give battle to the enemy, or to drive him south." McClellan paid no attention to the order. Four days later the Confederate general, Stuart, with 2000 cavalry and a battery, crossed into Maryland and made a tour around the Northern army, with the same insolent success which had attended his like enterprise on the Peninsula. On October 13 the President wrote to McClellan a letter, so admirable both in temper and in the soundness of its suggestions that it should be given entire: —

"MY DEAR SIR, — You remember my speaking to you of what I called your over-cautiousness. Are you not over-cautious when you assume that you cannot do what the enemy is constantly doing? Should you not claim to be at least his equal in prowess, and act upon the claim?

"As I understand, you telegraphed General Halleck that you cannot subsist your army at Winchester, unless the railroad from Harper's Ferry to that point be put in working order. But the enemy does now subsist his army at Winchester at a distance nearly twice as great from railroad transportation as you would have to do without the railroad last named. He now wagons from Culpepper Court House, which is just about twice as far as you would have to do from Harper's Ferry. He is certainly not more than half as well provided with wagons as you are. I certainly should be pleased for you to have the advantage of the railroad from Harper's Ferry to Winchester; but it wastes all the remainder of autumn to give it to you, and, in fact, ignores the question of *time*, which cannot and must not be ignored.

"Again, one of the standard maxims of war, as you know, is 'to operate upon the enemy's communications as much as possible without exposing your own.' You seem to act as if this applies *against* you, but cannot apply in your *favor*. Change positions with the enemy, and think you not he would break your communication with Richmond within the next twenty-four hours? You dread his going into Pennsylvania. But if he does so in full force, he gives up his communication to you absolutely, and you have nothing to do but to follow and ruin him; if he does so with less than full force, fall upon and beat what is left behind, all the easier.

"Exclusive of the water line, you are now nearer Richmond than the enemy is, by the route that you *can,* and he *must* take. Why can you not reach there before him, unless you admit that he is more than your equal on a march? His route is the arc of a circle, while yours is the chord. The roads are as good on yours as on his.

"You know I desired, but did not order you, to cross the Potomac below, instead of above, the Shenandoah and Blue Ridge. The idea was that this would at once menace the enemy's communications, which I would seize, if he would permit. If he should move northward, I would follow him closely, holding his communications. If he should prevent our seizing his communications, and move towards Richmond, I would press closely to him, fight him if a favorable opportunity should present, and at least try to beat him to Richmond on the inside track. I say, try; if we never try, we shall never succeed. If he makes a stand at Winchester, moving neither north nor south, I would fight him there, on the idea that if we cannot beat him when he bears the wastage of coming to us, we never can when we bear the wastage of going to him. This proposition is a simple truth, and is too important to be lost sight of for a moment. In coming to us, he tenders us an advantage which we should not waive. We should not so operate as to merely drive him away. As we must beat him somewhere, or fail finally, we can do it, if at all, easier near to us than far away. If we cannot beat the enemy where he now is, we never can, he again being within the intrenchments of Richmond.

"Recurring to the idea of going to Richmond on the inside track, the facility for supplying from the side away from the enemy is remarkable, as it were by the different spokes of a wheel extending from the hub towards the rim; and this, whether you moved directly by the chord or on the inside arc, hugging the Blue Ridge more closely. The chord line, as you see, carries you by Aldie, Haymarket, and Fredericksburg, and you see how turnpikes, railroads, and finally the Potomac, by Acquia Creek, meet you at all points from Washington. The same, only the lines lengthened a little, if you press closer to the Blue Ridge part of the way. The Gaps through the Blue Ridge, I understand to be about the following distances from Harper's Ferry, to wit: Vestala, five miles; Gregory's, thirteen; Snicker's, eighteen; Ashby's, twenty-eight; Manassas, thirty-eight; Chester, forty-five; and Thornton's, fifty-three. I should think it preferable to take the route nearest the enemy, disabling him to make an important move without your knowledge, and compelling him to keep his forces together for dread of you. The Gaps would enable you to attack if you should wish. For a great part of the way you would be practically between the enemy and both Washington and Richmond, enabling us to spare you the greatest number of troops from here. When, at length, running for Richmond ahead of him enables him to move this way, if he does so, turn and attack him in rear. But I think he should be engaged long before such point is reached. It is all easy if our troops march as well as the enemy, and it is unmanly to say they cannot do it. This letter is in no sense an order."

A general who failed to respond to such a spur as this was not the man for offensive warfare; and McClellan did not respond. Movement was as odious to him now as it ever had been, and by talking about shoes and overcoats, and by other dilatory pleas, he extended his delay until the close of the month. It was actually the second day of November before his army crossed the Potomac. Another winter of inaction seemed about to begin. It was simply unendurable. Though it was true that he had reorganized the army with splendid energy and skill, and had shown to the Northern soldiers in Virginia the strange and cheerful spectacle of the backs of General Lee's soldiers, yet it became a settled fact that he must give place to some new man. He and Pope were to be succeeded by a third experiment. Therefore, on November 5, 1862, the President ordered General McClellan to turn over the command of the army to General Burnside; and on November 7 this was done.

This action, taken just at this time, called forth a much more severe criticism than would have attended it if the removal had been made simultaneously with the withdrawal from the Peninsula. By what motive was Mr. Lincoln influenced? Not very often is the most eager search rewarded by the sure discovery of his opinions about persons. From what we know that he did, we try to infer why he did it, and we gropingly endeavor to apportion the several measures of influence between those motives which we choose to put by our conjecture into his mind; and after our toilful scrutiny is over we remain painfully conscious of the greatness of the chance that we have scarcely even approached the truth. Neither diary nor letters guide us; naught save reports of occasional pithy, pointed, pregnant remarks, evidence the most dubious, liable to be colored by the medium of the predilections of the hearer, and to be reshaped and misshaped by time, and by attrition in passing through many mouths. The President was often in a chatting mood, and then seemed not remote from his companion. Yet while this was the visible manifestation on the surface, he was the most reticent of men as to grave questions, and no confidant often heard his inmost thoughts. Especially it would be difficult to name an instance in which he told one man what he thought of another; a trifling criticism concerning some single trait was the utmost that he ever allowed to escape him; a full and careful estimate, never.

Such reflections come with peculiar force at this period in his career. What would not one give for his estimate of McClellan! It would be worth the whole great collection of characters sketched by innumerable friends and enemies for that much-discussed general. While others think that they know accurately the measure of McClellan's real value and usefulness, Lincoln really knew these things; but he never told his knowledge. We only see that he sustained McClellan for a long while in the face of vehement aspersions; yet that he never fully subjected his own convictions to the educational lectures of the general, and that he seemed at last willing to see him laid aside; then immediately in a crisis restored him to authority in spite of all opposition; and shortly afterward, as if utterly weary of him, definitively displaced him. Still, all these facts do not show what Lincoln thought of McClellan. Many motives besides his opinion of the man may have influenced him. The pressure of political opinion and of public feeling was very great, and might have turned him far aside from the course he would have pursued if it could have been neglected. Also other considerations have been suggested as likely to have weighed with him, —that McClellan could do with the army what no other man could do, because of the intense devotion of both officers and men to him; and that an indignity offered to McClellan might swell the dissatisfaction of the Northern Democracy to a point at which it would seriously embarrass the administration. These things may have counteracted, or may have corroborated, Mr. Lincoln's views concerning the man himself. He was an extraordinary judge of men in their relationship to affairs; moreover, of all the men of note of that time he alone was wholly dispassionate and non-partisan. Opinions tinctured with prejudices are countless; it is disappointing that the one opinion that was free from prejudice is unknown. [32]

[28] The consolidation, and the assignment of Pope to the command, bore date June 26, 1862.

[29] This campaign of General Pope has been the topic of very bitter controversy and crimination. In my brief account I have eschewed the view of Messrs. Nicolay and Hay, who seem to me if I may say it, to have written with the single-minded purpose of throwing everybody's blunders into the scale against McClellan, and I have adopted the view of Mr. John C. Ropes in his volume on *The Army under Pope*, in

the Campaigns of the Civil War Series. In his writing it is impossible to detect personal prejudice, for or against any one; and his account is so clear and convincing that it must be accepted, whether one likes his conclusions or not.

[30] *Own Story*, 466.

[31] Pope retained for a few days command of the army in camp outside the defenses

[32] McClure says: "I saw Lincoln many times during the campaign of 1864, when McClellan was his competitor for the presidency. I never heard him speak of McClellan in any other than terms of the highest personal respect and kindness." *Lincoln and Men of War-Times*, 207.

# CHAPTER IV
# THE AUTUMN ELECTIONS OF 1862, AND
# THE PROCLAMATION OF EMANCIPATION

The chapter which has been written on "Emancipation and Politics" shows that while loyalty to the Union operated as a bond to hold together the people of the North, slavery entered as a wedge to force them asunder. It was not long before the wedge proved a more powerful force than the bond, for the wedge was driven home by human nature; and it was inevitable that the men of conservative temperament and the men of progressive temperament should erelong be easily restored to their instinctive antagonism. Of those who had been stigmatized as "Northern men with Southern principles," many soon found their Southern proclivities reviving. These men, christened "Copperheads," became more odious to loyal Northerners than were the avowed Secessionists. In return for their venomous nickname and the contempt and hatred with which they were treated, they themselves grew steadily more rancorous, more extreme in their feelings. They denounced and opposed every measure of the government, harangued vehemently against the war and against all that was done to prosecute it, reviled with scurrilous and passionate abuse every prominent Republican, filled the air with disheartening forecasts of defeat, ruin, and woe, and triumphed whenever the miserable prophecies seemed in the way of fulfillment. General Grant truly described them as auxiliaries to the Confederate army, and said that the North would have been much better off with a hundred thousand of these men in the Southern ranks, and the rest of their kind at home thoroughly subdued, as the Unionists were at the South, than was the case as the struggle was actually conducted. In time the administration found itself forced, though reluctantly, to arrest and imprison many of the ringleaders in this Northern disaffection. Yet all the while the Copperheads resolutely maintained their affiliations with the Democratic party, and though they brought upon it much discredit which it did not deserve, yet they could not easily be ejected from it. Differences of opinion shaded into each other so gradually that to establish a line of division was difficult.

Impinging upon Copperheadism stood the much more numerous body of those who persistently asserted their patriotism, but with equal persistence criticised severely all the measures of the government. These men belonged to that well-known class which is happily described as being "for the law, but ag'in the enforcement of it." They were for the Union, but against saving it. They kept up a disapproving headshaking over pretty much everything that the President did. With much grandiloquent argument, in the stately, old-school style, they bemoaned the breaches which they charged him with making in the Constitution. They also hotly assumed the role of champions of General McClellan, and bewailed the imbecility of an administration which thwarted and deposed him. Protesting the purest and highest patriotism, they were more evasive than the outspoken Copperheads, and as their disaffection was less conspicuous and offensive, so also it was more insidious and almost equally hurtful. They constituted the true and proper body of Democracy.

In a fellowship, which really ought not to have existed, with these obstructionists, was the powerful and respectable body of war Democrats. These men maintained a stubborn loyalty to the old party, but prided themselves upon being as hearty and thorough-going war-men as any among the Republicans. A large proportion of the most distinguished generals, of the best regimental officers, of the most faithful soldiers in the field, were of this political faith. The only criticism that Republicans could reasonably pass upon them was, that they did not, in a political way, strengthen the hands of the government, that they would not uphold its authority by swelling its majorities, nor aid its prestige by giving it their good words.

Over against this Democracy, with its two very discordant wings, was arrayed the Republican party, which also was disturbed by the ill-will of those who should have been its allies; for while the moderate Abolitionists generally sustained the President, though only imperfectly satisfied with him, the extreme Abolitionists refused to be so reasonable. They were a very provoking body of pure moralists. They worried the President, condemned his policy, divided the counsels of the government, and introduced injurious personal enmities and partisanship with reckless disregard of probable consequences. To a considerable extent they had the same practical effect as if they had been avowed opponents of the Republican President. They wished immediately to place the war upon the footing of a crusade for the abolition of slavery. Among them were old-time Abolitionists, with whom this purpose was a religion, men who had hoped to see Seward the Republican President, and who said that Lincoln's friends in the nominating convention had represented a "superficial and only half-hearted Republicanism." Beside these men, though actuated by very different and much less honorable motives, stood many recruits, some even from the Democracy, who were so vindictive against the South that they desired to inflict abolition as a punishment.

All these critics and dissatisfied persons soon began to speak with severity, and sometimes with contempt, against the President. He had said that the war was for the Union; but they scornfully retorted that this was to reduce it to "a mere sectional strife for ascendency;" that "a Union, with slavery spared and reinstated, would not be worth the cost of saving it." It was true that to save the Union, without also removing the cause of disunion, might not be worth a very great price; yet both Union and abolition were in serious danger of being thrown away forever by these impetuous men who desired to pluck the fruit before it was ripe, or rather declared it to be ripe because they so wanted to pluck it.

It is not, here and now, a question of the merits and the usefulness of these men; undoubtedly their uncompromising ardor could not have been dispensed with in the great anti-slavery struggle; it was what the steam is to the engine, and if the motive power had been absent no one can say how long the United States might have lain dormant as a slave-country. But the question is of their present attitude and of its influence and effect in the immediate affairs of the government. Their demand was for an instant and sweeping proclamation of emancipation; and they were angry and denunciatory against the President because he would not give it to them. Of course, by their ceaseless assaults they hampered him and weakened his hands very seriously. It was as an exercise of the President's war-power that they demanded the proclamation; and the difficulty in the way of it was that Mr. Lincoln felt, and the great majority of Northern men were positive in the opinion, that such a proclamation at this time would not be an honest and genuine exercise of the war-power, that it would be only falsely and colorably so called, and that in real truth it would be a deliberate and arbitrary change of the war from a contest for Union to a contest for abolition. Mr. Lincoln could not *make* it a war measure merely by *calling* it so; it was no mere matter of political christening, but distinctly a very grave and substantial question of fact. It may be suspected that very many even of the Abolitionists themselves, had they spoken the innermost conviction of their minds, would have admitted that the character of the measure as a wise military transaction, pure and simple, was very dubious. It was certain that every one else in all the country which still was or ever had been the United States would regard it as an informal and misnamed but real change of base for the whole war. No preamble, no *Whereas*, in Mr. Lincoln's proclamation, reciting as a fact and a motive that which he would have known, and ninety-nine out of every hundred loyal men would have believed, not to be the true fact and motive, could make the rest of his proclamation lawful, or his act that of an honest ruler. Accordingly no pressure could drive him to the step; he preferred to endure, and long did endure, the abuse of the extreme Abolitionists, and all the mischief which their hostility could inflict upon his administration. Yet, in truth, there was not in the North an Abolitionist who thought worse of the institution of slavery than did the man who had repeatedly declared it to be "a moral, a social, and a political evil." Referring to these times, and the behavior of the Abolitionists, he afterward wrote: [33] —

"I am naturally anti-slavery. If slavery is not wrong, nothing is wrong. I cannot remember when I did not so think and feel, and yet I have never understood that the presidency conferred upon me an unrestricted right to act officially upon this judgment and feeling. It was in the oath I took that I would, to the best of my ability, preserve, protect, and defend the Constitution of the United States. I could not take the office without taking the oath. Nor was it my view that I might take an oath to get power, and break the oath in using the power. I understood, too, that in ordinary civil administration this oath even forbade me to practically indulge my primary abstract judgment on the moral question of slavery. I had publicly declared this many times, and in many ways. And I aver that, to this day, I have done no official act in mere deference to my abstract judgment and feeling on slavery. I did understand, however, that my oath to preserve the Constitution to the best of my ability imposed upon me the duty of preserving, by every indispensable means, that government,—that nation, of which that Constitution was the organic law. Was it possible to lose the nation and yet preserve the Constitution? By general law, life and limb must be protected, yet often a limb must be amputated to save a life; but a life is never wisely given to save a limb. I felt that measures, otherwise unconstitutional, might become lawful by becoming indispensable to the preservation of the Constitution through the preservation of the nation. Right or wrong, I assumed this ground, and now avow it. I could not feel that, to the best of my ability, I had even tried to preserve the Constitution, if, to save slavery or any minor matter, I should permit the wreck of government, country, and Constitution all together. When, early in the war, General Fremont attempted military emancipation, I forbade it, because I did not then think it an indispensable necessity. When, a little later, General Cameron, then secretary of war, suggested the arming of the blacks, I objected because I did not yet think it an indispensable necessity. When, still later, General Hunter attempted military emancipation, I again forbade it, because I did not yet think the indispensable necessity had come."

None could deny that the North could abolish slavery in the South only by beating the South in the pending war. Therefore, by his duty as

President of the Union and by his wishes as an anti-slavery man, Mr. Lincoln was equally held to win this fight. Differing in opinion from the Abolitionists, he believed that to turn it, at an early stage, into a war for abolition rather than to leave it a war for the Union would be to destroy all hope of winning. The step would alienate great numbers at the North. The "American Society for promoting National Unity" had lately declared that emancipation "would be rebellion against Providence and destruction to the colored race in our land;" and it was certain that this feeling was still widely prevalent in the loyal States. In July, 1862, General McClellan said, warningly, that a declaration of radical views on the slavery question would rapidly disintegrate and destroy the Union armies. Finally, it seemed hardly doubtful that fatal defections would take place in the Border States, even if they should not formally go over to the Confederacy. No man saw the value of those Border States as Mr. Lincoln did. To save or to lose them was probably to save or lose the war; to lose them and the war was to establish a powerful slave empire. Where did abolition come in among these events? It was not there!

Painfully, therefore, untiringly, with all the skill and tact in his power, Mr. Lincoln struggled to hold those invaluable, crucial States. His "border-state policy" soon came to be discussed as the most interesting topic of which men could talk wherever they came together. Savage were the maledictions which emancipationists uttered against it, and the intensity of their feeling is indicated by the fact that, though that policy was carried out, and though the nation, in due time, gathered the ripe and perfect fruit of it both in the integrity of the country and the abolition of slavery, yet even at the present day many old opponents of President Lincoln, survivors of the Thirty-seventh Congress, remain unshaken in the faith that his famous policy was "a cruel and fatal mistake."

By the summer of 1862 the opinions and the action of Mr. Lincoln in all these matters had brought him into poor standing in the estimation of many Republicans. The great majority of the politicians of the party and sundry newspaper editors, that is to say, those persons who chiefly make the noise and the show before the world, were busily engaged in condemning his policy. The headquarters of this disaffection were in Washington. It had one convert even within the cabinet, where the secretary of the treasury was thoroughly infected with the notion that the President was fatally inefficient, laggard, and unequal to the occasion. The feeling was also especially rife in congressional circles. Mr. Julian, than whom there can be no better witness, says: "No one at a distance could have formed any adequate conception of the hostility of Republican members toward Mr. Lincoln at the final adjournment [the middle of July], while it was the belief of many that our last session of Congress had been held in Washington. Mr. Wade said the country was going to hell, and that the scenes witnessed in the French Revolution were nothing in comparison with what we should see here." If most of the people at the North had not had heads more cool and sensible than was the one which rested upon the shoulders of the ardent "Ben" Wade, the alarming prediction of that lively spokesman might have been fulfilled. Fortunately, however, as Mr. Julian admits, "the feeling in Congress was far more intense than [it was] throughout the country." The experienced denizens of the large Northern cities read in a critical temper the tirades of journalist critics, who assumed to know everything. The population of the small towns and the village neighborhoods, though a little bewildered by the echoes of denunciation which reached them from the national capital, yet by instinct, or by a divine guidance, held fast to their faith in their President. Thus the rank and file of the Republican party refused to follow the field officers in a revolt against the general. No better fortune ever befell this very fortunate nation. If the anti-slavery extremists had been able to reinforce their own pressure by the ponderous impact of the popular will, and so had pushed the President from his "border-state policy" and from his general scheme of advancing only very cautiously along the anti-slavery line, it is hardly conceivable either that the Union would have been saved or that slavery would have been destroyed.

On August 19, 1862, the good, impulsive, impractical Horace Greeley published in his newspaper, the New York "Tribune," an address to the President, to which he gave an awe-inspiring title, "The Prayer of 20,000,000 of People." It was an extremely foolish paper, and its title, like other parts of it, was false. Only those persons who were agitators for immediate emancipation could say amen to this mad prayer, and they were far from being even a large percentage of "20,000,000 of people." Yet these men, being active missionaries and loud preachers in behalf of a measure in which they had perfect faith, made a show and exerted an influence disproportioned to their numbers. Therefore their prayer, [34] though laden with blunders of fact and reasoning, fairly expressed malcontent Republicanism. Moreover, multitudes who could not quite join in the prayer would read it and would be moved by it. The influence of the "Tribune" was enormous. Colonel McClure truly says that by means of it Mr. Greeley "reached the very heart of the Republican party in every State in the Union;" and perhaps he does not greatly exaggerate when he adds that through this same line of connection the great Republican editor "was in closer touch with the active loyal sentiment of the people than [was] even the President himself." For these reasons it seemed to Mr. Lincoln worth while to make a response to an assault which, if left unanswered, must seriously embarrass the administration. He therefore wrote:—

"DEAR SIR,—I have just read yours of the 19th instant, addressed to myself through the New York 'Tribune.'

"If there be in it any statements or assumptions of fact which I may know to be erroneous, I do not now and here controvert them.

"If there be any inferences which I believe to be falsely drawn, I do not now and here argue against them.

"If there be perceptible in it an impatient and dictatorial tone, I waive it in deference to an old friend, whose heart I have always supposed to be right.

"As to the policy 'I seem to be pursuing,' as you say, I have not meant to leave any one in doubt. I would save the Union. I would save it in the shortest way under the Constitution.

"The sooner the national authority can be restored, the nearer the Union will be,—the Union as it was.

"If there be those who would not save the Union, unless they could at the same time save slavery, I do not agree with them.

"If there be those who would not save the Union, unless they could at the same time destroy slavery, I do not agree with them.

"*My paramount object is to save the Union, and not either to save or destroy slavery.*

"If I could save the Union without freeing any slave, I would do it. And if I could save it by freeing all the slaves, I would do it. And if I could save it by freeing some, and leaving others alone, I would also do that.

"What I do about slavery and the colored race, I do because I believe it helps to save the Union, and what I forbear, I forbear because I do not believe it would help to save the Union.

"I shall do less whenever I believe what I am doing hurts the cause, and shall do more whenever I believe doing more will help the cause.

"I shall try to correct errors when shown to be errors, and I shall adopt new views so fast as they shall appear to be true views.

"I have here stated my purpose, according to my view of official duty, and I intend no modification of my oft-expressed personal wish, that all men everywhere could be free."

This reply, placing the Union before all else, did "more to steady the loyal sentiment of the country in a very grave emergency than anything that ever came from Lincoln's pen." It was, very naturally, "particularly disrelished by anti-slavery men," whose views were not modified by it, but whose temper was irritated in proportion to the difficulty of meeting it. Mr. Greeley himself, enthusiastic and woolly-witted, allowed this heavy roller to pass over him, and arose behind it unaware that he had been crushed. He even published a retort, which was discreditably abusive. A fair specimen of his rhetoric was his demand to be informed whether Mr. Lincoln designed to save the Union "by recognizing, obeying, and enforcing the laws, or by ignoring, disregarding, and in fact defying them." Now the precise fact which so incensed Mr. Greeley and all his comrades was that the President was studiously and stubbornly insisting upon "recognizing, obeying, and enforcing the laws;" and the very thing which they were crying for was a step which, according to his way of thinking, would involve that he should "ignore, disregard, and defy" them. They had not shrunk from taking this position, when pushed toward it. They had contemned the Constitution, and had declared that it should not be allowed to stand in the way of doing those things which, in their opinion, ought to be done. Their great warrior, the chieftain of their forces in the House of Representatives, Thaddeus Stevens, was wont to say, in his defiant iconoclastic style, that there was no longer any Constitution, and that he was weary of hearing this "never-ending gabble about the sacredness of the Constitution." Yet somewhat inconsistently these same men held as an idol and a leader Secretary Chase; and he at the close of 1860 had declared: "At all hazards and against all opposition, the laws of the Union should be enforced.... The question of slavery should not be permitted to influence my action, one way or the other." Later, perhaps he and his allies had forgotten these words. Still many persons hold to the opinion that the emancipationists did not give Mr. Lincoln fair play. [35]

On September 13 a body of clergymen from Chicago waited upon Mr. Lincoln to urge immediate and universal emancipation. The occasion was made noteworthy by his remarks to them.

"I am approached with the most opposite opinions and advice, and that by religious men, who are equally certain that they represent the Divine will. I am sure that either the one or the other class is mistaken in that belief, and perhaps, in some respect, both. I hope it will not be irreverent for me to say that, if it is probable that God would reveal his will to others on a point so connected with my duty, it might be supposed He would reveal it directly to me; for, unless I am more deceived in myself than I often am, it is my earnest desire to know the will of Providence in this matter. And if I can learn what it is, I will do it! These are not, however, the days of miracles, and I suppose it will be granted that I am not to expect a direct revelation. I must study the plain physical facts of the case, ascertain what is possible, and learn what appears to be wise and right. The subject is difficult, and good men do not agree.

... "What good would a proclamation of emancipation from me do, especially as we are now situated? I do not want to issue a document that the whole world will see must necessarily be inoperative, like the Pope's bull against the comet! Would my word free the slaves, when I cannot even enforce the Constitution in the rebel States? Is there a single court, or magistrate, or individual that would be influenced by it there? And what reason is there to think it would have any greater effect upon the slaves than the late law of Congress, which I approved, and which offers protection and freedom to the slaves of rebel masters who come within our lines? Yet I cannot learn that that law has caused a single slave to come over to us.

... "Now, then, tell me, if you please, what possible result of good would follow the issuing of such a proclamation as you desire? Understand, I raise no objections against it on legal or constitutional grounds, for, as commander-in-chief of the army and navy, in time of war, I suppose I have a right to take any measure which may best subdue the enemy; nor do I urge objections of a moral nature, in view of possible consequences of insurrection and massacre at the South. I view this matter as a practical war measure, to be decided on according to the advantages or disadvantages it may offer to the suppression of the rebellion.

... "Do not misunderstand me because I have mentioned these objections. They indicate the difficulties that have thus far prevented my action in some such way as you desire. I have not decided against a proclamation of liberty to the slaves, but hold the matter under advisement. And I can assure you that the subject is on my mind, by day and night, more than any other. Whatever shall appear to be God's will I will do. I trust that in the freedom with which I have canvassed your views I have not in any respect injured your feelings."

Whether or not the clerical advisers winced under the President's irony, at least they must have appreciated the earnestness and sincerity with which he considered the subject.

All this while that newspaper writers, religious teachers, members of Congress, and political busy-bodies generally were tirelessly enlightening Mr. Lincoln concerning what was right, what was wise, what was the will of the people, even what was the will of God, he was again quietly making good that shrewd Southerner's prophecy: he was "doing his own thinking;"

neither was he telling to anybody what this thinking was. Throngs came and went, and each felt called upon to leave behind him some of his own wisdom, a precept, advice, or suggestion, for the use of the President; perhaps in return he took away with him a story which was much more than full value for what he had given; but no one found out the working of the President's mind, and no one could say that he had influenced it. History is crowded with tales of despots, but it tells of no despot who thought and decided with the tranquil, taciturn independence which was now marking this President of the free American Republic. It is a little amusing for us, to-day, to know that while the emancipationists were angrily growling out their disgust at the ruler who would not abolish slavery according to their advice, the rough draft of the Emancipation Proclamation had already been written. It was actually lying in his desk when he was writing to Greeley that letter which caused so much indignation. It had been communicated to his cabinet long before he talked to those Chicago clergymen, and showed them that the matter was by no means so simple as they, in their one-sided, unworldly way, believed it to be.

It is said to have been on July 8 that the President wrote this rough draft, on board the steamboat which was bringing him back from his visit to McClellan at Harrison's Landing. He then laid it away for the days and events to bring ripeness. By his own statement he had for some time felt convinced that, if compensated emancipation should fail, emancipation as a war measure must ensue. Compensated emancipation had now been offered, urged, and ill received; therefore the question in his mind was no longer *whether*, but *when* he should exercise his power. This was more a military than a political question. His right to emancipate slaves was strictly a war-power; he had the right to exercise it strictly for the purpose of weakening the enemy or strengthening his own generals; he had not the right to exercise it in the cause of humanity, if it would not either weaken the enemy or strengthen his own side. If by premature exercise he should alienate great numbers of border-state men, while the sheet of paper with his name at its foot would be ineffectual to give actual liberty of action to a single black man in the Confederacy, he would aid the South and injure the North,—that is to say, he would accomplish precisely the reverse of that which alone could lawfully form the basis of his action. The question of *When*, therefore, was a very serious one. At what stage of the contest would a declaration of emancipation be hurtful to the Southern and beneficial to the Northern cause?

Schuyler Colfax well said that Mr. Lincoln's judgment, when settled, "was almost as immovable as the eternal hills." A good illustration of this was given upon a day about the end of July or beginning of August, 1862, when Mr. Lincoln called a cabinet meeting. To his assembled secretaries he then said, with his usual simple brevity, that he was going to communicate to them something about which he did not desire them to offer any advice, since his determination was taken; they might make suggestions as to details, but nothing more. After this imperious statement he read the preliminary proclamation of emancipation. The ministers listened in silence; not one of them had been consulted; not one of them, until this moment, knew the President's purpose; not even now did he think it worth while to go through any idle form of asking the opinion of any one of them. [36] He alone had settled the matter, and simply notified them that he was about to do the most momentous thing that had ever been done upon this continent since thirteen British colonies had become a nation. Such a presentation of "one-man-power" certainly stood out in startling relief upon the background of popular government and the great free republican system of the world!

One or two trifling verbal alterations were made. The only important suggestion came from Mr. Seward, who said that, in the "depression of the public mind consequent upon our repeated adverses," he feared that so important a step might "be viewed as the last measure of an exhausted government, a cry for help; the government stretching forth its hands to Ethiopia, instead of Ethiopia stretching forth her hands to the government." He dreaded that "it would be considered our last shriek on the retreat." Therefore he thought it would be well to postpone issuing the proclamation till it could come before the country with the support of some military success. Mr. Lincoln, who had not committed himself upon the precise point of time, approved this idea. In fact, he had already had in mind this same notion, that a victory would be an excellent companion for the proclamation. In July Mr. Boutwell had said to him that the North would not succeed until the slaves were emancipated, and Mr. Lincoln had replied: "You would not have it done now, would you? Had we not better wait for something like a victory?" This point being accordingly settled to the satisfaction of all, the meeting then dissolved, with the understanding that the secret was to be closely kept for the present; and Mr. Lincoln again put away his paper to await the coming of leaden-footed victory.

For the moment the prospects of this event were certainly sufficiently gloomy. Less than three weeks, however, brought the battle of Antietam. As a real "military success" this was, fairly speaking, unsatisfactory; but it had to serve the turn; the events of the war did not permit the North to be fastidious in using the word victory; if the President had imprudently been more exacting, the Abolitionists would have had to wait for Gettysburg. News of the battle reached Mr. Lincoln at the Soldiers' Home. "Here," he says, "I finished writing the second draft. I came to Washington on Saturday, called the cabinet together to hear it, and it was published on the following Monday, the 22d of September, 1862."

The proclamation was preliminary or monitory only, and it did not promise universal emancipation. It stated that, on January 1, 1863, "all persons held as slaves within any State or designated part of a State, the people whereof shall then be in rebellion against the United States, shall be then, thenceforward, and forever free;" also, that "the Executive will, on the first day of January aforesaid, by proclamation, designate the States and parts of States, if any, in which the people thereof respectively shall then be in rebellion against the United States."

The measure was entirely Mr. Lincoln's own. Secretary Chase reports that at the cabinet meeting on September 22 he said: "I must do the best I can, and bear the responsibility of taking the course which I feel I ought to take." It has been said that he acted under a severe specific pressure, emanating from the calling of the famous conference of governors at Altoona. This, however, is not true. On September 14 Governor Curtin invited the governors of loyal States to meet on September 24 to discuss the situation and especially the emergency created by the northward advance of General Lee. But that this meeting was more than a coincidence, or that the summons to it had any influence in the matter of the proclamation, is disproved by all that is known concerning it. [37] The connection with the battle is direct, avowed, and reasonable; that with the gubernatorial congress is supposititious and improbable. Governor Curtin says distinctly that the President, being informed by himself and two others that such a conference was in preparation, "did not attempt to conceal the fact that we were upon the eve of an emancipation policy," in response to which statement he received from his auditors the "assurance that the Altoona conference would cordially indorse such a policy." As matter of fact, at the meeting, most of the governors, in a sort of supplementary way, declared their approval of the proclamation; but the governors of New Jersey, Delaware, Maryland, Kentucky, and Missouri would not unite in this action. If further evidence were needed upon this point, it is furnished by the simple statement of President Lincoln himself. He said: "The truth is, I never thought of the meeting of the governors at all. When Lee came over the Potomac I made a resolve that, if McClellan drove him back, I would send the proclamation after him. The battle of Antietam was fought Wednesday, but I could not find out until Saturday whether we had won a victory or lost a battle. It was then too late to issue it on that day, and on Sunday I fixed it up a little, and on Monday I let them have it." Secretary Chase, in his Diary, under date of September 22, 1862, gives an account in keeping with the foregoing sketch, but casts about the proclamation a sort of superstitious complexion, as if it were the fulfillment of a religious vow. He says that at the cabinet meeting the President said: "When the rebel army was at Frederick, I determined, as soon as it should be driven out of Maryland, to issue a proclamation of emancipation, such as I thought most likely to be useful. I said nothing to any one; but I made the promise to myself, and (hesitating a little) to my Maker. The rebel army is now driven out, and I am going to fulfill that promise." About an event so important and so picturesque small legends will cluster and cling like little barnacles on the solid rock; but the rock remains the same beneath these deposits, and in this case the fact that the proclamation was determined upon and issued at the sole will and discretion of the President is not shaken by any testimony that is given about it. He regarded it as a most grave measure, as plainly it was; to a Southerner, who had begged him not to have recourse to it, he replied: "You must not expect me to give up this government without playing my last card." [38] So now, on this momentous twenty-second day of September, the President, using his own judgment in playing the great game, cast what he conceived to be his ace of trumps upon the table.

The measure took the country by surprise. The President's secret had been well kept, and for once rumor had not forerun execution. Doubtless the reader expects now to hear that one immediate effect was the conciliation of all those who had been so long reproaching Mr. Lincoln for his delay in taking this step. It would seem right and natural that the emancipationists should have rallied with generous ardor to sustain him. They did not. They remained just as dissatisfied and distrustful towards him as ever. Some said that he had been *forced* into this policy, some that he had drifted with the tide of events, some that he had waited for popular opinion at the North to give him the cue, instead of himself guiding that opinion. To show that he was false to the responsibility of a ruler, there were those who cited against him his own modest words: "I claim not to have controlled events, but confess plainly that events have controlled me." Others, however, put upon this language the more kindly and more honest interpretation, that Mr. Lincoln appreciated that both President and people were moved by the drift of events, which in turn received their own impulse from an agency higher than human and to which they must obediently yield. But whatever ingenious excuses were devised by extremists for condemning the man who had done the act, the Republican party faithfully supported the act itself. In the middle of December the House passed a resolution ratifying the President's policy as "well adapted to hasten the restoration of peace," and "well chosen as a war measure."

The President himself afterward declared his "conviction" that, had the proclamation been issued six months earlier, it would not have been sustained by public opinion; and certainly it is true that contemporaneous political occurrences now failed to corroborate the soundness of those assertions by which the irreconcilable emancipationist critics of Mr. Lincoln had been endeavoring to induce him to adopt their policy earlier. They themselves, as Mr. Wilson admits, "had never constituted more than an inconsiderable fraction" of the whole people at the North. He further says: "At the other extreme, larger numbers received it [the proclamation] with deadly and outspoken opposition; while between these extremes the great body even of Union men doubted, hesitated.... Its immediate practical effect did perhaps more nearly answer the apprehensions of the President than the expectations of those most clamorous for it. It did, as charged, very much 'unite the South and divide the North.'"

In the autumn of 1862 there took place the elections for Representatives to the Thirty-eighth Congress. The most ingenious sophist could hardly maintain that strenuous anti-slavery voters, who had been angry with the government for backwardness in the emancipation policy, ought now to manifest their discontent by voting the Democratic ticket. If there should be a Democratic reaction at the polls it could not possibly be construed otherwise than as a reaction against anti-slavery; it would undeniably indicate that Congress and the administration had been too hostile rather than too friendly towards that cause of the strife, that they had outstripped rather than fallen behind popular sympathy. It soon became evident that a formidable reaction of this kind had taken place, that dissatisfaction with the anti-slavery measures and discouragement at the military failures, together, were even imperiling Republican ascendency. Now all knew, though some might not be willing to say, that the loss of Republican ascendency meant, in fact, the speedy settlement of the war by compromise; and the South was undoubtedly in earnest in declaring that there could be no compromise without disunion. Therefore, in those elections of the autumn months in 1862 the whole question of Union or Disunion had to be fought out at the polls in the loyal States, and there was an appalling chance of its going against the Unionist party. "The administration," says Mr. Blaine, "was now subjected to a fight for its life;" and for a while the fortunes of that mortal combat wore a most alarming aspect.

The Democracy made its fight on the ground that the anti-slavery legislation of the Republican majority in the Thirty-seventh Congress had substantially made abolition the ultimate purpose of the war. Here, then, they said, was a change of base; were or were not the voters of the loyal States willing to ratify it? Already this ground had been taken in the platforms of the party in the most important Northern States, before Mr. Lincoln issued his proclamation. Was it unreasonable to fear that this latest and most advanced step would intensify that hostility, stimulate the too obvious reaction, and aggravate the danger which, against his judgment, [39] as it was understood, Congress had created? Was it not probable that Mr. Blair was correct when he warned the President that the proclamation would "cost the administration the fall elections"? Naturally it will be asked: if this was a reasonable expectation, why did the President seize this critical moment to ally the administration with anti-slavery? Mr. Blaine furnishes a probable explanation: "The anti-slavery policy of Congress had gone far enough to arouse the bitter hostility of all Democrats, who were not thoroughly committed to the war, and yet not far enough to deal an effective blow against the institution." The administration stood at a point where safety lay rather in defying than in evading the ill opinion of the malcontents, where the best wisdom was to commit itself, the party, and the nation decisively to the "bold, far-reaching, radical, and aggressive policy," from which it would be impossible afterward to turn back "without deliberately resolving to sacrifice our nationality." Presumably the President wished to show the people that their only choice now lay between slavery on the one hand and nationality on the other, so that, of the two things, they might take that one which they deemed the more worthy. The two together they could never again have. This theory tallies with the well-known fact that Mr. Lincoln was always willing to trust the people upon a question of right and wrong. He never was afraid to stake his chance upon the faith that what was intrinsically right would prove in the long run to be politically safe. While he was a shrewd politician in matters of detail, he had the wisdom always in a great question to get upon that side where the inherent morality lay. Yet, unfortunately, it takes time—time which cannot always be afforded—for right to destroy prejudice; the slow-grinding mill of God grinds sometimes so slowly that man cannot help fearing that for once the stint will not be worked out; and in this autumn of 1862 there was one of these crises of painful anxiety among patriots at the North.

Maine held her election early in September, and upon the vote for governor a Republican majority, which usually ranged from 10,000 to 19,000, was this year cut down to a little over 4000; also, for the first time in ten years, a Democrat secured a seat in the national House of Representatives. Then came the "October States." In that dreary month Ohio elected 14 Democrats and 5 Republicans; the Democrats casting, in the total, about 7000 more votes than the Republicans. Indiana sent 8 Democrats, 3 Republicans. In Pennsylvania the congressional delegation was divided, but the Democrats polled the larger vote by about 4000; whereas Mr. Lincoln had had a majority in the State of 60,000! In New York the famous Democratic leader, Horatio Seymour, was elected governor by a majority of nearly 10,000.

Illinois, the President's own State, showed a Democratic majority of 17,000, and her congressional delegation stood 11 Democrats to 3 Republicans. New Jersey turned from Republicanism to Democracy. Michigan reduced a Republican majority from 20,000 to 6000. Wisconsin divided its delegation evenly. [40] When the returns were all in, the Democrats, who had had only 44 votes in the House in the Thirty-seventh Congress, found that in its successor they would have 75. Even if the non-voting absentees in the army [41] had been all Republicans, which they certainly were not, such a reaction would have been appalling.

Fortunately some other Northern States—New England's six, and Iowa, Kansas, Minnesota, California, and Oregon—held better to their Republican faith. But it was actually the border slave States which, in these dark and desperate days, came gallantly to the rescue of the President's party. If the voters of these States had seen in him a radical of the stripe of the anti-slavery agitators, it is not imaginable that they would have helped him as they now did. Thus was his much maligned "border-state policy" at last handsomely vindicated; and thanks to it the frightened Republicans saw, with relief, that they could command a majority of about twenty votes in the House. Mr. Lincoln had saved the party whose leaders had turned against him.

Beneath the dismal shadow of these autumnal elections the Thirty-seventh Congress came together for its final session, December 1, 1862. The political situation was peculiar and unfortunate. There was the greatest possible need for sympathetic coöperation in the Republican party; but sympathy was absent, and coöperation was imperfect and reluctant. The majority of the Republican members of Congress obstinately maintained their alienation from the Republican President; an enormous popular defection from Republicanism had taken place in its natural strongholds; and Republican domination had only been saved by the aid of States in which Republican majorities had been attainable actually because a large proportion of the population was so disaffected as either to have enlisted in the Confederate service, or to have refrained from voting at elections held under Union auspices. Therefore, whether Mr. Lincoln looked forth upon the political or the military situation, he beheld only gloomy prospects. But having made fast to what he believed to be right, he would not, in panic, cast loose from it. In the face of condemnation he was not seen to modify his course in order to conciliate any portion of the people; but, on the contrary, in his message he returned to his plan which had hitherto been so coldly received, and again strenuously recommended appropriations for gradual, compensated emancipation and colonization. The scheme had three especial attractions for him: 1. It would be operative in those loyal States and parts of States in which military emancipation would not take effect. 2. In its practical result it would do away with slavery by the year 1900, whereas military emancipation would now free a great number of individuals, but would leave slavery, as an institution, untouched and liable to be revived and reinvigorated later on. 3. It would make emancipation come as a voluntary process, leaving a minimum of resentment remaining in the minds of slaveholders, instead of being a violent war measure never to be remembered without rebellious anger. This last point was what chiefly moved him. He intensely desired to have emancipation effected in such a way that good feeling between the two sections might be a not distant condition; the humanity of his temperament, his passion for reasonable dealing, his appreciation of the mischief of sectional enmity in a republic, all conspired to establish him unchangeably in favor of "compensated emancipation."

For the accomplishment of his purpose he now suggested three articles of amendment to the Constitution. He spoke earnestly; for "in times like the present," he said, "men should utter nothing for which they would not willingly be responsible through time and eternity." Beneath the solemnity of this obligation he made for his plan a very elaborate argument. Among the closing sentences were the following: —

"The plan would, I am confident, secure peace more speedily, and maintain it more permanently, than can be done by force alone; while all it would cost, considering amounts, and manner of payment, and times of payment, would be easier paid than will be the additional cost of the war, if we rely solely upon force. It is much, very much, that it would cost no blood at all.

... "Is it doubted, then, that the plan I propose, if adopted, would shorten the war, and thus lessen its expenditure of money and of blood? Is it doubted that it would restore the national authority and national prosperity, and perpetuate both indefinitely? Is it doubted that we here—Congress and Executive—can secure its adoption? Will not the good people respond to a united and earnest appeal from us? Can we, can they, by any other means so certainly or so speedily assure these vital objects? We can succeed only by concert. It is not 'Can *any* of us *imagine* better?' but; 'Can we *all do* better?' Object whatsoever is possible, still the question recurs, 'Can we do better?' The dogmas of the quiet past are inadequate to the stormy present. The occasion is piled high with difficulty, and we must rise with the occasion. As our case is new, so we must think anew and act anew. We must disenthrall ourselves, and then we shall save our country.

"Fellow citizens, *we* cannot escape history. We, of this Congress and this administration, will [shall] be remembered in spite of ourselves. No personal significance, or insignificance, can spare one or another of us. The fiery trial through which we pass will light us down, in honor or dishonor, to the latest generation. We *say* we are for the Union. The world will not forget that we say this. We know how to save the Union. The world knows we do know how to save it. We—even *we here*—hold the power and bear the responsibility. In *giving* freedom to the *slave* we *assure* freedom to the *free*,—honorable alike in what we give and what we preserve. We shall nobly save, or meanly lose, the last, best hope of earth. Other means may succeed; this could not fail. The way is plain, peaceful, generous, just,—a way which, if followed, the world will forever applaud, and God must forever bless."

Beautiful and impressive as was this appeal, it persuaded few or none. In fact, no effort on the President's part now, or at any time, could win much approval for his plan. Not many were ever pleased by it; but afterward, in the winter of 1863, many members of the Thirty-eighth Congress were willing, without believing in it, to give him a chance to try it in Missouri. Accordingly a bill then passed the House appropriating $10,000,000 to compensate slave-owners in that State, if abolition of slavery should be made part of its organic law. The Senate made the sum $15,000,000 and returned the bill to the House for concurrence. But the representatives from Missouri were tireless in their hostility to the measure, and finally killed it by parliamentary expedients of delay.

This was a great disappointment to Mr. Lincoln. While the measure was pending he argued strenuously with leading Missourians to induce them to put their State in the lead in what he hoped would then become a procession of slave States. But these gentlemen seemed to fear that, if they should take United States bonds in payment, they might awake some morning in these troublous times to find their promiser a bankrupt or a repudiationist. On the other hand, such was the force of habit that a slave seemed to them very tangible property. Mr. Lincoln shrewdly suggested that, amid present conditions, "*bonds* were better than *bondsmen*," and "two-legged property" was a very bad kind to hold. Time proved him to be entirely right; but for the present his argument, entreaty, and humor were all alike useless. Missouri would have nothing to do with "compensated emancipation;" and since she was regarded as a test case, the experiment was not tried elsewhere. So it came to pass afterward that the slaveholders parted with their slaves for nothing instead of exchanging them for the six per cent. bonds of the United States.

The first day of January, 1863, arrived, and no event had occurred to delay the issue of the promised proclamation. It came accordingly. By virtue of his power as commander-in-chief, "in time of actual armed rebellion,.... and as a fit and necessary war measure for suppressing said rebellion," the President ordered that all persons held as slaves in certain States and parts of States, which he designated as being then in rebellion, should be thenceforward free, and declared that the Executive, with the army and navy, would "recognize and maintain the freedom of said persons." The word "maintain" was inserted at Seward's suggestion, and somewhat against Mr. Lincoln's wish. He said that he had intentionally refrained from introducing it, because it was not his way to promise what he was not entirely *sure* that he could perform. The sentence invoking the favor of God was contributed by Secretary Chase. The paper was signed after the great public reception of New Year's Day. Mr. Lincoln, as he took the pen, remarked to Mr. Seward that his much-shaken hand was almost paralyzed, so that people who, in time to come, should see that signature would be likely to say: "He hesitated," whereas, in fact, his whole soul was in it. The publication took place late in the day, and the anti-slavery critics grumbled because it was not sent out in the morning.

The people at large received this important step with some variety of feeling and expression; but, upon the whole, approval seems to have far outrun the dubious prognostications of the timid and conservative class. For the three months which had given opportunity for thinking had produced the result which Mr. Lincoln had hoped for. It turned out that the mill of God had been grinding as exactly as always. Very many who would not have advised the measure now heartily ratified it. Later, after men's minds had had time to settle and the balance could be fairly struck, it appeared undeniable that the final proclamation had been of good effect; so Mr. Lincoln himself said.

It is worth noting that while many Englishmen spoke out in generous praise, the rulers of England took the contrary position. Earl Russell said that the measure was "of a very strange nature," "a very questionable kind," an act of "vengeance on the slave-owner," and that it did no more than "profess to emancipate slaves, where the United States authorities cannot make emancipation a reality." But the English people were strongly and genuinely anti-slavery, and the danger of English recognition of the Confederacy was greatly diminished when the proclamation established the policy of the administration.

The proclamation contained a statement that ex-slaves would be "received into the armed service of the United States." Up to this time not much had been done in the way of enlisting colored troops. The negroes themselves had somewhat disappointed their friends by failing to take the initiative, and it became evident that they must be stirred by influences outside their own race. The President now took the matter in hand, and endeavored to stimulate commanders of Southern departments to show energy concerning it. By degrees successful results were obtained. The Southerners formally declared that they would not regard either negro troops or their officers as prisoners of war; but that they would execute the officers as ordinary felons, and would hand over the negroes to be dealt with by the state authorities as slaves in insurrection. Painful and embarrassing questions of duty were presented by these menaces. To Mr. Lincoln the obvious policy of retaliation seemed abhorrent, and he held back from declaring that he would adopt it, in the hope that events might never compel him to do so. But on July 30 he felt compelled, in justice to the blacks and those who led them, to issue an order that for every Union soldier killed in violation of the laws of war a rebel soldier should be executed; and for every one enslaved a rebel soldier should be placed at hard labor on the public works. Happily, however, little or no action ever became necessary in pursuance of this order. The Southerners either did not in fact wreak their vengeance in fulfillment of their furious vows, or else covered their doings so that they could not be proved. Only the shocking incident of the massacre at Fort Pillow seemed to demand stern retaliatory measures, and even this was, too mercifully, allowed gradually to sink away into neglect. [42]

[33] To A.G. Hodges, April 4, 1864, N. and H. vi. 430; and see Lincoln to Chase, September 2, 1863; *ibid*. 434.

[34] "It was," says Mr. Arnold, "full of errors and mistaken inferences, and written in ignorance of many facts which it was the duty of the President to consider." *Life of Lincoln*, 254. But, *per contra*, Hon. George W. Julian says: "It was one of the most powerful appeals ever made in behalf of justice and the rights of man." *Polit. Recoil.* 220. Arnold and Julian were both members of the House, and both thorough-going Abolitionists. Their difference of opinion upon this letter of Mr. Greeley illustrates well the discussions which, like the internecine feuds of Christian sects, existed between men who ought to have stood side by side against the heretics and unbelievers.

[35] For views contrary to mine, see Julian, *Polit. Recoil.* 221.

[36] The story that some members of the cabinet were opposed to the measure was distinctly denied by the President. Carpenter, *Six Months in the White House*, 88.

[37] For interesting statements about this Altoona conference see McClure, *Lincoln and Men of War-Times*, 248-251.

[38] Blaine, i. 439.

[39] It was understood that he had not favored the principal anti-slavery measures of the Thirty-seventh Congress, on the ground measures of the Thirty-seventh Congress, on the ground that they were premature

[40] The foregoing-statistics have been taken from Mr. Elaine, *Twenty Years of Congress*, i. 441-444.

[41] Later, legislation enabled the soldiers in the field to vote; but at this time they could not do so.

[42] For account of these matters of retaliation and protection of negroes, see N. and H. vol. vi. ch. xxi.

# CHAPTER V
# BATTLES AND SIEGES: DECEMBER,
# 1862 — DECEMBER, 1863

The clouds of gloom and discouragement, which shut so heavily about the President in the autumn of 1862, did not disperse as winter advanced. That dreary season, when nearly all doubted and many despaired, is recognized now as an interlude between the two grand divisions of the drama. Before it, the Northern people had been enthusiastic, united, and hopeful; after it, they saw assurance of success within reach of a reasonable persistence. But while the miserable days were passing, men could not see into the mysterious future. Not only were armies beaten, but the people themselves seemed to be deserting their principles. The face and the form of the solitary man, whose position brought every part of this sad prospect fully within the range of his contemplation, showed the wear of the times. The eyes went deeper into their caverns, and seemed to send their search farther than ever away into a receding distance; the furrows sank far into the sallow face; a stoop bent the shoulders, as if the burden of the soul had even a physical weight. Yet still he sought neither counsel, nor strength, nor sympathy from any one; neither leaned on any friend, nor gave his confidence to any adviser; the problems were his and the duty was his, and he accepted both wholly. "I need success more than I need sympathy," he said; for it was the cause, not his own burden, which absorbed his thoughts. The extremists, who seemed to have more than half forgotten to hate the South in the intensity of their hatred of McClellan, had apparently cherished a vague faith that, if this procrastinating spirit could be exorcised, the war might then be trusted to take care of itself. But after they had accomplished their purpose they were confronted by facts which showed that in this matter, as in that of emancipation, the President's deliberation was not the unpardonable misdoing which they had conceived it to be. In spite of McClellan's insolent arrogance and fault-finding, his unreasonable demands, and his tedious squandering of invaluable time, Mr. Lincoln, being by nature a man who contemplated the consequence of an action, did not desire to make a vacancy till he could fill it with a better man. "I certainly have been dissatisfied," he said, "with Buell and McClellan; but before I relieved them I had great fears I should not find successors to them who would do better; and I am sorry to add I have seen little since to relieve those fears." One bloody and costly experiment had already failed at Manassas. Two others were soon to result even more disastrously; and still another leader was to be superseded, before the "man of destiny" came. McClellan had thrown away superb opportunities; but to turn him out was not to fill his place with an abler man.

On the evening of November 7, 1862, the dispatch came which relieved McClellan and put Burnside in command. The moment was not well chosen. McClellan seemed in an unusually energetic temper. He had Lee's army divided, and was conceivably on the verge of fighting it in detail. [43] On the other hand, Burnside assumed the charge with reluctance and self-distrust. A handsome, popular gentleman, of pleasing manners and with the prestige of some easily won successes, he had the misfortune to be too highly esteemed.

The change of commanders brought a change of scheme, which was now to advance upon Richmond by way of Fredericksburg. When this was submitted to the President he said that it might succeed if the movement was rapid, otherwise not. The half of this opinion which concerned success was never tested; the other half was made painfully good. Instead of rapidity there was great delay, with the result that the early days of December found Lee intrenching strongly upon the heights behind Fredericksburg on the south bank of the Rappahannock, having his army now reunited and reinforced to the formidable strength of 78,288 men "present for duty." Burnside lay upon the north bank, with 113,000 men, but having exchanged the promising advantages which had existed when he took command for very serious disadvantages. He had the burden of attacking a position which he had allowed his enemy not only to select but to fortify. Happily it is not our task to describe the cruel and sanguinary thirteenth day of December, 1862, when he undertook this desperate task. When that night fell at the close of a fearful combat, which had been rather a series of blunders than an intelligent plan, 10,208 Federal soldiers were known to be lying killed or wounded, while 2145 more were "missing." Such was the awful price which the brave Northern army had paid, and by which it had bought— nothing! Nothing, save the knowledge that General Burnside's estimate of his capacity for such high command was correct. Even the mere brutal comparison of "killed and wounded" showed that among the Confederates the number of men who had been hit was not quite half that of the Federal loss. The familiar principle, that in war a general should so contrive as to do the maximum of injury to his adversary with a minimum of injury to himself, had been directly reversed; the unfortunate commander had done the maximum of injury to himself with the minimum of injury to his foe.

The behavior of Burnside in so bitter a trial was such as to attract sympathy. Yet his army had lost confidence in his leadership, and therefore suffered dangerously in morale. Many officers whispered their opinions in Washington, and, as usual, Congress gave symptoms of a desire to talk. Influenced by these criticisms and menacings, on December 30 the President ordered Burnside not to enter again upon active operations without first informing him. Burnside, much surprised, hastened to see Mr. Lincoln, and learned what derogatory strictures were in circulation. After brief consideration he proposed to resign. But Mr. Lincoln said: "I do not yet see how I could profit by changing the command of the army of the Potomac; and, if I did, I should not wish to do it by accepting the resignation of your commission." So Burnside undertook further manoeuvres. These, however, did not turn out well, and he conceived that a contributing cause lay in the half-heartedness of some of his subordinates. Thereupon he designed against them a defensive or retaliatory move in the shape of an order dismissing from the service of the United States four generals, and relieving from command four others, and one colonel. This wholesale decapitation was startling, yet was, in fact, soundly conceived. In the situation, either the general, or those who had lost faith in the general, must go. Which it should be was conclusively settled by the length of the list of condemned. The President declined to ratify this, and Burnside's resignation inevitably followed. His successor was the general whose name led the list of those malcontent critics whom he had desired to displace, and was also the same who had once stigmatized McClellan as "a baby." Major-General Joseph Hooker, a graduate of West Point, was now given the opportunity to prove his own superiority.

The new commander was popularly known as "Fighting Joe." There was inspiration in the nickname, and yet it was not quite thus that a great commander, charged with weighty responsibility, should be appropriately described. Upon making the appointment, January 26, 1863, the President wrote a letter remarkable in many points of view:—

"GENERAL,—I have placed you at the head of the army of the Potomac. Of course, I have done this upon what appears to me to be sufficient reasons; and yet I think it best for you to know that there are some things in regard to which I am not quite satisfied with you. I believe you to be a brave and skillful soldier,—which, of course, I like. I also believe you do not mix politics with your profession,—in which you are right. You have confidence in yourself,—which is a valuable, if not an indispensable quality. You are ambitious,—which, within reasonable bounds, does good rather than harm; but I think that, during General Burnside's command of the army, you have taken counsel of your ambition and thwarted him as much as you could, in which you did a great wrong to the country, and to a most meritorious and honorable brother officer. I have heard, in such way as to believe it, of your recently saying that both the army and the government needed a dictator. Of course, it was not for this, but in spite of it, that I have given you the command. Only those generals who gain successes can set up as dictators. What I now ask of you is military success, and I will risk the dictatorship. The government will support you to the utmost of its ability,—which is neither more nor less than it has done and will do for all commanders. I much fear that the spirit which you have aided to infuse into the army, of criticising their commander and withholding confidence from him, will now turn upon you. I shall assist you as far as I can to put it down. Neither you nor Napoleon, if he were alive again, could get any good out of an army while such a spirit prevails in it. And now, beware of rashness. Beware of rashness, but, with energy and sleepless vigilance, go forward and give us victories."

Hooker was of that class of generals who show such capacity as lieutenants that they are supposed to be capable of becoming independent chiefs, until their true measure is ascertained by actual trial. In two months he had restored to good shape an army which he had found demoralized and depleted by absenteeism, and at the end of April he had under him about 124,500 men. He still lay on the north bank of the Potomac, facing Lee's army in its intrenchments about Fredericksburg. His plan of campaign, says General Doubleday, was "simple, efficacious, and should have been successful." Diverting the attention of Lee, he threw the chief part of his army across the Rappahannock several miles above Fredericksburg; then, marching rapidly to Chancellorsville, he threatened the left flank and rear of the Confederates. Pushing a short distance out upon the three roads which led from Chancellorsville to Fredericksburg, he came to the very edge and brink, as it were, of beginning a great battle with good promise of success. But just at this point his generals at the front were astounded by orders to draw back to Chancellorsville. Was it that he suddenly lost nerve in the crisis of his great responsibility? [44] Or was it possible that he did not appreciate the opportunity which he was throwing away? No one can say. Only the fact can be stated that he rejected the chance which offended Fortune never offers a second time. Back came the advanced columns, and took position at Chancellorsville, while Lee, who had not the Northern habit of repudiating fair opportunity, pressed close upon them.

On May 1 manoeuvring for position and some fighting took place. On Saturday, May 2, a brilliant flanking movement by "Stonewall" Jackson wrecked the Federal right. But the dangerous Southerner, accidentally shot by his own soldiers, was carried from the field a dying man. Upon Sunday,

May 3, there was a most sanguinary conflict. "The Federals fought like devils at Chancellorsville," said Mahone. Still it was again the sad and wearisome story of brave men so badly handled that their gallantry meant only their own slaughter. The President had expressly urged Hooker to be sure to get all his troops at work. Yet he actually let 37,000 of them stand all day idle, not firing a shot, while their comrades were fighting and falling and getting beaten. On May 4, Hooker, whose previous "collapse" had been aggravated by a severe personal hurt, "seemed disposed to be inactive;" and Lee seized the chance to turn upon Sedgwick, who was coming up in the rear of the Confederates, and to drive him across the river. General Hooker now made up his mind that he had been beaten; and though a majority of his corps commanders were otherwise minded and were for renewing the conflict, he returned to the northern bank, leaving behind him his wounded soldiers, 14 guns, and 20,000 stand of arms. Another ghastly price had been paid to settle another experiment and establish the value of another general. The North lost in killed and wounded 12,197 men, with 5000 others "missing," and found out that General Hooker was not the man to beat General Lee. The Confederate loss was 10,266 killed and wounded, 2753 missing.

The days in which the news from Chancellorsville was spreading among the cities and villages of the North were the darkest of the war. In those countless households, by whose generous contributions the armies had been recruited, the talk began to be that it was folly, and even cruelty, to send brave and patriotic citizens to be slaughtered uselessly, while one leader after another showed his helpless incompetence. The disloyal Copperheads became more bodeful than ever before; while men who would have hanged a Copperhead as gladly as they would have shot a Secessionist felt their hearts sink before the undeniable Southern prestige. But the truth was that Pope and Burnside and Hooker, by their very defeats, became the cause of victory; for the elated Southerners, beginning to believe that their armies were invincible, now clamored for "invasion" and the capture of Washington. Apparently General Lee, too, had drunk the poison of triumph, and dreamed of occupying the national capital, Baltimore, and Philadelphia, and dictating the terms of peace to a disheartened North. The fascinating scheme—the irretrievable and fatal blunder—was determined upon.

To carry out this plan Swell's corps was covertly moved early in June into the Shenandoah Valley. Hooker, anticipating some such scheme, had suggested to Mr. Lincoln that, if it were entered upon, he should like to cross the river and attack the Southern rear corps in Fredericksburg. The President suggested that the intrenched Southerners would be likely to worst the assailants, while the main Southern army "would in some way be getting an advantage northward." "In one word," he wrote, "I would not take any risk of being entangled upon the river, like an ox jumped half over a fence and liable to be torn by dogs front and rear, without a fair chance to gore one way or kick the other." Yet, very soon, when the attenuation of Lee's line became certain, Lincoln sent to Hooker one of his famous dispatches: "If the head of Lee's army is at Martinsburg, and the tail of it on the plank road between Fredericksburg and Chancellorsville, the animal must be very slim somewhere. Could you not break him?" But the "animal" was moving rapidly, and the breaking process did not take place.

Hooker now conceived a plan seductive by its audacity and its possible results. He proposed by a sudden movement to capture Richmond, presumably garrisoned very scantily, and to get back before Lee could make any serious impression at the North. It *might* have been done, and, if done, it would more than offset all the dreary past; yet the risk was great, and Mr. Lincoln could not sanction it. He wrote: "I think Lee's army, and not Richmond, is your sure objective point. If he comes towards the Upper Potomac, follow on his flank and on his inside track, shortening your lines while he lengthens his; fight him, too, when opportunity offers. If he stays where he is, *fret him, and fret him.*"

This was good strategy and was adopted for the campaign. Ewell's corps crossed the Upper Potomac, and on June 22 was in Pennsylvania. The corps of Longstreet and Hill quickly followed, and Lee's triumphant army, at least 70,000 strong, marched through the Cumberland Valley to Chambersburg and Carlisle, gathering rich booty of herds and grain as they went, with Harrisburg as an immediate objective, Philadelphia in no remote distance, Baltimore and Washington in a painfully distinct background. The farmers of western Pennsylvania, startled by the spectacle of gray-coated cavalry riding northward towards their state capital, cumbered the roads with their wagons. The President called from the nearest States 120,000 militia. General Hooker, released from his waiting attitude by the development of his adversary's plan, manoeuvred well. He crossed the Potomac at Edwards' Ferry, June 25-26, and drew his forces together at Frederick. It was then decided to move northward and to keep Lee as well to the westward as possible, thereby reserving, for the bearing of future events, the questions of cutting the Confederate communications or bringing on a battle.

An unfortunate element in these critical days was that Halleck and Hooker disliked each other, and that their ideas often clashed. Mr. Lincoln was at last obliged to say to Hooker: "To remove all misunderstanding, I now place you in the strict military relation to General Halleck of a commander of one of the armies to the general-in-chief of all the armies. I have not intended differently; but as it seems to be differently understood, I shall direct him to give you orders, and you to obey them." At the same time he wrote him a "private" letter, endeavoring to allay the ill-feeling. He closed it with words of kindness, of modesty, and with one of his noble appeals for subjection of personal irritation and for union of effort on behalf of the country:—

"I believe you are aware that, since you took command of the army, I have not believed you had any chance to effect anything till now. As it looks to me, Lee's now returning towards Harper's Ferry gives you back the chance that I thought McClellan lost last fall. Quite possibly I was wrong both then and now; but, in the great responsibility resting upon me, I cannot be entirely silent. Now, all I ask is that you will be in such mood that we can get into our action the best cordial judgment of yourself and General Halleck, with my poor mite added, if, indeed, he and you shall think it entitled to any consideration at all."

The breach, however, could not be closed. Hooker, finding his army seriously weakened by the withdrawal of the two years' and the nine months' troops, asked for the garrison of Harper's Ferry, which seemed useless where it was. Halleck refused it, and, June 27, Hooker requested to be relieved of the command. His request was instantly granted, and Major-General George G. Meade was appointed in his place. Swinton says that command was given to Meade "without any lets or hindrances, the President expressly waiving all the powers of the executive and the Constitution, so as to enable General Meade to make, untrammeled, the best dispositions for the emergency." One would like to know the authority upon which so extraordinary a statement is based; probably it is a great exaggeration, and the simple fact would prove to be that, since the situation was such that new developments were likely to occur with much suddenness, the President wisely and even necessarily placed the general in full control, free from requirements of communication and consultation. But to represent that Mr. Lincoln abdicated his constitutional functions is absurd! Be this as it may, the fact is that the appointment brought no change of plan. For three days the armies manoeuvred and drew slowly together. Finally it was betwixt chance and choice that the place and hour of concussion were determined. The place was the village of Gettysburg, and the time was the morning of July 1.

Then ensued a famous and most bloody fight! During three long, hot days of midsummer those two great armies struggled in a desperate grapple, and with not unequal valor, the Confederates fiercely assailing, the Federals stubbornly holding, those historic ridges, and both alike, whether attacking or defending, whether gaining or losing ground, always falling in an awful carnage of dead and wounded. It was the most determined fighting that had yet taken place at the East, and the names of Cemetery Ridge, Little Round

Top, and Culp's Hill are written deep in blood in American memories. When the last magnificent charge of the Southerners was hurled back in the afternoon of July 3, the victory was decided. The next day Lee began to send away his trains, his wounded and prisoners. It is indeed true that during the day he held his army in position on Seminary Ridge, hoping that Meade would attack, and that, with an exchange of their relative parts of assailants and defenders, a change of result also might come about. But Meade made no advance, and with the first hours of darkness on the evening of July 4 the Southern host began its retreat.

The losses at Gettysburg were appalling. The estimate is 2834 killed, 13,709 wounded, 6643 missing, a total of 23,186 on the Federal side; the figures were only a trifle less on the Confederate side. But if such bloodshed carried grief into many a Northern household, at least there was not the cruel thought that life and limb, health and usefulness, had been sacrificed through incompetence and without advantage to the cause. It was true that the Northern general ought to have won, for he commanded more troops, [45] held a very strong defensive position, and fought a strictly defensive battle. But such had been the history of the war that when that which *ought* to be done *was* done, the people felt that it was fair cause for rejoicing. Later there was fault-finding and criticism; but that during so many days so many troops on unfamiliar ground should be handled in such a manner that afterward no critic can suggest that something might have been done better, hardly falls among possibilities. The fact was sufficient that a most important and significant victory had been won. On the battlefield a stone now undertakes to mark the spot and to name the hour where and when the flood tide of rebellion reached its highest point, and where and when it began its slow and sure ebb. Substantially that stone tells the truth. Nevertheless the immediately succeeding days brought keen, counteracting disappointment. Expectation rose that the shattered army of Lee would never cross the Potomac; and the expectation was entirely reasonable, and ought to have been fulfilled. But Meade seemed to copy McClellan after Antietam. Spurred on by repeated admonitions from the President and General Halleck, he did, on July 10, catch up with the retreating army, which was delayed at Williamsport on the north bank of the river by the unusually high water. He camped close by it, and received strenuous telegrams urging him to attack. But he did not, [46] and on the night of July 13 the Southern general successfully placed the Potomac between himself and his too tardy pursuer. Bitter then was the resentment of every loyal man at the North. For once the President became severe and sent a dispatch of such tenor that General Meade replied by an offer to resign his command. This Mr. Lincoln did not accept. Yet he was too sorely pained not to give vent to words which in fact if not in form conveyed severe censure. He was also displeased because Meade, in general orders, spoke of "driving the invaders from our soil;" as if the whole country was not *our soil*! Under the influence of so much provocation, he wrote to General Meade a letter reproduced from the manuscript by Messrs. Nicolay and Hay. It is true that on cooler reflection he refrained from sending this missive, but it is in itself sufficiently interesting to deserve reading:—"I have just seen your dispatch to General Halleck, asking to be relieved of your command because of a supposed censure of mine. I am very grateful to you for the magnificent success you gave the cause of the country at Gettysburg; and I am sorry now to be the author of the slightest pain to you. But I was in such deep distress myself that I could not restrain some expression of it. I have been oppressed nearly ever since the battle of Gettysburg by what appeared to be evidences that yourself and General Couch and General Smith were not seeking a collision with the enemy, but were trying to get him across the river without another battle. What these evidences were, if you please, I hope to tell you at some time when we shall both feel better. The case, summarily stated, is this: You fought and beat the enemy at Gettysburg; and, of course, to say the least, his loss was as great as yours. He retreated; and you did not, as it seemed to me, pressingly pursue him; but a flood in the river detained him till, by slow degrees, you were again upon him. You had at least twenty thousand veteran troops directly with you, and as many more raw ones within supporting distance, all in addition to those who fought with you at Gettysburg, while it was not possible that he had received a single recruit; and yet you stood and let the flood run down, bridges be built, and the enemy move away at his leisure without attacking him. And Couch and Smith,—the latter left Carlisle in time, upon all ordinary calculation, to have aided you in the last battle at Gettysburg, but he did not arrive. At the end of more than ten days, I believe twelve, under constant urging, he reached Hagerstown from Carlisle, which is not an inch over fifty-five miles, if so much; and Couch's movement was very little different.

"Again, my dear general, I do not believe you appreciate the magnitude of the misfortune involved in Lee's escape. He was within your easy grasp, and to have closed upon him would, in connection with our other late successes, have ended the war. As it is, the war will be prolonged indefinitely. If you could not safely attack Lee last Monday, how can you possibly do so south of the river, when you can take with you very few more than two thirds of the force you then had in hand? It would be unreasonable to expect, and I do not expect [that] you can now effect much. Your golden opportunity is gone, and I am distressed immeasurably because of it.

"I beg you will not consider this a prosecution or persecution of yourself. As you had learned that I was dissatisfied, I have thought it best to kindly tell you why."

There was an odd coincidence during this momentous first week in July. During the preceding winter Mr. Lincoln had been exceedingly bothered by certain Democrats, notably that gentleman of unsavory repute, Fernando Wood, who had urged upon him all sorts of foolish schemes for "compromising" or "settling the difficulties,"—phrases which were euphemisms of the peace Democracy to disguise a concession of success to the South. The President endured these sterile suggestions with his wonted patience. But toward the close of June, Alexander H. Stephens, Vice-President of the Confederacy, was seized with the notion that, if he should go to Washington on a personal mission to Mr. Lincoln, purporting to be about prisoners of war, he might then "indirectly ... turn attention to a general adjustment." Accordingly he set forth on his way to Fortress Monroe; but very inopportunely for his purposes it fell out that the days of his journey were the very days in which General Lee was getting so roughly worsted at Gettysburg. So it happened that it was precisely on the day of the Southern retreat, July 4, that he notified the admiral in Hampton Roads that he was the "bearer of a communication in writing from Jefferson Davis, commander-in-chief of the land and naval forces of the Confederate States, to Abraham Lincoln, commander-in-chief of the land and naval forces of the United States;" and he asked for leave to proceed to Washington. But his ingenious phraseology was of no avail. Mr. Lincoln said: "The request of A.H. Stephens is inadmissible. The customary agents and channels are adequate for all needful communication and conference between the United States forces and the insurgents." Thus the shrewd instinct of the Northerner brought to naught a scheme conceived in the spirit of the old-time Southern politics, a scheme which was certainly clever, but which, without undue severity, may also be called a little artful and insidious; for Mr. Stephens himself afterward confessed that it had, for its ulterior purpose, "not so much to act upon Mr. Lincoln and the then ruling authorities at Washington as through them, when the correspondence should be published, upon the great mass of the people in the Northern States." The notion, disseminated among the people, that Mr. Lincoln would not listen to proposals for peace, would greatly help malcontents of the Fernando Wood school.

It is necessary now to turn from the Eastern field of operations to the Middle and Western parts of the country, where, however, the control exercised by Mr. Lincoln was far less constant than at the East. After the series of successes which culminated at Corinth, the Federal good fortune rested as if to recuperate for a while. A large part of the powerful army there gathered was carried away by Buell, and was soon given occupation by General Bragg. For Jefferson Davis had long chosen to fancy that Kentucky was held in an unwilling subjection to the Union, and from this thralldom he now designed to relieve her, and to make the Ohio River the frontier of Secession. Accordingly cavalry raids in considerable force were made, Cincinnati was threatened, and General Bragg, with a powerful army, started northward from Gainesville. At the same time the Federals left Murfreesboro', and the two armies raced for Louisville. Bragg, with a handsome start, should have won, but on September 29, 1862, Buell entered the city ahead. The winning of the goal, however, was not the end. Two hostile armies, which had come so far and got so close together, were bound to have a fight. This took place at Perryville, October 8, with the result that on the next day Bragg began a rapid retreat. He had brought 20,000 stand of arms for the Kentuckians who were to flock to his camp; but they had not flocked, and the theory of Kentuckian disloyalty was no longer tenable.

So soon as Bragg was out of Kentucky, Halleck, probably at the instigation of the President, recurred to the project of a campaign in Eastern Tennessee. Buell said that it was not feasible, and since by this opinion he placed himself at odds with the authorities at Washington, he asked to be relieved from his command. At the close of October, Major-General William S. Rosecrans succeeded him. But the new commander would not, any more than his predecessor, fall in with Halleck's schemes, and what Cist contemptuously describes as "Halleck's brilliant paper campaign into East Tennessee" did not take place.

General Rosecrans took command of the army at Bowling Green, November 2, 1862. Bragg fell back to Murfreesboro', in Tennessee, and the city of Nashville, now in Federal possession, became the gage of battle. On December 26 Rosecrans moved out from that city towards Murfreesboro', and on January 2, 1863, the battle of Stone's River took place. It was desperately contested, and the losses were heavy. At the close of the day the advantage rested with the Confederates; but it was inconsiderable, and both sides considered the battle only begun. On the next day, however, Bragg found such dangerous demoralization among his troops that he decided to withdraw. Although he always persisted in describing himself as the victor in the engagement, yet he now left his wounded in the hospitals, and fell back to Shelbyville. In these positions, not far apart, the two armies lay for a long while watching each other; there were a few raids and small encounters, but substantially, during the first six months of 1863, quietude reigned in the region which they dominated.

But quietude was not what the government wished, and Mr. Lincoln and General Halleck soon fell into much the same relationship with

Rosecrans which they had previously occupied towards McClellan. Whenever Rosecrans had taken the field he had shown himself a skillful strategist and an able commander in battle; but his propensity seemed to be to remain in quarters, and thence to present extravagant exactions, and to conduct endless disputes with the President and the general-in-chief. He seemed like a restive horse, the more he was whipped and spurred the more immovably he retained his balking attitude. Mr. Lincoln was sorely tried by this obstinacy, and probably had been pushed nearly to the limits of his patience, when at last Rosecrans stirred. It was on June 24 that he set his army in motion to settle with Bragg those conclusions which had been left open for half a year. With this purpose he moved upon Shelbyville, but when he arrived there he found that Bragg had gone back to Tullahoma; and when he pushed on to Tullahoma, Bragg had left there also. Thus it came to pass that on the same famous Fourth of July on which Lee started to get out of Pennsylvania, Bragg in like manner was getting over the southern boundary line of Tennessee and putting the mountain range between himself and the pursuing Federal commander. The converging lines of Federal good luck came together on this great day of the nation, in a way that touches the superstitious chord; for still farther west another and a momentous event was taking place.

General Grant, at Corinth, had been pondering a great scheme which he meant to undertake so soon as his scanty army should be sufficiently reinforced. If Richmond had an artificial value as a token of final triumph, the Mississippi River had scarcely less value of a practical character. Vicksburg and Port Hudson cut out a mid-section of about 200 miles of the great stream, which section still remained under Confederate control. Vicksburg was General Grant's objective point. Even to conceive the capture of this stronghold seemed in itself evidence of genius; no mere pedant in warfare could have had the conception. Every difficulty lay in the way of the assailant. The Confederates had spared no skill, no labor, no expense in fortifying the town; yet after all had been done that military science could do, human achievement counted for little in comparison with the surpassing arrangements of Nature. If what she intended could be inferred from what she had done, she clearly had designed this town to be through all time a veritable "virgin fortress;" she had made for its resting-place a great bluff, which jutted insolently out into the channel of the Mississippi River, and upon the summit of which the cluster of buildings resembled rather an eyrie of eagles than a place of human habitation; the great stream, as if confounded by the daring obstruction, before it could recover its interrupted course spread itself far over the surrounding country in a tangle of bayous and a vast expanse of unwholesome, impassable swamp; the high ridges which lay inland around the place were intersected by frequent long, deep, and precipitous ravines, so that by this side also hostile approach had apparently been rendered impossible. Nevertheless, that one of the Northern generals to whom nothing ever seemed impossible, having cast the eye of desire upon this especial spot, now advanced upon it, and began operations in his silent, enduring, pertinacious way, which no men and no intrenchments could permanently withstand. His lieutenant, Sherman, made one desperate assault,—not, as it seemed, because there was a possibility of taking the place, but rather to demonstrate that it could not be taken. Then slower and more toilsome methods were tried. It was obvious that a siege must be resorted to; yet it was not easy to get near enough even to establish a siege.

General Grant had early decided that the city would remain impregnable until by some means he could get below it on the river and approach it from the landward side. Ingenious schemes of canals were tried, and failed. Time passed; the month of April was closing, and all that had been done seemed to amount to nothing better than an accumulation of evidence that the Confederacy had one spot which the Federals could never touch. At last ingenuity was laid aside for sheer daring. The fleet, under Admiral Porter, transported the army down-stream, athwart the hostile batteries, and set it ashore on the east bank, below the fortifications. Yet this very success seemed only to add peril to difficulty. The Confederates, straining every nerve to save the place, were gathering a great force in the neighborhood to break up the besieging army. With a base of supplies which was substantially useless, in a hostile country, with a powerful army hovering near him, and an unapproachable citadel as his objective, Grant could save himself from destruction only by complete and prompt success. Desperate, indeed, was the occasion, yet all its exorbitant requirements were met fully, surely, and swiftly by the commander and the gallant troops under him. In the task of getting a clear space, by driving the Confederates from the neighborhood for a considerable distance around, the army penetrated eastward as far as Jackson, fighting constantly and living off the country. Then, returning westward, they began the siege, which, amid hardship and peril and infinite difficulty, was pushed with the relentless vigor of the most relentless and most vigorous leader of the war. At last, on July 3, General Pemberton, commanding within the city, opened negotiations for a surrender. He knew that an assault would be made the next day, and he knew that it must succeed; he did not want to illustrate the Fourth of July by so terrible a Confederate loss, so magnificent a Federal gain. Yet he haggled over the terms, and by this delay brought about a part of that which he had wished to avoid. It was due to his fretfulness about details, that the day on which the

Southern army marched out and stacked their arms before the fortifications of Vicksburg, and on which the Northern army, having generously watched the operation without a cheer, then marched in and took possession of the place, was that same Fourth of July on which two other defeated generals were escaping from two other victorious Northern armies.

In a military point of view this campaign and siege have been pronounced by many competent critics the greatest achievement of the war; but the magnificent and interesting story must, with regret, be yielded to the biographer of Grant; it does not belong to the biographer of Lincoln. The whole enterprise was committed to Grant to be handled by him without let or hindrance, and it was conducted by him from beginning to end without interference, and almost even without suggestion. Yet this very fact was greatly to the credit of the administration. In the outset the President passed judgment upon the man; and it was a correct judgment. Afterward he stood to it gallantly. In the middle of the business, when the earlier expedients went wrong, a great outcry against Grant arose. Editors and politicians, even the secretary of the treasury himself, began to hound the President with importunate demands for the displacement of a general whom they fervently alleged to be another of the incompetents; in short, there was the beginning of just such a crusade as that which had been made against McClellan. But by this time the President had had opportunity to measure the military capacity of editors and politicians, and he was not now so much disquieted by their clamor as he once had been. He simply, in his quiet way, paid no attention to them whatsoever. Only when one of them reiterated the gossip about Grant being drunk at Shiloh, he made his famous reply, that he should like to send to some other generals a barrel of the whiskey which Grant drank. In a word, the detractors of the silent general made little impression on the solitary President, who told them shortly and decisively: "I can't spare this man; he fights." They wholly failed to penetrate the protecting fence which the civilian threw around the soldier, and within the shelter of which that soldier so admirably performed the feat which more than any other illustrates the national arms. Certainly the President comes in for his peculiar share of the praise. When the news came to Mr. Lincoln he wrote to General Grant this letter:—

"July 16, 1863.

"My DEAR GENERAL,—I do not remember that you and I ever met personally. I write this now as a grateful acknowledgment for the almost inestimable services you have done the country.

"I wish to say a word further. When you reached the vicinity of Vicksburg, I thought you should do what you finally did,—march the troops across the neck, run the batteries with the transports, and thus go below; and I never had any faith, except in a general hope that you knew better than I, that the Yazoo Pass expedition and the like would succeed.

"When you got below and took Port Gibson, Grand Gulf, and vicinity, I thought you should go down the river and join General Banks; and when you turned northward, east of the Big Black, I feared it was a mistake. I now wish to make a personal acknowledgment that you were right and I was wrong."

Immediately after the ceremony of surrender was over Sherman marched away with a strong force to find and fight Johnston's army. But that general, shunning the conflict, moved so far southward into Mississippi that pursuit was imprudent during the hot season.

While Grant was finishing the siege of Vicksburg, General Banks was besieging Port Hudson, which lay at the southern end of the rebel section of the river. The fall of the northern post rendered the southern one untenable, and it was surrendered on July 9. Henceforth the great river was a safe roadway for unarmed craft flying the stars and stripes.

It is time now to go back to Tennessee. By the close of the first week in July, 1863, the Confederate force was established in Chattanooga, and thus the hostile armies were "placed back in the relative positions occupied by them prior to Bragg's advance into Kentucky, a little less than one year previous." But though the Southern general had reached his present position by a retreat at the end of a disappointing enterprise, the issue of final success was still an open one between him and Rosecrans, with many advantages on his side. He had a large army in the heart of a mountainous region, with the opportunity to post it in positions which ought to be impregnable. Moreover, he received fresh troops under Johnston; and later the inaction of Meade in Virginia encouraged Lee to send to him a considerable force under Longstreet, himself no small reinforcement. These arrived just on the eve of the impending battle.

Meantime Mr. Lincoln was sorely exercised at his inability to make his generals carry out his plans. He desired that Burnside should move down from the north and unite with Rosecrans, and that then the combined force should attack Bragg promptly. But Rosecrans lay still for about six weeks, to repair losses and fatigue, and again played the part of the restive steed, responding to the President's spur only with fractious kickings. It was August 16 when he moved, but then he showed his usual ability in action. The march was difficult; yet, on September 6, he had his whole force across the Tennessee and in the mountains south of Chattanooga. Burnside, meanwhile, had advanced to Knoxville, but had stopped there, and was now, greatly to Mr. Lincoln's bewilderment and annoyance, showing activity in every direction except precisely that in which he was directed to move.

At last, after much fruitless manoeuvring, the collision took place, and for two days there was fierce and stubborn fighting on the famous battlefield of Chickamauga. On the second day, September 20, Longstreet, commanding the Confederate left, thoroughly defeated the Federal right and centre and sent them in precipitate flight to Chattanooga. Rosecrans, overwhelmed amid the rush of fugitives, and thinking that all was lost, also hastened thither to take charge of the fragments. In truth all would have been lost, had it not been for Thomas. This able and resolute commander won in this fight the rhetorical but well merited name of "the Rock of Chickamauga." Under him the Federal left stood immovable, though furiously assailed by odds, and tried by the rout of their comrades. At nightfall these troops, still in position, covered the withdrawal to Chattanooga.

Rosecrans, badly demoralized, gave the President to understand that there had been a terrible disaster, and the President, according to his custom in such trying moments, responded with words of encouragement and an instant effort to restore morale. Mr. Lincoln always cheered his generals in the hour of disaster, which he seemed to regard only as the starting-point for a new advance, the incentive to a fresh exertion. Yet, in fact, there had not been a disaster, but only a moderate worsting of the Federal army, resulting in its retirement a trifling distance to the place whence its opponents had just marched out. The issue between the two generals was still as open after Rosecrans's misfortune as it had been after the previous misfortunes of Bragg. Already there was a new question, who would win that coming battle which plainly was close at hand. The curtain had only gone down on an act; the drama itself had not been played out.

Bragg advanced to besiege Chattanooga, and Rosecrans's communications were so imperfect that his troops were put on short rations. On the other hand, Mr. Lincoln bestirred himself vigorously. He promptly sent Sherman from the West, and Hooker from the East, each with considerable reinforcements, en route for the beleaguered town. Also he saw plainly that, whether by fault or misfortune, the usefulness of Rosecrans was over, and on October 16 he put Thomas in place of Rosecrans, [47] and gave to General Grant the command of the Military Division of the Mississippi, including the Departments of the Ohio, the Cumberland, and the Tennessee. Grant at once telegraphed to Thomas to hold Chattanooga at all hazards; to which Thomas replied: "We will hold the town till we starve!" Grant well knew that they were already getting very hungry. He showed his usual prompt energy in relieving them; and a little fighting soon opened a route by which sufficient food came into the place.

It was now obvious that the decisive conflict between the two armies, which had so long been striving for the advantage of strategic position, and fighting in hostile competition, was at last to occur. Each had its distinctive advantage. The Federals were led by Grant, with Sherman, Thomas, Sheridan, and Hooker as his lieutenants, — a list which may fairly recall Napoleon and his marshals. On the other hand, the Southerners, lying secure in intrenched positions upon the precipitous sides and lofty summits of Lookout Mountain and Missionary Ridge, seemed invulnerably placed. It does not belong to this narrative to describe the terrific contest in which these two combatants furiously locked horns on November 24 and 25. It was Hooker's brave soldiers who performed the conspicuous feat which was conclusive of victory. Having, by command, stormed the first line of rifle-pits on the ascent, upon the Confederate left, they suddenly took the control into their own hands; without orders they dashed forward, clambered upward in a sudden and resistless access of fighting fury, and in an hour, emerging above the mists which shrouded the mid-mountain from the anxious view of General Grant, they planted the stars and stripes on top of Lookout Mountain. They had fought and won what was poetically christened "the battle above the clouds." Sherman, with seven divisions, had meanwhile been making desperate and bloody assaults upon Missionary Ridge, and had gained the first hilltop; but the next one seemed impregnable. It was, however, not necessary for him to renew the costly assault; for Hooker's victory, which was quickly followed by a handsome advance by Sheridan, on Sherman's right, so turned the Confederate position as to make it untenable.

The Northerners were exasperated to find, among the Confederate troops who surrendered as captives in these two battles, prisoners of war taken at Vicksburg and Port Hudson, who had been paroled and never exchanged.

On the eve of this battle Longstreet had started northward to cut off and destroy Burnside in Knoxville, and no sooner was the actual fighting over than Grant sent Sherman in all haste to Burnside's assistance. Thereupon Longstreet fell back towards Virginia, and came to a resting-place midway, where he afterward lay unharmed and unharming for many months. Thus at last the long-deferred wish of the President was fulfilled, and the chief part of East Tennessee was wrested from Confederate occupation. Among the loyal inhabitants the great rejoicing was in proportion to the sufferings which they had so long been undergoing.

Meanwhile, since Gettysburg, no conspicuous event had attracted attention in Virginia. The President had been disappointed that Meade had not fought at Williamsport, but soon afterward he gave decisive advice against forcing a fight at a worse place in order to cure the blunder of having let go the chance to fight at the right place. About the middle of September, however, when Lee had reduced his army by leaves of absence and by dispatching Longstreet to reinforce Bragg, Mr. Lincoln thought it a good time to attack him. Meade, on the other hand, now said that he did not feel strong enough to assault, and this although he had 90,000 men "between him and Washington," and by his estimate the whole force of the enemy, "stretching as far as Richmond," was only 60,000. "For a battle, then," wrote Mr. Lincoln, "General Meade has three men to General Lee's two. Yet, it having been determined that choosing ground and standing on the defensive gives so great advantage that the three cannot safely attack the two, the three are left simply standing on the defensive also. If the enemy's 60,000 are sufficient to keep our 90,000 away from Richmond, why, by the same rule, may not 40,000 of ours keep their 60,000 away from Washington, leaving us 50,000 to put to some other use?... I can perceive no fault in this statement, unless we admit we are not the equal of the enemy man for man." But when, a few days later, Stanton proposed to detach 30,000 men from Meade to Rosecrans, Mr. Lincoln demurred, and would agree only to let go 13,000, whom Hooker took with him to Chattanooga. Probably he did not wish to diminish the Federal strength in Virginia.

Late in October, Lee, overestimating the number of troops thus withdrawn, endeavored to move northward; but Meade outmanoeuvred and outmarched him, and he fell back behind the Rapidan. General Meade next took his turn at the aggressive. Toward the close of November he crossed the Rapidan with the design of flanking and attacking Lee. But an untoward delay gave the Southerners time to intrench themselves so strongly that an attack was imprudent, and Meade returned to the north bank of the stream. The miscarriage hurt his reputation with the people, though he was not to blame for it.

Now, as the severe season was about to begin, all the armies both of the North and of the South, on both sides of the mountain ranges, turned gladly into winter quarters. Each had equal need to rest and recuperate after hard campaigns and bloody battles. For a while the war news was infrequent and insignificant; and the cessation in the thunder of cannon and the rattle of musketry gives opportunity again to hear the voices of contending politicians. For a while we must leave the warriors and give ear to the talkers.

[43] Palfrey, *The Antietam and Fredericksburg,* 132.

[44] Swinton says: "The moment he confronted his antagonist he seemed to suffer a collapse of all his powers." *Army of Potomac,* 280.

[45] But, says Swinton, there was less disproportion than usual; for the great army which Hooker had had before Chancellorsville had been greatly reduced, both by casualties and by the expiration of terms of service. On May 13 he reported that his "marching force of infantry" was "about 80,000 men." A little later the cavalry was reported at 4677. *Army of Potomac,* 310.

[46] Swinton says that whether Meade should have attacked or not, "will probably always remain one of those questions about which men will differ." He inclines to think that Meade was right. *Army of Potomac, 369, 370.*

[47] Grant disliked Rosecrans, and is said to have asked for this change.

# CHAPTER VI
# SUNDRIES

It has been pleasant to emerge from the dismal winter of 1862-63 into the sun-gleam of the Fourth of July of the latter year. But it is necessary to return for a while into that dusky gloom, for the career of a "war president" is by no means wholly a series of campaigns. Domestic politics, foreign relations, finance, make their several demands.

Concerning one of these topics, at least, there is little to be said. One day, in a period of financial stress, Mr. Chase expressed a wish to introduce to the President a delegation of bankers, who had come to Washington to discuss the existing condition with regard to money. "Money!" exclaimed Mr. Lincoln, "I don't know anything about 'money'! I never had enough of my own to fret me, and I have no opinion about it any way." Accordingly, throughout his administration he left the whole subject in the hands of the secretary of the treasury. The tariffs and internal revenue bills, the legal tender notes, the "five-twenties," the "ten-forties," and the "seven-thirties," all the loans, the national banking system, in short, all the financial schemes of the administration were adopted by Mr. Lincoln upon the recommendation of Mr. Chase, with little apparent study upon his own part. Satisfied of the ability of his secretary, he gave to all the Treasury measures his loyal support. In return, he expected the necessary funds to be forthcoming; for he had implicit confidence in the willingness of the people to pay the bills of the Union; and he expected the secretary to arrange methods by which they could do so with reasonable convenience. Mr. Chase was cast for the role of magician, familiar with those incantations which could keep the Treasury ever full. It was well thus, for in fact no word or incident in Mr. Lincoln's life indicates that he had any capacity whatsoever in financiering. To live within his income and pay his dues with a minute and careful punctuality made the limit of his dealings and his interest in money matters.

Foreign affairs, less technical, could not in like easy manner be committed to others, and in these Mr. Lincoln and Mr. Seward labored together. The blackest cloud was the Trent affair, yet after that had passed the sky by no means became clear. In the spring of 1862 the Oreto went out from Liverpool to become the rebel privateer Florida. Before her departure Mr. Adams complained concerning her to the English government, but was assured that the vessel was designed for the Sicilian fruit trade! As it is not diplomatic to say that gentlemen in office are telling lies, the American minister could push the matter no farther. The Florida, therefore, escaped, not to conduct commerce with Sicily, but to destroy the commerce of the United States. At the same time that she was fitting out, a mysterious craft, oddly known only as the "290," was also building in the Liverpool docks, and against her Mr. Adams got such evidence that the queen's ministers could not help deciding that she must be detained. Unfortunately, however, and by a strange, if not a significant chance, they reached this decision on the day after she had sailed! She became the notorious Alabama. Earl Russell admitted that the affair was "a scandal," but this did not interfere with the career of Captain Semmes. In these incidents there was both cause and provocation for war, and hot-headed ones cried out for it, while prudent men feared it. But the President and the secretary were under the bonds of necessity to keep their official temper. Just at this juncture England would have found it not only very easy, but also very congenial to her real sympathies, to play for the South a part like that which France had once played for certain thirteen revolted colonies, and thereby to change a rebellion into a revolution. So Mr. Lincoln and Mr. Seward, not willing to give the unfriendly power this opportunity, only wrote down in the national ledger sundry charges against Great Britain, which were afterward paid, not promptly, yet in full!

Another provoking thing was the placing of

Confederate loans in London. This could not be interfered with. The only comfort was that the blockaded South had much difficulty in laying hands upon the proceeds of the bonds which English friends of the Slave Empire were induced to buy. Yet time, always the faithful auxiliary of the North, took care of this matter also. When the news of Gettysburg and Vicksburg came, the investors, who had scarcely finished writing the cheques with which to pay their subscriptions, were obliged to face a drop of thirty per cent, in the market price of their new securities. For many years after the war was over British strong boxes wasted space in accommodating these absurd documents, while the idea of their worthlessness was slowly filtering through the minds of their owners.

Another thing, which did no harm at all, but was exceedingly vexatious, was the constant suggestion of European mediation. For a couple of years, at least, the air was full of this sort of talk. Once, in spite of abundant discouragement, the French emperor actually committed the folly of making the proposal. It came inopportunely on February 3, 1863, after the defeat of Fredericksburg, like a carrion bird after a battle. It was rejected very decisively, and if Napoleon III. appreciated Mr. Seward's dispatch, he became aware that he had shown gross lack of discernment. Yet he was not without some remarkable companions in this incapacity to understand that which he was observing, as if from aloft, with an air of superior wisdom. One would think that the condition of feeling in the United States which had induced Governor Hicks, in the early stage of the rebellion, to suggest a reference to Lord Lyons, as arbitrator, had long since gone by. But it had not; and it is the surprising truth that Horace Greeley had lately written to M. Mercier, the French minister at Washington, suggesting precisely the step which the emperor took; and there were other less conspicuous citizens who manifested a similar lack of spirit and intelligence.

All this, however, was really of no serious consequence. Talk about mediation coming from American citizens could do little actual injury, and from foreigners it could do none. If the foreigners had only been induced to offer it by reason of a friendly desire to help the country in its hour of stress, the rejection might even have been accompanied with sincere thanks. Unfortunately, however, it never came in this guise; but, on the contrary, it always involved the offensive assumption that the North could never restore the integrity of the Union by force. Northern failure was established in advance, and was the unconcealed, if not quite the avowed, basis of the whole transaction. Now though mere unfriendliness, not overstepping the requirements of international law, could inflict little substantial hurt, yet there was something very discouraging in the unanimity and positiveness with which all these experienced European statesmen assumed the success of the Confederacy as the absolutely sure outcome; and in this time of extreme trial to discourage was to injure. Furthermore, the undisguised pleasure with which this prospect was contemplated was sorely trying to men oppressed by the burdens of anxiety and trouble which rested on the President and his ministers. The man who had begun life as a frontiersman had need of much moral courage to sustain him in the face of the presagings, the condemnations, and the hostility of nearly all the sage and well-trained statesmen of Europe. In those days the United States had not yet fully thrown off a certain thralldom of awe before European opinion. Nevertheless, at whatever cost in the coin of self-reliance, the President and the secretary maintained the courage of their opinions, and never swerved or hesitated in the face of foreign antipathy or contempt. The treatment inflicted upon them was only so much added to the weight under which they had to stand up.

Rebellion and foreign ill-will, even Copperheadism, presented difficulties and opposition which were in a certain sense legitimate; but that loyal Republicans should sow the path of the administration thick with annoyances certainly did seem an unfair trial. Yet, on sundry occasions, some of which have been mentioned, these men did this thing, and they did it in the very uncompromising and exasperating manner which is the natural emanation from conscientious purpose and intense self-faith. An instance occurred in December, 1862. The blacker the prospect became, the more bitter waxed the extremists. Such is the fashion of fanatics, who are wont to grow more warm as their chances seem to grow more desperate; and some of the leaders of the anti-slavery wing of the Republican party were fanatics. These men by no means confined their hostility to the Democratic McClellan; but extended it to so old and tried a Republican as the secretary of state himself. It had already come to this, that the new party was composed of, if not split into, two sections of widely discordant views. The conservative body found its notions expressed in the cabinet by Seward; the radical body had a mouthpiece in Chase. The conservatives were not aggressive; but the radicals waged a genuine political warfare, and denounced Seward, not, indeed, with the vehemence which was considered to be appropriate against McClellan, yet very strenuously. Finally this hostility reached such a pass that, at a caucus of Republican senators, it was actually voted to demand the dismission of this long-tried and distinguished leader in the anti-slavery struggle. Later, in place of this blunt vote, a more polite equivalent was substituted, in the shape of a request for a reconstruction of the cabinet. Then a committee visited the President and pressed him to have done with the secretary, whom they thought lukewarm. Meanwhile, Seward had heard of what was going forward, and, in order to free Mr. Lincoln from embarrassment, he had already tendered his resignation before the committee arrived.

The crisis was serious. The recent elections indicated that even while, as now, the government represented all the sections of Republicanism, still the situation was none too good; but if it was to be controlled by the extremist wing of a discordant party, the chance that it could endure to the end the tremendous strain of civil war was reduced almost to hopelessness. The visitors who brought this unwelcome suggestion to the President received no immediate response or expression of opinion from him, but were invited to come again in the evening; they did so, and were then much surprised to meet all the members of the cabinet except Mr. Seward. An outspoken discussion ensued, in which Mr. Chase found his position embarrassing, if not equivocal. On the following morning, he, with other members of the cabinet, came again for further talk with the President; in his hand he held a written resignation of his office. He "tendered" it, yet "did not advance to deliver it," whereupon the President stepped forward and took it "with alacrity." [48]

Having now in his hands the resignations of the chiefs of the two principal factions of the party, the President had made the first step towards relieving the situation of dangerous one-sidedness. At once he took the next step by sending to each this note:—

December 20, 1862.

HON. WILLIAM H. SEWARD and HON. SALMON P. CHASE:

*Gentlemen,*—You have respectively tendered me your resignations as secretary of state and secretary of the treasury of the United States. I am apprised of the circumstances which render this course personally desirable to each of you; but, after most anxious consideration, my deliberate judgment is, that the public interest does not admit of it.

I therefore have to request that you will resume the duties of your departments respectively.

Your obedient servant,

A. LINCOLN.

The next morning Mr. Seward wrote briefly: "I have cheerfully resumed the functions of this department, in obedience to your command." Mr. Chase seemed to hesitate. On December 20, in the afternoon, he had written a letter, in which he had said that he thought it desirable that his resignation should be accepted. He gave as his reason that recent events had "too rudely jostled the unity" of the cabinet; and he intimated that, with both himself and Seward out of it, an improved condition might be reached. He had not, however, actually dispatched this, when the President's note reached him. He then, though feeling his convictions strengthened, decided to hold back the letter which he had prepared and "to sleep on" the matter. Having slept, he wrote, on the morning of December 22, a different letter, to the effect that, though reflection had not much, if at all, changed his original opinion as to the desirability of his resignation, yet he would conform to the judgment and wishes of the President. If Mr. Chase was less gracious than Mr. Seward in this business, it is to be remembered that he was very much more dissatisfied with the President's course than was Mr. Seward, who, indeed, for the most part was not dissatisfied at all.

Thus a dangerous crisis was escaped rather than overcome. For though after the relief given by this plain speaking the situation did not again become quite so strained as it had previously been, yet disagreement between men naturally prudent and men naturally extremist was inevitable. Nevertheless it was something that the two sections had encountered each other, and that neither had won control of the government. The President had restrained dissension within safe limits and had saved himself from the real or apparent domination of a faction. When it was all over, he said: "Now I can ride; I have got a pumpkin in each end of my bag." Later on he repeated: "I do not see how it could have been done better. I am sure it was right. If I had yielded to that storm and dismissed Seward, the thing would all have slumped over one way, and we should have been left with a scanty handful of supporters." Undoubtedly he had managed very skillfully a very difficult affair, but he ought never to have been compelled to arrange such quarrels in the camp of his own party.

Those counties of Virginia which lay west of the Alleghanies contained a population which was, by an overwhelming majority, strenuously loyal. There had long been more of antagonism than of friendship between them and the rest of the State, and now, as has been already mentioned, the secession of Virginia from the Union stimulated them, in turn, to secede from Virginia. In the summer of 1861 they took measures to form themselves into a separate State; and in April, 1862, they adopted a state Constitution by a vote of 18,862 yeas against 514 nays. A bill for the admission of "West Virginia" was passed by the Senate in July, and by the House in December, and was laid before the President for signature. There were nice questions of constitutional law about this, and some doubt also as to whether the move was altogether well advised. Mr. Lincoln asked the opinions of the cabinet as to whether he should sign the bill. Three said Yea, and three Nay; and it was noteworthy that the three who thought it expedient also thought it constitutional, and that the three who thought it inexpedient also thought it unconstitutional. Mr. Lincoln, not much assisted, then decided in the affirmative, and signed the bill December 31, 1862. A statement of the reasons [49] which led him to this decision concludes thus: "It is said that the admission of West Virginia is secession, and tolerated only because it is *our* secession. Well, if we call it by that name, there is still difference enough between secession against the Constitution and secession in favor of the Constitution." Mr. Elaine says that the creation of this State was sustained by "legal fictions;" and Thaddeus Stevens declared that it was a measure entirely outside of any provision of the Constitution, yet said that he should vote for it in accordance with his general principle: that none of the States in rebellion were entitled to the protection of the Constitution. The Republicans themselves were divided in their views as to the lawfulness of the measure. However the law may have stood, it is evident to us, looking backward, that for practical purposes the wisdom of the President's judgment cannot be impugned. The measure was the amputation of so much territory from that which the Confederates, if they should succeed, could claim as their own; and it produced no inconvenience at all when, instead of succeeding, they failed.

Many causes conspired to induce an obstreperous outbreak of "Copperheadism" in the spring of 1863. The Democratic successes in the elections of the preceding autumn were in part a premonition of this, in part also a cause. Moreover, reaction was inevitable after the intense outburst of patriotic enthusiasm which had occurred during the earlier part of the war. But more than all this, Mr. Lincoln wrote, and every one knew, that, "if the war fails, the administration fails," and thus far the war had been a failure. So the grumblers, the malcontents, and the Southern sympathizers argued that the administration also, at least so far as it had gone, had been a failure; and they fondly conceived that their day of triumph was dawning.

That which was due, punctually arrived. There now came into prominence those secret societies which, under a shifting variety of names, continued to scheme and to menace until the near and visible end of the war effected their death by inanition. The Knights of the Golden Circle, The Order of American Knights, the Order of the Star, The Sons of Liberty, in turn enlisted recruits in an abundance which is now remembered with surprise and humiliation,—sensations felt perhaps most keenly by the sons of those who themselves belonged to the organizations. Mr. Seward well said: "These persons will be trying to forget, years hence, that they ever opposed this war." These societies gave expression to a terrible blunder, for Copperheadism was even more stupid than it was vicious. But the fact of their stupidity made them harmless. Their very names labeled them. Men who like to enroll themselves in Golden Circles and in Star galaxies seldom accomplish much in exacting, especially in dangerous, practical affairs. Mr. Lincoln took this sensible view of these associations. His secretaries, who doubtless speak from personal knowledge, say that his attitude "was one of good-humored contempt."

As a rule these "Knights" showed their valor in the way of mischief, plotting bold things, but never doing them. They encouraged soldiers to desert; occasionally they assassinated an enrolling officer; they maintained communications with the Confederates, to whom they gave information and occasionally also material aid; they were tireless in caucus work and wire-pulling; in Indiana, in 1863, they got sufficient control of the legislature to embarrass Governor Morton quite seriously; they talked much about establishing a Northwestern Confederacy; a few of them were perhaps willing to aid in those cowardly efforts at incendiarism in the great Northern cities, also in the poisoning of reservoirs, in the distribution of clothing infected with disease, and in other like villainies which were arranged by Confederate emissaries in Canada, and some of which were imperfectly carried out in New York and elsewhere; they also made great plans for an uprising and for the release of Confederate prisoners in Ohio, Illinois, and Indiana. But no actual outbreak ever occurred; for when they had come close to the danger line, these associates of mediaeval tastes and poetic appellatives always stopped short.

The President was often urged to take decisive measures against these devisers of ignoble treasons. Such men as Governor Morton and General Rosecrans strove to alarm him. But he said that the "conspiracy merited no special attention, being about an equal mixture of puerility and malice." He had perfect information as to all the doings and plottings, and as to the membership, of all the societies, and was able to measure accurately their real power of hurtfulness; he never could be induced to treat them with a severity which was abundantly deserved, but which might not have been politic and would certainly have added to the labor, the expense, and the complications of the government. "Nothing can make me believe," he once charitably said, "that one hundred thousand Indiana Democrats are disloyal!" His judgment was proved to be sound; for had many of these men been in grim earnest in their disloyalty, they would have achieved something. In fact these bodies were unquestionably composed of a small infusion of genuine traitors, combined with a vastly larger proportion of bombastic fellows who liked to talk, and foolish people who were tickled in their shallow fancy by the element of secrecy and the fineness of the titles.

The man whose name became unfortunately preeminent for disloyalty at this time was Clement L. Vallandigham, a Democrat, of Ohio. General Burnside was placed in command of the Department of the Ohio, March 25, 1863, and having for the moment no Confederates to deal with, he turned his attention to the Copperheads, whom he regarded with even greater animosity. His Order No. 38, issued on April 13, brought these hornets about his ears in impetuous fury; for, having made a long schedule of their favorite offenses, which he designed for the future severely to proscribe, he closed it by saying that "the habit of declaring sympathy for the enemy will not be allowed in this Department;" and he warned persons with treasonable tongues that, unless they should keep that little member in order, they might expect either to suffer death as traitors, or to be sent southward within the lines of "their friends." Now Mr. Vallandigham had been a member of Congress since 1856, and was at present a prominent candidate for any office which the Democrats of his State or of the United States might be able to fill; he was the popular and rising leader of the Copperhead wing of the Democracy. Such was his position that it would have been ignominious for him to allow any Union general to put a military gag in his mouth. Nor did he. On the contrary, he made speeches which at that time might well have made Unionists mad with rage, and which still seem to have gone far beyond the limit of disloyalty which any government could safely tolerate. Therefore on May 4 he was arrested by a company of soldiers, brought to Cincinnati, and thrown into jail. His friends gathered in anger, and a riot was narrowly avoided. At once, by order of General Burnside, he was tried by a military commission. He was charged with "publicly expressing sympathy for those in arms against the government of the United States, and declaring disloyal sentiments and opinions, with the object and purpose of weakening the power of the government in its efforts to suppress an unlawful rebellion." Specifications were drawn from a speech delivered by him on or about May 1. The evidence conclusively sustained the indictment, and the officers promptly pronounced him guilty, whereupon he was sentenced by Burnside to confinement in Fort Warren. An effort to obtain his release by a writ of habeas corpus was ineffectual.

The rapidity of these proceedings had taken every one by surprise. But the Democrats throughout the North, rapidly surveying the situation, seized the opportunity which perhaps had been too inconsiderately given them. The country rang with plausible outcries and high-sounding oratory concerning military usurpation, violation of the Constitution, and stifling freedom of speech. It was painfully obvious that this combination of rhetoric and argument troubled the minds of many well-affected persons. If the President had been consulted in the outset, it is thought by some that he would not have allowed matters to proceed so far. Soon afterward, in his reply to the New York Democrats, he said: "In my own discretion, I do not know whether I would have ordered the arrest of Mr. Vallandigham." On the other hand, Mr. Blaine states that Burnside "undoubtedly had confidential instructions in regard to the mode of dealing with the rising tide of disloyalty which, beginning in Ohio, was sweeping over the West."

In a very short time the violence of the fault-finding reached so excessive a measure that Burnside offered his resignation; but Mr. Lincoln declined to accept it, saying that, though all the cabinet regretted the necessity for the arrest, "some perhaps doubting there was a real necessity for it, yet, being done, all were for seeing you through with it." This seems to have been his own position. In fact it was clear that, whether what had been done was or was not a mistake, to undo it would be a greater mistake. Accordingly Mr. Lincoln only showed that he felt the pressure of the criticism and denunciation by commuting the sentence, and directing that Vallandigham should be released from confinement and sent within the Confederate lines,—which was, indeed, a very shrewd and clever move, and much better than the imprisonment. Accordingly the quasi rebel was tendered to and accepted by a Confederate picket, on May 25. He protested vehemently, declared his loyalty, and insisted that his character was that of a prisoner of war. But the Confederates, who had no objection whatsoever to his peculiar methods of demonstrating "loyalty" to their opponents, insisted upon treating him as a friend, the victim of an enemy common to themselves and him; and instead of exchanging him as a prisoner, they facilitated his passage through the blockade on his way to Canada. There he arrived in safety, and thence issued sundry manifestoes to the Democracy. On June 11 the Democratic Convention of Ohio nominated him as their candidate for governor, and it seems that for a while they really expected to elect him.

In the condition of feeling during the months in which these events were occurring, they undeniably subjected the government to a very severe strain. They furnished the Democrats with ammunition far better than any which they had yet found, and they certainly used it well. Since the earliest days of the war there had never been quite an end of the protestation against arbitrary military arrests and the suspension of the sacred writ of habeas corpus, and now the querulous outcry was revived with startling vehemence. Crowded meetings were held everywhere; popular orators terrified or enraged their audiences with pictures of the downfall of freedom, the jeopardy of every citizen; resolutions and votes without number expressed the alarm and anger of the great assemblages; learned lawyers lent their wisdom to corroborate the rhetoricians, and even some Republican newspapers joined the croaking procession of their Democratic rivals. Erelong the assaults appeared to be producing effects so serious and widespread that the President was obliged to enter into the controversy. On May 16 a monster meeting of "the Democrats of New York" was told by Governor Seymour that the question was: "whether this war is waged to put down rebellion at the South, or to destroy free institutions at the North." Excited by such instigation, the audience passed sundry damnatory resolutions and sent them to the President.

Upon receiving these, Mr. Lincoln felt that he must come down into the arena, without regard to official conventionality. On June 12 he replied by a full presentation of the case, from his point of view. He had once more to do the same thing in response to another address of like character which was sent to him on June 11 by the Democratic State Convention of Ohio. In both cases the documents prepared by the remonstrants were characterized, to more than the usual degree, by that dignified and *ore rotundo* phraseology, that solemnity in the presentation of imposing generalities, which are wont to be so dear to committees charged with drafting resolutions. The replies of the President were in striking contrast to this rhetorical method alike in substance and in form; clear, concise, and close-knit, they were models of good work in political controversy, and like most of his writing they sorely tempt to liberal transcription, a temptation which must unfortunately be resisted, save for a few sentences. The opening paragraph in the earlier paper was cleverly put:—

"The resolutions are resolvable into two propositions,—first, the expression of a purpose to sustain the cause of the Union, to secure peace through victory, and to support the administration in every constitutional and lawful measure to suppress the rebellion; and, secondly, a declaration of censure upon the administration for supposed unconstitutional action, such as the making of military arrests. And, from the two propositions, a third is deduced, which is, that the gentlemen composing the meeting are resolved on doing their part to maintain our common government and country, despite the folly or wickedness, as they may conceive, of any administration. This position is eminently patriotic, and, as such, I thank the meeting, and congratulate the nation for it. My own purpose is the same, so that the meeting and myself have a common object, and can have no difference, except in the choice of means or measures for effecting that object."

Later on followed some famous sentences:—

"Mr. Vallandigham avows his hostility to the war on the part of the Union; and his arrest was made because he was laboring, with some effect, to prevent the raising of troops, to encourage desertion from the army, and to leave the rebellion without an adequate military force to suppress it. He was not arrested because he was damaging the political prospects of the administration or the personal interests of the commanding general, but because he was damaging the army, upon the existence and vigor of which the life of the Nation depends....

"I understand the meeting whose resolutions I am considering to be in favor of suppressing the rebellion by military force, by armies. Long experience has shown that armies cannot be maintained unless desertion shall be punished by the severe penalty of death.

"The case requires, and the law and the Constitution sanction, this punishment. Must I shoot a simple-minded soldier boy who deserts, while I must not touch a hair of a wily agitator who induces him to desert? This is none the less injurious when effected by getting a father, or brother, or friend, into a public meeting, and there working upon his feelings until he is persuaded to write the soldier boy that he is fighting in a bad cause, for a wicked administration of a contemptible government, too weak to arrest and punish him if he shall desert. I think that, in such a case, to silence the agitator, and save the boy, is not only constitutional, but withal a great mercy."

The Ohio Democrats found themselves confronted with this:—

"Your nominee for governor ... is known to you and to the world to declare against the use of an army to suppress the rebellion. Your own attitude therefore encourages desertion, resistance to the draft, and the like, because it teaches those who incline to desert and to escape the draft to believe it is your purpose to protect them, and to hope that you will become strong enough to do so."

The arguments of the President called out retort rather than reply, for in fact they really could not be answered, and they were too accurately put to be twisted by sophistry; that they reached the minds of the people was soon made evident. The Democratic managers had made a fatal blunder in arraying the party in a position of extreme hostility to the war. Though there were at the North hosts of grumblers who were maliciously pleased at all embarrassments of the administration, and who were willing to make the prosecution of the war very difficult, there were not hosts who were ready to push difficulty to the point of impossibility. On the other hand the fight was made very shrewdly by the Union men of Ohio, who nominated John Brough, a "war Democrat," as their candidate. Then the scales fell from the eyes of the people; they saw that in real fact votes for Brough or for Vallandigham were, respectively, votes for or against the Union. The campaign became a direct trial of strength on this point. Freedom of speech, habeas corpus, and the kindred incidents of the Vallandigham case were laid aside as not being the genuine and fundamental questions. It was one of those instances in which the common sense of the multitude suddenly takes control, brushes away confusing details, and gets at the great and true issue. The result was that Vallandigham was defeated by a majority of over 100,000 votes; and thus a perilous crisis was well passed. This incident had put the Republican ascendency in extreme peril, but when the administration emerged from the trial with a success so brilliant, it was thereafter much stronger than if the test had never been made. The strain was one of that kind to which the war was subjecting the whole nation, a strain which strengthens rather than weakens the body which triumphantly encounters it. The credit for the result was generally admitted to be chiefly due to Mr. Lincoln's effective presentation of the Republican position.

As the second year of the war drew towards its close, the administration had to face a new and grave difficulty in the recruitment of the army. Serious errors which had been made in calling and enlisting troops now began to bear fruit. Under the influence of the first enthusiasm a large proportion of the adult male population at the North would readily have enlisted "for the war;" but unfortunately that opportunity had not been seized by the government, and it soon passed, never to return. That the President and his advisers had been blameworthy can hardly be said; but whether they had been blameworthy or excusable became an immaterial issue, when they found that the terms of enlistment were soon to expire, and also that just when the war was at its hottest, the patriotism of the people seemed at its coldest. Defeats in the field and Copperheadism at home combined in their dispiriting and deadly work. Voluntary enlistment almost ceased. Thereupon Congress passed an act "for enrolling and calling out the national forces." All able-bodied citizens between twenty and forty-five years of age were to "perform military duty in the service of the United States, when called on by the President for that purpose." [50] This was strenuous earnest, for it portended a draft.

The situation certainly was not to be considered without solicitude when, in a war which peculiarly appealed to patriotism, compulsion must be used to bring involuntary recruits to maintain the contest. Yet the relaxation of the patriotic temper was really not so great as this fact might seem to indicate. Besides many partial and obvious explanations, one which is less obvious should also be noted. During two years of war the people, notoriously of a temperament readily to accept new facts and to adapt themselves thereto, had become accustomed to a state of war, and had learned to regard it as a *condition*, not normal and permanent, yet of indefinite duration. Accordingly they were now of opinion that the government must charge itself with the management of this condition, that is to say, with the conduct of the war, as a strict matter of business, to be carried on like all other public duties and functions. In the first months of stress every man had felt called upon to contribute, personally, his own moral, financial, and even physical support; but that crisis had passed, and it was now conceived that the administration might fairly be required to arrange for getting men and money and supplies in the systematic and business-like fashion in which, as history taught, all other governments had been accustomed to get these necessaries in time of war.

At any rate, however it was to be explained or commented upon, the fact confronted Mr. Lincoln that he must institute enrollment and drafting. The machinery was arranged and the very disagreeable task was entered upon early in the summer of 1863. If it was painful in the first instance for the President to order this, the process was immediately made as hateful as possible for him. Even loyal and hearty "war-governors" seemed at once to accept as their chief object the protection of the people of their respective States from the operation of the odious law. The mercantile element was instantly and fully accepted by them. The most patriotic did not hesitate to make every effort to have the assigned quotas reduced; they drew jealous comparisons to show inequalities; and they concocted all sorts of schemes for obtaining credits. Not marshaling recruits in the field, but filling quotas upon paper, seemed a legitimate purpose; for the matter had become one of figures, of business, of competition, and all the shrewdness of the Yankee mind was at once aroused to gain for one's self, though at the expense of one's neighbors. Especially the Democratic officials were viciously fertile in creating obstacles. The fact that the Act of Congress was based on the precedent of an Act of the Confederate Congress, passed a year before, did not seem in the least to conciliate the Copperheads. Governor Seymour of New York obtained a discreditable preeminence in thwarting the administration. He gathered ingenious statistics, and upon them based charges of dishonest apportionments and of fraudulent discrimination against Democratic precincts. He also declared the statute unconstitutional, and asked the President to stay all proceedings under it until it could be passed upon by the Supreme Court of the United States,—an ingenuous proposition, which he neglected to make practicable by arranging with General Lee to remain conveniently quiescent while the learned judges should be discussing the methods of reinforcing the Northern armies.

In a word, Mr. Lincoln was confronted by every difficulty that Republican inventiveness and Democratic disaffection could devise. Yet the draft must go on, or the war must stop. His reasonableness, his patience, his capacity to endure unfair trials, received in this business a demonstration more conspicuous than in any other during his presidency. Whenever apportionments, dates, and credits were questioned, he was liberal in making temporary, and sometimes permanent allowances, preferring that any error in exactions should be in the way of moderation. But in the main business he was inflexible; and at last it came to a direct issue between himself and the malcontents, whether the draft should go on or stop. In the middle of July the mob in New York city tested the question. The drafting began there on Saturday morning, July 11. On Monday morning, July 13, the famous riot broke out. It was an appalling storm of rage on the part of the lower classes; during three days terror and barbarism controlled the great city, and in its streets countless bloody and hideous massacres were perpetrated. Negroes especially were hanged and otherwise slain most cruelly. The governor was so inefficient that he was charged, of course extravagantly, with being secretly in league with the ringleaders. A thousand or more lives, as it was roughly estimated, were lost in this mad and brutal fury, before order was again restored. The government gave the populace a short time to cool, and then sent 10,000 troops into the city and proceeded with the business without further interruption. A smaller outbreak took place in Boston, but was promptly suppressed. In other places it was threatened, but did not occur. In spite of all, the President continued to execute the law. Yet although by this means the armies might be kept full, the new men were very inferior to those who had responded voluntarily to the earlier calls. Every knave in the country adopted the lucrative and tolerably safe occupation of "bounty-jumping," and every worthless loafer was sent to the front, whence he escaped at the first opportunity to sell himself anew and to be counted again. The material of the army suffered great depreciation, which was only imperfectly offset by the improvement of the military machine, whereby a more effective discipline, resembling that of European professionalism, was enforced. [51]

[48] N. and H. vi. 268; this account is derived from their twelfth chapter.

[49] N. and H. vi. 309, from MS.

[50] The act was signed by the President, March 3, 1863.

[51] Concerning the deterioration of the army, in certain particulars, see an article, "The War as we see it now," by John C. Ropes, *Scribner's Magazine*, June, 1891.

# CHAPTER VII
# THE TURN OF THE TIDE

The winter of 1862-63 was for the Rebellion much what the winter of Valley Forge was for the Revolution. It passed, however, and the nation still clung fast to its purpose. The weak brethren who had become dismayed were many, but the people as a whole was steadfast. This being so, ultimate success became assured. Wise and cool-headed men, in a frame of mind to contemplate the situation as it really was, saw that the tide was about at its turning, and that the Union would not drift away to destruction in this storm at any rate. They saw that the North *could* whip the South, if it chose; and it was now sufficiently evident that it would choose,—that it would endure, and would finish its task. It was only the superficial observers who were deceived by the Virginian disasters, which rose so big in the foreground as partially to conceal the real fact,—that the Confederacy was being at once strangled and starved to death. The waters of the Atlantic Ocean and of the Gulf of Mexico were being steadily made more and more inaccessible, as one position after another along the coast gradually passed into Federal hands. The Mississippi River, at last a Union stream from its source to its mouth, now made a Chinese wall for the Confederacy on the west. Upon the north the line of conflict had been pushed down to the northern borders of Mississippi and Georgia, and the superincumbent weight of the vast Northwest lay with a deadly pressure upon these two States.

It was, therefore, only in Virginia that the Confederates had held their own, and here, with all their victories, they had done no more than just hold their own. They had to recognize, also, that from such battlefields as Fredericksburg and Chancellorsville they gathered no sustenance, however much they might reap in the way of glory. Neither had they gained even any ground, for the armies were still manoeuvring along the same roads over which they had been tramping and swaying to and fro for more than two years. By degrees the Southern resources in the way of men, money, food, and supplies generally, were being depleted. The Confederacy was like a lake, artificially inclosed, which was fed by no influx from outside, while it was tapped and drained at many points.

On the other hand, within the North, affairs were coming into a more satisfactory condition. It was true that all the military successes of July had not discouraged the malcontents; and during the summer they had been busily preparing for the various state elections of the autumn, which they hoped would strongly corroborate their congressional triumphs of 1862. But when the time came they were exceedingly disappointed. The law now, fairly enough, permitted soldiers in the field to vote, and this was, of course, a reinforcement for the Republican party; but even among the voters at home the Democratic reaction of the preceding year had spent its force. In October Pennsylvania gave Governor Curtin, the Republican candidate for reëlection, a majority of 15,000. In the same month, under the circumstances described in the preceding chapter, Ohio buried Vallandigham under a hostile majority of more than 100,000. The lead thus given by the "October States" was followed by the "November States." In New York no governor was to be elected; but the Republican state ticket showed a majority of 30,000, whereas the year before Seymour had polled a majority of 10,000. The Northwest fell into the procession, though after a hard fight. A noteworthy feature of the struggle, which was fierce and for a time doubtful in Illinois, was a letter from Mr. Lincoln. He was invited to attend a mass meeting at Springfield, and with reluctance felt himself obliged to decline; but in place of a speech, which might not have been preserved, the good fortune of posterity caused him to write this letter:—

August 26, 1863.

HON. JAMES C. CONKLING:

*My dear Sir,*—Your letter inviting me to attend a mass meeting of unconditional Union men, to be held at the capital of Illinois, on the third day of September, has been received. It would be very agreeable for me thus to meet my old friends at my own home, but I cannot just now be absent from here as long as a visit there would require.

The meeting is to be of all those who maintain unconditional devotion to the Union, and I am sure my old political friends will thank me for tendering, as I do, the nation's gratitude to those other noble men whom no partisan malice or partisan hope can make false to the nation's life.

There are those who are dissatisfied with me. To such I would say: you desire peace, and you blame me that we do not have it. But how can we attain it? There are but three conceivable ways: First, to suppress the rebellion by force of arms. This I am trying to do. Are you for it? If you are, so far we are agreed. If you are not for it, a second way is to give up the Union. I am against this. Are you for it? If you are, you should say so plainly. If you are not for *force*, nor yet for *dissolution*, there only remains some imaginable *compromise*.

I do not believe that any compromise embracing the maintenance of the Union is now possible. All that I learn leads to a directly opposite belief. The strength of the rebellion is its military, its army. That army dominates all the country and all the people within its range. Any offer of terms made by any man or men within that range, in opposition to that army, is simply nothing for the present; because such man or men have no power whatever to enforce their side of a compromise, if one were made with them.

To illustrate: suppose refugees from the South and peace men of the North get together in convention, and frame and proclaim a compromise embracing a restoration of the Union. In what way can that compromise be used to keep Lee's army out of Pennsylvania? Meade's army can keep Lee's army out of Pennsylvania, and, I think, can ultimately drive it out of existence. But no paper compromise, to which the controllers of Lee's army are not agreed, can at all affect that army. In an effort at such compromise we would [should] waste time, which the enemy would improve to our disadvantage, and that would be all.

A compromise, to be effective, must be made either with those who control the rebel army, or with the people, first liberated from the domination of that army by the success of our own army. Now, allow me to assure you that no word or intimation from that rebel army, or from any of the men controlling it, in relation to any peace compromise, has ever come to my knowledge or belief. All charges and insinuations to the contrary are deceptive and groundless. And I promise you that if any such proposition shall hereafter come, it shall not be rejected and kept a secret from you. I freely acknowledge myself to be the servant of the people, according to the bond of service, the United States Constitution; and that, as such, I am responsible to them. But to be plain, you are dissatisfied with me about the negro. Quite likely there is a difference of opinion between you and myself upon that subject. I certainly wish that all men could be free, while you, I suppose, do not. Yet I have neither adopted nor proposed any measure which is not consistent with even your views, provided that you are for the Union. I suggested compensated emancipation, to which you replied: you wished not to be taxed to buy negroes. But I had not asked you to be taxed to buy negroes, except in such a way as to save you from greater taxation to save the Union exclusively by other means.

You dislike the emancipation proclamation, and perhaps would have it retracted. You say it is unconstitutional. I think differently. I think the Constitution invests its commander-in-chief with all the law of war in time of war. The most that can be said, if so much, is, that slaves are property. Is there, has there ever been, any question that by the law of war, property, both of enemies and friends, may be taken when needed? And is it not needed whenever it helps us and hurts the enemy? Armies, the world over, destroy enemies' property when they cannot use it, and even destroy their own to keep it from the enemy.

... But the proclamation, as law, either is valid or is not valid. If it is not valid it needs no retraction. If it is valid, it cannot be retracted, any more than the dead can be brought to life. Some of you profess to think its retraction would operate favorably for the Union. Why better after the retraction than before the issue? There was more than a year and a half of trial to suppress the rebellion before the proclamation was issued, the last one hundred days of which passed under an explicit notice that it was coming, unless averted by those in revolt returning to their allegiance. The war has certainly progressed as favorably for us since the issue of the proclamation as before. I know, as fully as one can know the opinion of others, that some of the commanders of our armies in the field, who have given us our most important victories, believe the emancipation policy and the use of colored troops constitute the heaviest blows yet dealt to the rebellion, and that at least one of those important successes could not have been achieved, when it was, but for the aid of black soldiers.

Among the commanders who hold these views are some who have never had an affinity with what is called "abolitionism," or with "Republican party politics," but who hold them purely as military opinions. I submit their opinions as entitled to some weight against the objections often urged that emancipation and arming the blacks are unwise as military measures, and were not adopted as such in good faith.

You say that you will not fight to free negroes. Some of them seem willing to fight for you; but no matter. Fight you, then, exclusively to save the Union. I issued the proclamation on purpose to aid you in saving the Union. Whenever you shall have conquered all resistance to the Union, if I shall urge you to continue fighting it will be an apt time then for you to declare you will not fight to free negroes. I thought that, in your struggle for the Union, to whatever extent the negroes should cease helping the enemy, to that extent it weakened the enemy in his resistance to you. Do you think differently?

I thought that whatever negroes can be got to do as soldiers, leaves just so much less for white soldiers to do in saving the Union. Does it appear otherwise to you? But negroes, like other people, act upon motives. Why should they do anything for us, if we will do nothing for them? If they stake their lives for us, they must be prompted by the strongest motive, even the promise of freedom. And the promise, being made, must be kept.

The signs look better. The Father of Waters again goes unvexed to the sea. Thanks to the great Northwest for it; nor yet wholly to them. Three hundred miles up they met New England, Empire, Keystone, and Jersey, hewing their way right and left. The sunny South, too, in more colors than one, also lent a helping hand. On the spot their part of the history was jotted down in black and white. The job was a great national one, and let none be slighted who bore an honorable part in it. And while those who have cleared the great river may well be proud, even that is not all. It is hard to say that anything has been more bravely or well done than at Antietam, Murfreesboro', Gettysburg, and on many fields of less note. Nor must Uncle Sam's web-feet be forgotten. At all the watery margins they have been present, not only on the deep sea, the broad bay, and the rapid river, but also up the narrow muddy bayou, and wherever the ground was a little damp, they have been and made their tracks. Thanks to all. For the great Republic,—for the principle it lives by and keeps alive,—for man's vast future,—thanks to all.

Peace does not appear so distant as it did. I hope it will come soon, and come to stay, and so come as to be worth the keeping in all future time. It will then have been proved that among free men there can be no successful appeal from the ballot to the bullet, and that they who take such appeal are sure to lose their case and pay the cost. And there will be some black men who can remember that with silent tongue, and clinched teeth, and steady eye, and well-poised bayonet, they have helped mankind on to this great consummation; while I fear there will be some white men unable to forget that with malignant heart and deceitful speech they have striven to hinder it.

Still, let us not be over-sanguine of a speedy final triumph. Let us be quite sober. Let us diligently apply the means, never doubting that a just God, in his own good time, will give us the rightful result.

Yours very truly,

A. LINCOLN.

This was a fair statement of past facts and of the present condition; and thus the plain tokens of the time showed that the menace of disaffection had been met and sufficiently conquered. The President had let the nation see the strength of his will and the immutability of his purpose. He had faced bullying Republican politicians, a Democratic reaction, Copperheadism, and mob violence, and by none of these had he been in the least degree shaken or diverted from his course. On the contrary, from so many and so various struggles he had come out the victor, a real ruler of the country.

He had shown that whenever and by whomsoever, and in whatever part of the land he was pushed to use power, he would use it. Temporarily the great republic was under a "strong government," and Mr. Lincoln was the strength. Though somewhat cloaked by forms, there was for a while in the United States a condition of "one-man power," and the people instinctively recognized it, though they would on no account admit it in plain words. In fact every malcontent knew that there was no more use in attempting to resist the American President than in attempting to resist a French emperor or a Russian czar; there was even less use, for while the President managed on one plausible ground or another to have and to exercise all the power that he needed, he was sustained by the good-will and confidence of a majority of the people, which lay as a solid substratum beneath all the disturbance on the surface. It was well that this was so, for a war conducted by a cabinet or a congress could have ended only in disaster. This peculiar character of the situation may not be readily admitted; it is often convenient to deny and ignore facts in order to assert popular theories; and that there was a real *master* in the United States is a proposition which many will consider it highly improper to make and very patriotic to contradict. None the less, however, it is true, and by the autumn of 1863 every intelligent man in the country *felt* that it was true. Moreover, it was because this was true, and because that master was immovably persistent in the purpose to conquer the South, that the conquest of the South could now be discerned as substantially a certainty in the future.

Some other points should also be briefly made here. The war is to be divided into two stages. The first two years were educational; subsequently the fruits of that education were attained. The men who had studied war as a profession, but had had no practical experience, found much to learn in warfare as a reality after the struggle began. But before the summer of 1863 there were in the service many generals, than whom none better could be desired. "Public men" were somewhat slow in discovering that their capacity to do pretty much everything did not include the management of campaigns. But by the summer of 1863 these "public" persons made less noise in the land than they had made in the days of McClellan; and though political considerations could never be wholly suppressed, the question of retaining or displacing a general no longer divided parties, or superseded, and threatened to wreck, the vital question of the war. Moreover, as has been remarked in another connection, the nation began to appreciate that while war was a science so far as the handling of armies in the field was concerned, it was strictly a business in its other aspects. By, and in fact before, the summer of 1863 this business had been learned and was being efficiently conducted.

Time and experience had done no less for the President than for others. A careful daily student of the topography of disputed regions, of every proposed military movement, of every manoeuvre, every failure, every success, he was making himself a skillful judge in the questions of the campaigns. He had also been studying military literature. Yet as his knowledge and his judgment grew, his modesty and his abstention from interference likewise grew. He was more and more chary of endeavoring to control his generals. The days of such contention as had thwarted the plans of McClellan without causing other plans to be heartily and fully adopted had fortunately passed, never to return. Of course, however, this was in part due to the fact that the war had now been going on long enough to enable Mr. Lincoln to know pretty well what measure of confidence he could place in the several generals. He had tried his experiments and was now using his conclusions. Grant, Sherman, Sheridan, Thomas, Hancock, and Meade were no longer undiscovered generals; while Fremont, McClellan, Halleck— and perhaps two or three more might be named—may be described in a counter-phrase as generals who were now quite thoroughly discovered. The President and the country were about to get the advantage of this acquired knowledge.

A consequence of these changed conditions, of the entrance upon this new stage of the war, becomes very visible in the life of Mr. Lincoln. The disputation, the hurly-burly, the tumultuous competition of men, opinions, and questions, which made the first eighteen months of his presidency confusing and exciting as a great tempest on the sea, have gone by. For the future his occupation is rather to keep a broad, general supervision, to put his controlling touch for the moment now here, now there. He ceases to appear as an individual contestant; his personality, though not less important, is less conspicuous; his influence is exerted less visibly, though not less powerfully. In short, the business-like aspect affects him and his functions as it does all else that concerns the actual conduct of the war; he too feels, though he may not formulate, the change whereby a crisis has passed into a condition. This will be seen from the character of the remainder of this narrative. There are no more controversies which call for other chapters like those which told of the campaigns of McClellan. There are no more fierce intestine dissensions like those which preceded the Proclamation of Emancipation,—at least not until the matter of reconstruction comes up, and reconstruction properly had not to do with the war, but with the later period. In a word, the country had become like the steed who has ceased fretfully to annoy the rider, while the rider, though exercising an ever-watchful control, makes less apparent exertion.

By one of the odd arrangements of our governmental machine, it was not until December 7, 1863, that the members of the Thirty-eighth Congress met for the first time to express those political sentiments which had been in vogue more than a year before that time, that is to say during the months of October and November, 1862, when these gentlemen had been elected, at the close of the summer's campaign. It has been said and shown that a very great change in popular feeling had taken place and made considerable advance during this interval. The autumn of 1863 was very different from the autumn of 1862! A Congress coming more newly from the people would have been much more Republican in its complexion. Still, even as it was, the Republicans had an ample working majority, and moreover were disturbed by fewer and less serious dissensions among themselves than had been the case occasionally in times past. McClellan and the Emancipation Proclamation had not quite yet been succeeded by any other questions of equal potency for alienating a large section of the party from the President. Not that unanimity prevailed by any means; that was impossible under the conditions of human nature. The extremists still distrusted Mr. Lincoln, and regarded him as an obstruction to sound policies. Senator Chandler of Michigan, a fine sample of the radical Republican, instructed him that, by the elections, Conservatives and traitors had been buried together, and begged him not to exhume them, since they would "smell worse than Lazarus did after he had been buried three days." Apparently he ranked Seward among these defunct and decaying Conservatives; certainly he regarded the secretary as a "millstone about the neck" of the President. [52] Still, in spite of such denunciations, times were not in this respect so bad as they had been, and the danger that the uncompromising Radicals would make wreck of the war was no longer great.

Another event, occurring in this autumn of 1863, was noteworthy because through it the literature of our tongue received one of its most distinguished acquisitions. On November 19 the national military cemetery at Gettysburg was to be consecrated; Edward Everett was to deliver the oration, and the President was of course invited as a guest. Mr. Arnold says that it was actually while Mr. Lincoln was "in the cars on his way from the White House to the battlefield" that he was told that he also would be expected to say something on the occasion; that thereupon he jotted down in pencil the brief address which he delivered a few hours later. [53] But that the composition was quite so extemporaneous seems doubtful, for Messrs. Nicolay and Hay transcribe the note of invitation, written to the President on November 2 by the master of the ceremonies, and in it occurs this sentence: "It is the desire that, after the oration, you, as Chief Executive of the Nation, formally set apart these grounds to their sacred use, by a few appropriate remarks." Probably, therefore, some forethought went to the preparation of this beautiful and famous "Gettysburg speech." When Mr. Everett sat down, the President arose and spoke as follows: [54] —

"Fourscore and seven years ago our fathers brought forth on this continent a new nation, conceived in liberty, and dedicated to the proposition that all men are created equal. Now we are engaged in a great civil war, testing whether that nation, or any nation so conceived and so dedicated, can long endure. We are met on a great battlefield of that war. We have come to dedicate a portion of that field as a final resting-place for those who here gave their lives that that nation might live. It is altogether fitting and proper that we should do this. But in a larger sense we cannot dedicate, we cannot consecrate, we cannot hallow, this ground. The brave men, living and dead, who struggled here have consecrated it far above our poor power to add or detract. The world will little note, nor long remember, what we say here, but it can never forget what they did here. It is for us, the living, rather, to be dedicated here to the unfinished work which they who fought here have thus far so nobly advanced. It is rather for us to be here dedicated to the great task remaining before us;—that from these honored dead, we take increased devotion to that cause for which they gave the last full measure of devotion;—that we here highly resolve that these dead shall not have died in vain, that this nation, under God, shall have a new birth of freedom, and that government of the people, by the people, for the people, shall not perish from the earth."

[52] N. and H. vii. 389.

[53] Arnold, *Lincoln*, 328. This writer gives a very vivid description of the delivery of the speech, derived in part from Governor Dennison, afterward the postmaster-general, who was present on the occasion.

[54] Mr. Arnold says that in an unconscious and absorbed manner, Mr. Lincoln "adjusted his spectacles" and read his address.

# CHAPTER VIII
# RECONSTRUCTION

In his inaugural address President Lincoln said: "The union of these States is perpetual.... No State, upon its own mere motion, can lawfully get out of the Union; resolves and ordinances to that effect are legally void." In these words was imbedded a principle which later on he showed his willingness to pursue to its logical conclusions concerning the reconstruction of the body politic. If no State, by seceding, had got itself out of the Union, there was difficulty in maintaining that those citizens of a seceding State, who had not disqualified themselves by acts of treason, were not still lawfully entitled to conduct the public business and to hold the usual elections for national and state officials, so soon as the removal of hostile force should render it physically possible for them to do so. Upon the basis of this principle, the resumption by such citizens of a right which had never been lost, but only temporarily interfered with by lawless violence, could reasonably be delayed by the national government only until the loyal voters should be sufficient in number to relieve the elections from the objection of being colorable and unreal. This philosophy of "reconstruction" seemed to Mr. Lincoln to conform with law and good sense, and he was forward in meeting, promoting, almost even in creating opportunities to apply it. From the beginning of the war he had been of opinion that the framework of a state government, though it might be scarcely more than a skeleton, was worth preservation. It held at least the seed of life. So after West Virginia was admitted into statehood, the organization which had been previously established by the loyal citizens of the original State was maintained in the rest of the State, and Governor Pierpoint was recognized as the genuine governor of Virginia, although few Virginians acknowledged allegiance to him, and often there were not many square miles of the Old Dominion upon which the dispossessed ruler could safely set his foot. For the present he certainly was no despot, but in the future he might have usefulness. He preserved continuity; by virtue of him, so to speak, there still was a State of Virginia.

Somewhat early in the war large portions of Tennessee, Louisiana, and Arkansas were recovered and kept by Union forces, and beneath such protection a considerable Union sentiment found expression. The President, loath to hold for a long time the rescued parts of these States under the sole domination of army officers, appointed "military governors." [55] The anomalous office found an obscure basis among those "war powers" which, as a legal resting-place, resembled a quicksand, and as a practical foundation were undeniably a rock; the functions and authority of the officials were as uncertain as anything, even in law, possibly could be. Legal fiction never reached a droller point than when these military governorships were defended as being the fulfillment by the national government "of its high constitutional obligation to guarantee to every State in this Union *a republican form of government!*" [56] Yet the same distinguished gentleman, who dared gravely to announce this ingenious argument, drew a picture of facts which was in itself a full justification of almost any scheme of rehabilitation; he said: "The state government has disappeared. The Executive has abdicated; the Legislature has dissolved; the Judiciary is in abeyance." In this condition of chaos Mr. Lincoln was certainly bound to prevent anarchy, without regard to any comicalities which might creep into his technique. So these hermaphrodite officials, with civil duties and military rank, were very sensibly and properly given a vague authority in the several States, as from time to time these were in part redeemed from rebellion by the Union armies. So soon as possible they were bidden, in collaboration with the military commanders in their respective districts, to make an enrollment of loyal citizens, with a view to holding elections and organizing state governments in the customary form. The President was earnest, not to say pertinacious, in urging forward these movements. On September 11, 1863, immediately after the battle of Chattanooga, he wrote to Andrew Johnson that it was "the nick of time for reinaugurating a loyal state government" in Tennessee; and he suggested that, as touching this same question of "time when," it was worth while to "remember that it cannot be known who is next to occupy the position I now hold, nor what he will do." He warned the governor that reconstruction must not be so conducted "as to give control of the State, and its representation in Congress, to the enemies of the Union.... It must not be so. You must have it otherwise. Let the reconstruction be the work of such men only as can be trusted for the Union. Exclude all others; and trust that your government, so organized, will be recognized here as being the one of republican form to be guaranteed to the State." [57]

At the same time these expressions by no means indicated that the President intended to have, or would connive at, any sham or colorable process. Accordingly, when some one suggested a plan for setting up as candidates in Louisiana certain Federal officers, who were not citizens of that State, he decisively forbade it, sarcastically remarking to Governor Shepley: "We do not particularly want members of Congress from there to enable us to get along with legislation here. What we do want is the conclusive evidence that respectable citizens of Louisiana are willing to be members of Congress, and to swear support to the Constitution, and that other respectable citizens there are willing to vote for them and send them. To send a parcel of Northern men here as representatives, elected, as would be understood (and perhaps really so), at the point of the bayonet, would be disgraceful and outrageous." Again he said that he wished the movement for the election of members of Congress "to be a movement of the people of the district, and not a movement of our military and quasi-military authorities there. I merely wish our authorities to give the people a chance,—to protect them against secession interference." These instructions were designed as genuine rules of action, and were not to be construed away. Whatever might be said against the theory which the President was endeavoring to establish for state restoration, no opponent of that theory was to be given the privilege of charging that the actual conduct of the proceedings under it was not rigidly honest. In December, 1862, two members of Congress were elected in Louisiana, and in February, 1863, they were admitted to take seats in the House for the brief remnant of its existence. This was not done without hesitation, but the fact that it was done at all certainly was in direct line with the President's plan. Subsequently, however, other candidates for seats, coming from rehabilitated States, were not so fortunate.

As reorganizations were attempted the promoters generally desired that the fresh start in state life should be made with new state Constitutions. The conventions chosen to draw these instruments were instructed from Washington that the validity of the Emancipation Proclamation and of all the legislation of Congress concerning slavery must be distinctly admitted, if their work was to receive recognition. Apart from this, so strenuous were the hints conveyed to these bodies that they would do well to arrange for the speedy abolition of slavery, that no politician would have been so foolish as to offer a constitution, or other form of reorganization, without some provision of this sort. This practical necessity sorely troubled many, who still hoped that some happy turn of events would occur, whereby they would be able to get back into the Union with the pleasant and valuable group of their slaves still about them, as in the good times of yore. Moreover, in other matters there were clashings between the real military commanders and the quasi-military civilian officials; and it was unfortunately the case that, in spite of Mr. Lincoln's appeal to loyal men to "eschew cliquism" and "work together," there were abundant rivalries and jealousies and personal schemings. All these vexations were dragged before the President to harass him with their pettiness amid his more conspicuous duties; they gave him infinite trouble, and devoured his time and strength. Likewise they were obstacles to the advancement of the business itself, and, coming in addition to the delays inevitable upon elections and deliberations, they ultimately kept all efforts towards reconstruction dallying along until a late period in the war. Thus it was February 22, 1864, when the state election was held in Louisiana; and it was September 5 in the same year when the new Constitution, with an emancipation clause, was adopted. It was not until January, 1865, that, in Tennessee, a convention made a constitution, for purposes of reconstruction, and therein abolished slavery.

Pending these doings and before practical reconstruction had made noticeable progress, Mr. Lincoln sent in, on December 8, 1863, his third annual message to Congress. To this message was appended something which no one had anticipated,—a proclamation of amnesty. In this the President recited his pardoning power and a recent act of Congress specially confirmatory thereof, stated the wish of certain repentant rebels to resume allegiance and to restore loyal state governments, and then offered, to all who would take a prescribed oath, full pardon together with "restoration of all rights and property, except as to slaves, and ... where rights of third parties shall have intervened." The oath was simply to "support, protect, and defend" the Constitution and the Union, and to abide by and support all legislation and all proclamations concerning slavery made during the existing rebellion. There were, of course, sundry exceptions of persons from this amnesty; but the list of those excepted was a moderate and reasonable one. He also proclaimed that whenever in any seceded State "a number of persons not less than one tenth in number of the votes cast in such State at the presidential election of the year of our Lord one thousand eight hundred and sixty, each having taken the oath aforesaid and not having since violated it, and being a qualified voter by the election law of the State existing immediately before the so-called act of secession, and excluding all others, shall reëstablish a state government which shall be republican, and in no wise contravening said oath, such shall be recognized as the true government of the State, and the State shall receive thereunder the benefits of the constitutional provision which declares that 'the United States shall guarantee to every State in this Union a republican form of government, and shall protect each of them against invasion; and, on application of the legislature, or the executive (when the legislature cannot be convened), against domestic violence.'"

Also further: "that any provision that may be adopted by such state government, in relation to the freed people of such State, which shall recognize and declare their permanent freedom, provide for their education, and which may yet be consistent, as a temporary arrangement, with their present condition as a laboring, landless, and homeless class, will not be objected to by the national executive. And it is suggested as not improper that, in constructing a loyal state government in any State, the name of the State, the boundary, the subdivisions, the constitution, and the general code of laws, as before the rebellion, be maintained, subject only to the modifications made necessary by the conditions hereinbefore stated, and such others, if any, not contravening said conditions, and which may be deemed expedient by those framing the new state government."

Concerning this proclamation, the message which communicated it noted: that it did not transcend the Constitution; that no man was coerced to take the oath; and that to make pardon conditional upon taking it was strictly lawful; that a test of loyalty was necessary, because it would be "simply absurd" to guarantee a republican form of government in a State "constructed in whole, or in preponderating part, from the very element against whose hostility and violence it is to be protected;" that the pledge to maintain the laws and proclamations as to slavery was a proper condition, because these had aided and would further aid the Union cause; also because "to now abandon them would be not only to relinquish a lever of power, but would also be a cruel and astounding breach of faith."

He continued: "But why any proclamation, now, upon the subject? This question is beset with the conflicting views that the step might be delayed too long or be taken too soon. In some States the elements for resumption seem ready for action, but remain inactive, apparently for want of a rallying point,—a plan of action. Why shall A adopt the plan of B rather than B that of A? And if A and B should agree, how can they know but that the general government here will reject their plan? By the proclamation a plan is presented which may be accepted by them as a rallying point, and which they are assured in advance will not be rejected here. This may bring them to act sooner than they otherwise would.

"The objection to a premature presentation of a plan by the national executive consists in the danger of committals on points which could be more safely left to further developments.

"Care has been taken to so shape the document as to avoid embarrassments from this source. Saying that, on certain terms, certain classes will be pardoned, with rights restored, it is not said that other classes or other terms will never be included. Saying that reconstruction will be accepted if presented in a specified way, it is not said it will never be accepted in any other way.

"The movements, by state action, for emancipation in several of the States, not included in the emancipation proclamation, are matters of profound gratulation. And while I do not repeat in detail what I have heretofore so earnestly urged upon this subject, my general views and feelings remain unchanged; and I trust that Congress will omit no fair opportunity of aiding these important steps to a great consummation.

"In the midst of other cares, however important, we must not lose sight of the fact that the war power is still our main reliance. To that power alone we can look yet for a time, to give confidence to the people in the contested regions, that the insurgent power will not again overrun them. Until that confidence shall be established, little can be done anywhere for what is called reconstruction.

"Hence our chiefest care must be directed to the army and navy, who have thus far borne their harder part so nobly and well. And it may be esteemed fortunate that in giving the greatest efficiency to these indispensable arms, we do also honorably recognize the gallant men, from commander to sentinel, who compose them, and to whom, more than to others, the world must stand indebted for the home of freedom disenthralled, regenerated, enlarged, and perpetuated."

This step, this offer of amnesty and pardon, and invitation to state reconstruction, took every one by surprise. As usual the President had been "doing his own thinking," reaching his own conclusions and acting upon them with little counsel asked from any among the multitudes of wise men who were so ready to furnish it. For a moment his action received a gratifying welcome of praise and approval. The first impulsive sentiment was that of pleasure because the offer was in so liberal, so conciliatory, so forgiving a spirit; moreover, people were encouraged by the very fact that the President thought it worth while to initiate reconstruction; also many of the more weak-kneed, who desired to see the luring process tried, were gratified by a generous measure. Then, too, not very much thought had yet been given, at least by the people in general, to actual processes of reconstruction; for while many doubted whether there would ever be a chance to reconstruct at all, very few fancied the time for it to be nearly approaching. Therefore the President occupied vacant ground in the minds of most persons.

But in a short time a very different temper was manifested among members of Congress, and from them spread forth and found support among the people. Two reasons promoted this. One, which was avowed with the frankness of indignation, was a jealousy of seeing so important a business preempted by the executive department. The other was a natural feeling of mingled hostility and distrust towards rebels, who had caused so much blood to be shed, so much cost to be incurred. In this point of view, the liberality which at first had appeared admirable now began to be condemned as extravagant, unreasonable, and perilous.

Concerning the first of these reasons, it must be admitted that it was entirely natural that Congress should desire to take partial or, if possible, even entire charge of reconstruction. Which department had the better right to the duty, or how it should be distributed between the legislative and executive departments, was uncertain, and could be determined only by inference from the definite functions of each as established by the Constitution. The executive unquestionably had the power to pardon every rebel in the land; yet it was a power which might conceivably be so misused as to justify impeachment. The Senate and the House had the power to give or to refuse seats to persons claiming to have been elected to them. Yet they could not dare to exercise this power except for a cause which was at least colorable in each case. Furthermore, the meaning of "recognition" was vague. Exactly what was "recognition" of a state government, and by what specific process could it be granted or withheld? The executive might recognize statehood in some matters; Congress might refuse to recognize it in other matters. Every one felt that disagreement between the two departments would be most unfortunate and even dangerous; yet it was entirely possible; and what an absurd and alarming condition might be created, if the President, by a general amnesty, should reinstate the ex-rebels of a State as citizens with all their rights of citizenship, and Congress should refuse to seat the senators and representatives elected by these constituents on the alleged ground of peril to the country by reason of their supposed continuing disloyalty. Even worse still might be the case; for the Senate and the House might disagree. There was nothing in law or logic to make this consummation impossible.

People differed much in feeling as well as opinion upon this difficult subject, this problem which was solved by no law. Treason is a crime and must be made odious, said Andrew Johnson, sternly uttering the sentiments of many earnest and strenuous men in Congress and in the country. Others were able to eliminate revengefulness, but felt that it was not safe in the present, nor wise for the future, to restore to rebels all the rights of citizenship upon the moment when they should consent to abandon rebellion, more especially when all knew and admitted that the abandonment was made not in penitence but merely in despair of success. It was open to extremists to argue that the whole seceded area might logically, as conquered lands, be reduced to a territorial condition, to be recarved into States at such times and upon such conditions as should seem proper. But others, in agreement with the President, insisted that if no State could lawfully secede, it followed that no State could lawfully be deprived of statehood. These persons reinforced their legal argument with the sentimental one that lenity was the best policy. As General Grant afterward put it: "The people who had been in rebellion must necessarily come back into the Union, and be incorporated as an integral part of the nation. Naturally the nearer they were placed to an equality with the people who had not rebelled, the more reconciled they would feel with their old antagonists, and the better citizens they would be from the beginning. They surely would not make good citizens if they felt that they had a yoke around their necks." The question, in what proportions mercy and justice should be, or safely could be, mingled, was clearly one of discretion. In the wide distance betwixt the holders of extreme opinions an infinite variety of schemes and theories was in time broached and held. Very soon the gravity of the problem was greatly enhanced by its becoming complicated with proposals for giving the suffrage to negroes. Upon this Mr. Lincoln expressed his opinion that the privilege might be wisely conferred upon "the very intelligent, and especially those who have fought gallantly in our ranks," though apparently he intended thus to describe no very large percentage. Apparently his confidence in the civic capacity of the negro never became very much greater than it had been in the days of the joint debates with Douglas.

Congress took up the matter very promptly, and with much display of feeling. Early in May, 1864, Henry Winter Davis, a vehement opponent of the President, introduced a bill, of which the anti-rebel preamble was truculent to the point of being amusing. His first fierce *Whereas* declared that the Confederate States were waging a war so glaringly unjust "that they have no right to claim the mitigation of the extreme rights of war, which are accorded by modern usage to an enemy who has a right to consider the war a just one." But Congress, though hotly irritated, was not quite willing to say, in terms, that it would eschew civilization and adopt barbarism, as its system for the conduct of the war; and accordingly it rejected Mr. Davis's fierce exordium. The words had very probably only been used by him as a sort of safety valve to give vent to the fury of his wrath, so that he could afterward approach the serious work of the bill in a milder spirit; for in fact the actual effective legislation which he proposed was by no means unreasonable. After military resistance should be suppressed in any rebellious State, the white male citizens were to elect a convention for the purpose of reëstablishing a state government. The new organization must disfranchise prominent civil and military officers of the Confederacy, establish the permanent abolition of slavery, and prohibit the payment by the new State of any indebtedness incurred for Confederate purposes. After Congress should have expressed its assent to the work of the convention, the President was to recognize by proclamation the reorganized State. This bill, of course, gave to the legislative department the whole valuable control in the matter of recognition, leaving to the President nothing more than the mere empty function of issuing a proclamation, which he would have no right to hold back; but in other respects its requirements were entirely fair and unobjectionable, from any point of view, and it finally passed the House by a vote of 74 to 59. The Senate amended it, but afterward receded from the amendment, and thus the measure came before Mr. Lincoln on July 4, 1864. Congress was to adjourn at noon on that day, and he was at the Capitol, signing bills, when this one was brought to him. He laid it aside. Zachariah Chandler, senator from Michigan, a dictatorial gentleman and somewhat of the busybody order, was watchfully standing by, and upon observing this action, he asked Mr. Lincoln, with some show of feeling, whether he was not going to sign that bill. Mr. Lincoln replied that it was a "matter of too much importance to be swallowed in that way." Mr. Chandler warned him that a veto would be very damaging at the Northwest, and said: "The important point is that one prohibiting slavery in the reconstructed States." "This is the point," said Mr. Lincoln, "on which I doubt the authority of Congress to act." "It is no more than you have done yourself," said the senator. "I conceive," replied Mr. Lincoln, "that I may in an emergency do things on military grounds which cannot be done constitutionally by Congress." A few moments later he remarked to the members of the cabinet: "I do not see how any of us now can deny and contradict what we have always said: that Congress has no constitutional power over slavery in the States.... This bill and the position of these gentlemen seem to me, in asserting that the insurrectionary States are no longer in the Union, to make the fatal admission that States, whenever they please, may of their own motion dissolve their connection with the Union. Now we cannot survive that admission, I am convinced. If that be true, I am not President; these gentlemen are not Congress. I have laboriously endeavored to avoid that question ever since it first began to be mooted.... It was to obviate this question that I earnestly favored the movement for an amendment to the Constitution abolishing slavery.... I thought it much better, if it were possible, to restore the Union without the necessity for a violent quarrel among its friends as to whether certain States have been in or out of the Union during the war,—a merely metaphysical question, and one unnecessary to be forced into discussion." [58] So the bill remained untouched at his side.

A few days after the adjournment, having then decided not to sign the bill, he issued a proclamation in which he said concerning it, that he was "unprepared by a formal approval of [it] to be inflexibly committed to any single plan of restoration;" that he was also "unprepared to declare that the free-state constitutions and governments, already adopted and installed in Arkansas and Louisiana, [should] be set aside and held for naught, thereby repelling and discouraging the loyal citizens, who have set up the same, as to further effort;" also that he was unprepared to "declare a constitutional competency in Congress to abolish slavery in the States." Yet he also said that he was fully satisfied that the system proposed in the bill was "*one* very proper plan" for the loyal people of any State to adopt, and that he should be ready to aid in such adoption upon any opportunity. In a word, his objection to the bill lay chiefly in the fact that it established one single and exclusive process for reconstruction. The rigid exclusiveness seemed to him a serious error. Upon his part, in putting forth his own plan, he had taken much pains distinctly to keep out this characteristic, and to have it clearly understood that his proposition was not designed as "a procrustean bed, to which exact conformity was to be indispensable;" it was not *the only* method, but only *a* method.

So soon as it was known that the President would not sign the bill, a vehement cry of wrath broke from all its more ardent friends. H.W. Davis and B.F. Wade, combative men, and leaders in their party, who expected their opinion to be respected, published in the New York "Tribune" an address "To the Supporters of the Government." In unbridled language they charged "encroachments of the executive on the authority of Congress." They even impugned the honesty of the President's purpose in words of direct personal insult; for they said: "The President, by preventing this bill from becoming a law, holds the electoral votes of the rebel States at the dictation of his personal ambition.... If electors for president be allowed to be chosen in either of those States [Louisiana or Arkansas], a sinister light will be cast on [his] motives." They alleged that "a more studied outrage on the legislative authority of the people has never been perpetrated." They stigmatized this "rash and fatal act" as "a blow at the friends of the administration, at the rights of humanity, and at the principles of republican government." They warned Mr. Lincoln that, if he wished the support of Congress, he must "confine himself to his executive duties, — to obey and execute, not make the laws; to suppress by arms armed rebellion, and leave political reorganization to Congress." If they really meant what they said, or any considerable part of it, they would have been obliged to vote "Guilty" had the House of Representatives seen fit to put these newspaper charges of theirs into the formal shape of articles of impeachment against the President.

To whatever "friends" Mr. Lincoln might have dealt a "blow," it is certain that these angry gentlemen, whether "friends" or otherwise, were dealing him a very severe blow at a very critical time; and if its hurtfulness was diminished by the very fury and extravagance of their invective, they at least were entitled to no credit for the salvation thus obtained. They were exerting all their powerful influence to increase the chance, already alarmingly great, of making a Democrat the next President of the United States. Nevertheless Mr. Lincoln, with his wonted imperturbable fixedness when he had reached a conviction, did not modify his position in the slightest degree.

Before long this especial explosion spent its force, and thereafter very fortunately the question smouldered during the rest of Mr. Lincoln's lifetime, and only burst forth into fierce flame immediately after his death, when it became more practical and urgent as a problem of the actually present time. The last words, however, which he spoke in public, dealt with the matter. It was on the evening of April 11, and he was addressing in Washington a great concourse of citizens who had gathered to congratulate him upon the brilliant military successes, then just achieved, which insured the immediate downfall of the Confederacy. In language as noteworthy for moderation as that of his assailants had been for extravagance, he then reviewed his course concerning reconstruction and gave his reasons for still believing that he had acted for the best. Admitting that much might justly be said against the reorganized government of Louisiana, he explained why he thought that nevertheless it should not be rejected. Concede, he said, that it is to what it should be only what the egg is to the fowl, "we shall sooner have the fowl by hatching the egg than by smashing it." He conceived that the purpose of the people might be fairly stated to be the restoration of the proper practical relations between the seceded States and the Union, and he therefore argued that the question properly took this shape: Whether Louisiana could "be brought into proper practical relation with the Union *sooner* by *sustaining* or by *discarding* her new state government." [59]

By occurrences befalling almost immediately after Mr. Lincoln's death his opinions were again drawn into debate, when unfortunately he could neither explain nor develop them further than he had done. One of the important events of the war was the conference held on March 28, 1865, at Hampton Roads, between the President, General Grant, General Sherman, and Admiral Porter, and at which no other person was present. It is sufficiently agreed that the two generals then declared that one great final battle must yet take place; and that thereupon Mr. Lincoln, in view of the admitted fact that the collapse of the rebellion was inevitably close at hand, expressed great aversion and pain at the prospect of utterly useless bloodshed, and asked whether it could not by some means be avoided. It is also tolerably certain that Mr. Lincoln gave very plainly to be understood by his remarks, and also as usual by a story, his desire that Jefferson Davis and a few other of the leading rebels should not be captured, but rather should find it possible to escape from the country. It is in other ways well known that he had already made up his mind not to conclude the war with a series of hangings after the historic European fashion of dealing with traitors.

He preferred, however, to evade rather than to encounter the problem of disposing of such embarrassing captives, and a road for them out of the country would be also a road for him out of a difficulty. What else was said on this occasion, though it soon became the basis of important action, is not known with accuracy; but it may be regarded as beyond a doubt that, in a general way, Mr. Lincoln took a very liberal tone concerning the terms and treatment to be accorded to the rebels in the final arrangement of the surrendering, which all saw to be close at hand. It is beyond doubt that he spoke, throughout the conference, in the spirit of forgetting and forgiving immediately and almost entirely.

From this interview General Sherman went back to his army, and received no further instructions afterward, until, on April 18, he established with General Johnston the terms on which the remaining Confederate forces should be disbanded. This "Memorandum or basis of agreement," [60] then entered into by him, stipulated for "the recognition by the executive of the United States, of the several state governments, on their officers and legislatures taking the oaths prescribed by the Constitution of the United States;" also that the inhabitants of the Southern States should "be guaranteed, so far as the executive can, their political rights and franchises, as well as their rights of person and property;" also that the government would not "disturb any of the people by reason of the late war," if they should dwell quiet for the future; and, in short, that there should be "a general amnesty," so far as it was within the power of the executive of the United States to grant it, upon the return of the South to a condition of peace.

No sooner were these engagements reported in Washington than they were repudiated. However they might have accorded with, or might have transcended, the sentiments of him who had been president only a few days before, they by no means accorded with the views of Andrew Johnson, who was president at that time, and still less with the views of the secretary of war, who well represented the vengeful element of the country. Accordingly Mr. Stanton at once annulled them by an order, which he followed up by a bulletin containing ten reasons in support of the order. This document was immediately published in the newspapers, and was so vituperative and insulting towards Sherman [61] that the general, who naturally did not feel himself a fitting object for insolence at this season of his fresh military triumphs, soon afterward showed his resentment; at the grand parade of his army, in Washington, he conspicuously declined, in the presence of the President and the notabilities of the land, to shake the hand which Secretary Stanton did not hesitate then and there to extend to him,—for Stanton had that peculiar and unusual form of meanness which endeavors to force a civility after an insult. But however General Sherman might feel about it, his capitulation had been revoked, and another conference became necessary between the two generals, which was followed a little later by still another between Generals Schofield and Johnston. At these meetings the terms which had been established between Generals Grant and Lee were substantially repeated, and by this "military convention" the war came to a formal end on April 26, 1865.

By this course of events General Sherman was, of course, placed in a very uncomfortable position, and he defended himself by alleging that the terms which he had made were in accurate conformity with the opinions, wishes, and programme expressed by Mr. Lincoln on March 28. He reiterates this assertion strongly and distinctly in his "Memoirs," and quotes in emphatic corroboration Admiral Porter's account of that interview. [62] The only other witness who could be heard on this point was General Grant; he never gave his recollection of the expressions of President Lincoln concerning the matters in dispute; but on April 21 he did write to General Sherman that, after having carefully read the terms accorded to Johnston he felt satisfied that they "could not possibly be approved." [63] He did not, however, say whether or not they seemed to him to contravene the policy of the President, as he had heard or understood that policy to be laid down in the famous interview. In the obscurity which wraps this matter, individual opinions find ample room to wander; it is easy to believe that what General Sherman undertook to arrange was in reasonable accordance with the broad purposes of the President; but it certainly is not easy to believe that the President ever intended that so many, so momentous, and such complex affairs should be conclusively disposed of, with all the honorable sacredness attendant upon military capitulations, by a few hasty strokes of General Sherman's pen. The comprehensiveness of this brief and sudden document of surrender was appalling! Mr. Lincoln had never before shown any inclination to depute to others so much of his own discretionary authority; his habit was quite the other way.

It is not worth while to discuss much the merits or demerits of President Lincoln's schemes for reconstruction. They had been only roughly and imperfectly blocked out at the time of his death; and in presenting them he repeatedly stated that he did not desire to rule out other schemes which might be suggested; on the contrary, he distinctly stated his approval of the scheme developed in the bill introduced by Senator Davis and passed by Congress. Reconstruction, as it was actually conducted later on, was wretchedly bungled, and was marked chiefly by bitterness in disputation and by clumsiness in practical arrangements, which culminated in that miserable disgrace known as the regime of the "carpet-baggers." How far Lincoln would have succeeded in saving the country from these humiliating processes, no one can say; but that he would have strenuously disapproved much that was done is not open to reasonable doubt. On the other hand, it is by no means certain that his theories, at least so far as they had been developed up to the time of his death, either could have been, or ought to have been carried out. This seems to be generally agreed. Perhaps they were too liberal; perhaps he confided too much in a sudden change of heart, an immediate growth of loyalty, among persons of whom nearly all were still embittered, still believed that it was in a righteous cause that they had suffered a cruel defeat.

But if the feasibility of Mr. Lincoln's plan is matter of fruitless disputation, having to do only with fancied probabilities, and having never been put to the proof of trial, at least no one will deny that it was creditable to his nature. A strange freak of destiny arranged that one of the most obstinate, sanguinary wars of history should be conducted by one of the most humane men who ever lived, and that blood should run in rivers at the order of a ruler to whom bloodshed was repugnant, and to whom the European idol of military glory seemed a symbol of barbarism. During the war Lincoln's chief purpose was the restoration of national unity, and his day-dream was that it should be achieved as a sincere and hearty reunion in feeling as well as in fact. As he dwelt with much earnest aspiration upon this consummation, he perhaps came to imagine a possibility of its instant accomplishment, which did not really exist. His longing for a genuinely reunited country was not a pious form of expression, but an intense sentiment, and an end which he definitely expected to bring to pass. Not improbably this frame of mind induced him to advance too fast and too far, in order to meet with welcoming hand persons who were by no means in such a condition of feeling that they could grasp that hand in good faith, or could fulfill at once the obligations which such a reconciliation would have imposed upon them, as matter of honor, in all their civil and political relations. The reaction involved in passing from a state of hostilities to a state of peace, the deep gratification of seeing so mortal a struggle determined in favor of the national life, may have carried him somewhat beyond the limitations set by the hard facts of the case, and by the human nature alike of the excited conquerors and the impenitent conquered. On the other hand, however, it is dangerous to say that Mr. Lincoln made a mistake in reading the popular feeling or in determining a broad policy. If he did, he did so for the first time. Among those suppositions in which posterity is free to indulge, it is possible to fancy that if he, whom all now admit to have been the best friend of the South living in April, 1865, had continued to live longer, he might have alleviated, if he could not altogether have prevented, the writing of some very painful chapters in the history of the United States.

NOTE.—In writing this chapter, I have run somewhat ahead of the narrative in point of time; but I hope that the desirability of treating the topic connectedly, as a whole, will be obvious to the reader.

[55] These appointments were as follows: Andrew Johnson, Tennessee, February 23, 1862; Edward Stanley, North Carolina, May 19, 1862; Col. G.F. Shepley, Louisiana, June 10, 1862.

[56] So said Andrew Johnson, military governor of Tennessee, March 18, 1862.

[57] In a contest in which emancipation was indirectly at stake, in Maryland, he expressed his wish that "all loyal qualified voters" should have the privilege of voting.

[58] N. and H. ix. 120-122, quoting from the diary of Mr. John Hay.

[59] He had used similar language in a letter to General Canby, December 12, 1864; N. and H. ix. 448; also in his letter to Trumbull concerning the Louisiana senators, January 9, 1865; *ibid.* 454. Colonel McClure, on the strength of conversations with Lincoln, says that his single purpose was "the speedy and cordial restoration of the dissevered States. He cherished no resentment against the South, and every theory of reconstruction that he ever conceived or presented was eminently peaceful and looking solely to reattaching the estranged people to the government." *Lincoln and Men of War-Times,* 223.

[60] Sherman, *Memoirs,* ii. 356.

[61] Grant stigmatizes this as "cruel and harsh treatment ... unnecessarily ... inflicted," *Mem.* ii. 534, and as "infamous," Badeau, *Milit. Hist. of Grant,* iii. 636 n.

[62] Sherman, *Memoirs,* ii. 328. The admiral says that, if Lincoln had lived, he "would have shouldered all the responsibility" for Sherman's action, and Secretary Stanton would have "issued no false telegraphic dispatches." See also Senator Sherman's corroborative statement; McClure, *Lincoln and Men of War-Times,* 219 n.

[63] Sherman, *Memoirs,* ii. 360.

# CHAPTER IX
# RENOMINATION

In a period of fervid political feeling it was natural that those Republicans who were dissatisfied with President Lincoln should begin, long before the close of his term of office, to seek consolation by arrangements for replacing him by a successor more to their taste. Expressions of this purpose became definite in the autumn of 1863. Mr. Arnold says that the coming presidential election was expected to bring grave danger, if not even anarchy and revolution. [64] Amid existing circumstances, an opposition confined to the legitimate antagonism of the Democracy would, of course, have brought something more than the customary strain inherent in ordinary times in government by party; and it was unfortunate that, besides this, an undue gravity was imported into the crisis by the intestinal dissensions of the Republicans themselves. It seemed by no means impossible that these disagreements might give to the friends of peace by compromise a victory which they really ought not to have. Republican hostility to Mr. Lincoln was unquestionably very bitter in quality, whatever it might be in quantity. It was based in part upon the discontent of the radicals and extremists, in part upon personal irritation. In looking back upon those times there is now a natural tendency to measure this opposition by the weakness which it ultimately displayed when, later on, it was swept out of sight by the overwhelming current of the popular will. But this weakness was by no means so visible in the winter of 1863-64. On the contrary, the cry for a change then seemed to come from every quarter, and to come loudly; for it was echoed back and forth by the propagandists and politicians, and as these persons naturally did most of the talking and writing in the country, so they made a show delusively out of proportion to their following among the people.

The dislike toward the President flourished chiefly in two places, and with two distinct bodies of men. One of these places was Missouri, which will be spoken of later on. The other was Washington, where the class of "public men" was for the most part very ill-disposed towards him. [65] Mr. Julian, himself a prominent malcontent, bears his valuable testimony to the extent of the disaffection, saying that, of the "more earnest and thorough-going Republicans in both Houses of Congress, probably not one in ten really favored" [66] the renomination of Mr. Lincoln. In fact, there were few of them whom the President had not offended. They had brought to him their schemes and their policies, had made their arguments and demands, and after all had found the President keeping his counsel to himself and acting according to his own judgment. This seemed exasperatingly unjustifiable in a country where anybody might happen to be president without being a whit abler than any other one who had not happened to fall into the office. In a word, the politicians had, and hated, a master. Mr. Chase betrayed this when he complained that there was no "administration, in the true sense of the word;" by which he understood, "a president conferring with his cabinet and *taking their united judgments*." The existence of that strange moat which seems to isolate the capital and the political coteries therein gathered, and to shut out all knowledge of the feelings of the constituent people, is notorious, and certainly was never made more conspicuous than in this business of selecting the Republican candidate for the campaign of 1864. When Congress came together the political scheming received a strong impetus. Everybody seemed to be opposed to Mr. Lincoln. Thaddeus Stevens, the impetuous leader of the House of Representatives, declared that, in that body, Arnold of Illinois was the only member who was a political friend of the President; and the story goes that the President himself sadly admitted the fact. Visitors at Washington, who got their impressions from the talk there, concluded that Mr. Lincoln's chance of a second term was small.

This opposition, which had the capital for its headquarters and the politicians for its constituents, found a candidate ready for use. Secretary Chase was a victim to the dread disease of presidential ambition. With the usual conventional expressions of modesty he admitted the fact. Thereupon general talk soon developed into political organization; and in January, 1864, a "Committee of prominent Senators, Representatives, and Citizens," having formally obtained his approval, set about promoting his interests in business-like fashion.

The President soon knew what was going forward; but he gave no sign of disquietude; on the contrary, he only remarked that he hoped the country would never have a worse president than Mr. Chase would be. Not that he was indifferent to renomination and reëlection. That would have been against nature. His mind, his soul, all that there was of force and feeling in him had been expended to the uttermost in the cause and the war which were still pending. At the end of that desperate road, along which he had dared stubbornly and against so much advice to lead the nation, he seemed now to discern the goal. That he should be permitted to guide to the end in that journey, and that his judgment and leadership should receive the crown of success and approval, was a reward, almost a right, which he must intensely desire and which he could not lose without a disappointment that outruns expression. Yet he was so self-contained that, if he had cared not at all about the issue, his conduct would have been much the same that it was.

Besides his temperament, other causes promoted this tranquillity. What Mr. Lincoln would have been had his career fallen in ordinary times, amid commonplace political business, it is difficult to say. The world never saw him as the advocate or assailant of a tariff, or other such affair. From the beginning he had bound himself fast to a great moral purpose, which later became united with the preservation of the national life. Having thus deliberately exercised his judgment in a question of this kind, he seemed ever after content to have intrusted his fortunes to the movement, and always to be free from any misgiving as to its happy conclusion. Besides this, it is probable that he accurately measured the narrow limits of Mr. Chase's strength. No man ever more shrewdly read the popular mind. A subtle line of communication seemed to run between himself and the people. Nor did he know less well the politicians. His less sagacious friends noted with surprise and anxiety that he let the work of opposition go on unchecked. In due time, however, the accuracy of his foresight was vindicated; for when the secretary's friends achieved a sufficient impetus they tumbled over, in manner following:—

Mr. Pomeroy, senator from Kansas, was vindictive because the President had refused to take his side in certain quarrels between himself and his colleague. Accordingly, early in 1864, he issued a circular, stating that the efforts making for Mr. Lincoln's nomination required counter action on the part of those unconditional friends of the Union who disapproved the policy of the administration. He said that Mr. Lincoln's reëlection was "practically impossible;" that it was also undesirable, on account of the President's "manifest tendency towards compromises and temporary expedients of policy," and for other reasons. Therefore, he said, Mr. Chase's friends had established "connections in all the States," and now invited "the hearty coöperation of all those in favor of the speedy restoration of the Union upon the basis of universal freedom." The document, designed to be secret, of course was quickly printed in the newspapers. [67] This was awkward; and Mr. Chase at once wrote to the President a letter, certainly entirely fair, in which he expressed his willingness to resign. Mr. Lincoln replied kindly. He said that he had heard of the Pomeroy circular, but had not read it, and did not expect to do so. In fact, he said, "I have known just as little of these things as my friends have allowed me to know." As to the proposed resignation, that, he said, "is a question which I will not allow myself to consider from any standpoint other than my judgment of the public service, and in that view I do not perceive occasion for a change." There was throughout a quiet undertone of indifference to the whole business, which was significant enough to have puzzled the secretary, had he noticed it; for it was absolutely impossible that Mr. Lincoln should be really indifferent to dangerous competition. The truth was that the facts of the situation lay with the President, and that the enterprise, which was supposed by its friends to be only in its early stage, was really on the verge of final disposition. Mr. Chase had said decisively that he would not be a candidate unless his own State, Ohio, should prefer him. To enlighten him on this point the Republican members of the Ohio legislature, being in much closer touch with the people than were the more dignified statesmen at Washington, met on February 25, and in the name of the people and the soldiers of their State renominated Mr. Lincoln. The nail was driven a stroke deeper into the coffin by Rhode Island. Although Governor Sprague was Mr. Chase's son-in-law, the legislature of that State also made haste to declare for Mr. Lincoln. So the movement in behalf of Mr. Chase came suddenly and utterly to an end. Early in May he wrote that he wished no further consideration to be given to his name; and his wish was respected. After this collapse Mr. Lincoln's renomination was much less opposed by the politicians of Washington. Being naturally a facile class, and not so narrowly wedded to their own convictions as to be unable to subordinate them to the popular will or wisdom, they now for the most part gave their superficial and uncordial adhesion to the President. They liked him no better than before, but they respected a sagacity superior to their own, bowed before a capacity which could control success, and, in presence of the admitted fact of his overwhelming popularity, they played the part which became wise men of their calling.

However sincerely Mr. Chase might resolve to behave with magnanimity beneath his disappointment, the disappointment must rankle all the same. It was certainly the case that, while he professed friendship towards Mr. Lincoln personally, he was honestly unable to appreciate him as a president. Mr. Chase's ideal of a statesman had outlines of imposing dignity which Mr. Lincoln's simple demeanor did not fill out. It was now inevitable that the relationship between the two men should soon be severed. The first strain came because Mr. Lincoln would not avenge an unjustifiable assault made by General Blair upon the secretary. Then Mr. Chase grumbled at the free spending of the funds which he had succeeded in providing with so much skill and labor. "It seems as if there were no limit to expense.... The spigot in Uncle Abe's barrel is made twice as big as the bung-hole," he complained. Then ensued sundry irritations concerning appointments in the custom-houses, one of which led to an offer of resignation by the secretary. On each occasion, however, the President placated him by allowing him to have his own way. Finally, in May and June, 1864, occurred the famous imbroglio concerning the choice of a successor to Mr. Cisco, the assistant treasurer at New York. Though Mr. Chase again managed to prevail, yet he was made so angry by the circumstances of the case, that he again sent in his resignation, which this time was accepted. For, as Mr. Lincoln said: "You and I have reached a point of mutual embarrassment in our official relation, which it seems cannot be overcome or longer sustained consistently with the public service." This occurrence, taking place on June 29-30, at the beginning of the difficult political campaign of that anxious summer, alienated from the President's cause some friends in a crisis when all the friends whom he could muster seemed hardly sufficient.

The place of Mr. Chase was not easy to fill. Mr. Lincoln first nominated David Tod of Ohio. This was very ill received; but fortunately the difficulty which might have been caused by it was escaped, because Governor Tod promptly declined. The President then named William Pitt Fessenden, senator from Maine, and actually forced the office upon him against that gentleman's sincere wish to escape the honor. A better choice could not have been made. Mr. Fessenden was chairman of the Committee on Finance, and had filled the position with conspicuous ability; every one esteemed him highly; the Senate instantly confirmed him, and during his incumbency in office he fully justified these flattering opinions.

There were other opponents of the President who were not so easily diverted from their purpose as the politicians had been. In Missouri an old feud was based upon his displacement of Fremont; the State had ever since been rent by fierce factional quarrels, and amid them this grievance had never been forgotten or forgiven. Emancipation by state action had been chief among the causes which had divided the Union citizens into Conservatives and Radicals. Their quarrel was bitter, and in vain did Mr. Lincoln repeatedly endeavor to reconcile them. The Radicals claimed his countenance as a matter of right, and Mr. Lincoln often privately admitted that between him and them there was close coincidence of feeling. Yet he found their specific demands inadmissible; especially he could not consent to please them by removing General Schofield. So they, being extremists, and therefore of the type of men who will have every one against them who is not for them, turned vindictively against him. They found sympathizers elsewhere in the country, sporadic instances of disaffection rather than indications of an epidemic; but in their frame of mind they easily gained faith in the existence of a popular feeling which was, in fact, the phantasm of their own heated fancy. As spring drew on they cast out lines of affiliation.

Their purpose was not only negatively against Lincoln, but positively for Fremont. Therefore they made connection with the Central Fremont Club, a small organization in New York, and issued a call for a mass convention at Cleveland on May 31. They expressed their disgust for the "imbecile and vacillating policy" of Mr. Lincoln, and desired the "immediate extinction of slavery ... by congressional action," contemning the fact that Congress had no power under the Constitution to extinguish slavery. Their call was reinforced by two or three others, of which one came from a "People's Committee" of St. Louis, representing Germans under the lead of B. Gratz Brown.

The movement also had the hearty approval of Wendell Phillips, who was very bitter and sweeping in his denunciations of an administration which he regarded "as a civil and military failure." Lincoln's reëlection, he said, "I shall consider the end of the Union in my day, or its reconstruction on terms worse than disunion." But Mr. Phillips's friendship ought to have been regarded by the Fremonters as ominous, for it was his custom always to act with a very small minority. Moreover he had long since ceased to give voice to the intelligence of his party or even fairly to represent it. How far it had ever been proper to call the Abolitionists a party may be doubted; before the war they had been compressed into some solidity by encompassing hostility; but they would not have been Abolitionists at all had they not been men of exceptional independence both in temper and in intellect. They had often dared to differ from each other as well as from the mass of their fellow citizens, and they had never submitted to the domination of leaders in the ordinary political fashion. The career of Mr. Lincoln had of course been watched by them keenly, very critically, and with intense and various feeling. At times they had hopefully applauded him, and at times they had vehemently condemned what had seemed to them his halting, half-hearted, or timid action. As the individual members of the party had often changed their own minds about him, so also they had sometimes and freely disagreed with each other concerning his character, his intentions, his policies. In the winter and spring of 1864, however, it seemed that, by slow degrees, observation, their own good sense, and the development of events had at last won the great majority of the party to repose a considerable measure of confidence in him, both in respect of his capacity and of his real anti-slavery purposes. Accordingly in the present discussions such men as Owen Lovejoy, [68] William Lloyd Garrison, and Oliver Johnson came out fairly for him,—not, indeed, because he was altogether satisfactory to them, but because he was in great part so; also because they easily saw that as matter of fact his personal triumph would probably lead to abolition, that he was the only candidate by whom the Democracy could be beaten, and that if the Democracy should not be beaten, abolition would be postponed beyond human vision. Lovejoy said that, to his personal knowledge, the President had "been just as radical as any of his cabinet," and in view of what the Abolitionists thought of Chase, this was a strong indorsement. The old-time charge of being impractical could not properly be renewed against these men, now that they saw that events which they could help to bring about were likely to bring their purpose to the point of real achievement in a near future. In this condition of things they were found entirely willing to recognize and accept the best practical means, and their belief was clear that the best practical means lay in the renomination and reëlection of Abraham Lincoln. Their adhesion brought to him a very useful assistance, and beyond this it also gave him the gratification of knowing that he had at last won the approval of men whose friendly sympathy he had always inwardly desired. Sustained by the best men in the party, he could afford to disregard the small body of irreconcilable and quarrelsome fault-finders, who went over to Fremont, factious men, who were perhaps unconsciously controlled more by mere contradictoriness of temperament than by the higher motives which they proclaimed.

At Cleveland on the appointed day the "mass convention" assembled, only the mass was wanting. It nominated Fremont for the presidency and General John Cochrane for the vice-presidency; and thus again the Constitution was ignored by these malcontents; for both these gentlemen were citizens of New York, and therefore the important delegation from that State could lawfully vote for only one of them. Really the best result which the convention achieved was that it called forth a bit of wit from the President. Some one remarked to him that, instead of the expected thousands, only about four hundred persons had assembled. He turned to the Bible which, say Nicolay and Hay, "commonly lay on his desk," [69] and read the verse: "And every one that was in distress, and every one that was in debt, and every one that was discontented, gathered themselves unto him; and he became a captain over them: and there were with him about four hundred men." [70]

The Fremonters struck no responsive chord among the people. The nomination was received by every one with the same tranquil indifference, tinged with ridicule, which the President had shown. In vain did Fremont seek to give to his candidacy a serious and dignified character. Very few persons cared anything about it, except the Democrats, and their clamorous approval was as unwelcome as it was significant. Under this humiliation the unfortunate candidate at last decided to withdraw, and so notified his committee about the middle of September. He still stood by his principles, however, and asserted that Mr. Lincoln's administration had been "politically, militarily, and financially a failure;" that the President had paralyzed the generous unanimity of the North; and that, by declaring that "slavery should be protected," he had "built up for the South a strength which otherwise they could have never attained." The nation received the statement placidly and without alarm.

A feeble movement in New York to nominate General Grant deserves mention, chiefly for the purpose of also mentioning the generous manner in which the general decisively brushed it aside. Mr. Lincoln quietly said that if Grant would take Richmond he might also have the presidency. But it was, of course, plain to every one that for the present it would be ridiculous folly to take Grant out of his tent in order to put him into the White House.

During this same troubled period a few of the Republican malcontents went so far as to fancy that they could put upon Mr. Lincoln a pressure which would induce him to withdraw from the ticket. They never learned the extreme absurdity of their design, for they never got enough encouragement to induce them to push it beyond the stage of preliminary discussion.

All these movements had some support from newspapers in different parts of the country. Many editors had the like grievance against Mr. Lincoln which so many politicians had. For they had told him what to do, and too often he had not done it. Horace Greeley, it is needless to say, was conspicuous in his unlimited condemnation of the President.

The first indications of the revolt of the politicians and the radicals against Mr. Lincoln were signals for instant counteracting activity among the various bodies which more closely felt the popular impulse. State conventions, caucuses, of all sizes and kinds, and gatherings of the Republican members of state legislatures, overstepped their regular functions to declare for the renomination of Mr. Lincoln. Clubs and societies did the same. Simon Cameron, transmitting to the President a circular of this purport, signed by every Unionist member of the Pennsylvania legislature, said: "Providence has decreed your reëlection;" and if it is true that the *vox populi* is also the *vox Dei*, this statement of the political affiliations of Providence was entirely correct. Undoubtedly the number of the President's adherents was swelled by some persons who would have been among the disaffected had they not been influenced by the reflection that a change of administration in the present condition of things must be disastrous. This feeling was expressed in many metaphors, but in none other so famous as that uttered by Mr. Lincoln himself: that it was not wise to swap horses while crossing the stream. The process was especially dangerous in a country where the change would involve a practical interregum of one third of a year. The nation had learned this lesson, and had paid dearly enough for the schooling, too, in the four months of its waiting to get rid of Buchanan, after it had discredited him and all his ways. In the present crisis it was easy to believe that to leave Mr. Lincoln to carry on for four months an administration condemned by the people, would inflict a mortal injury to the Union cause. Nevertheless, though many persons not wholly satisfied with him supported him for this reason, the great majority undeniably felt implicit faith and intense loyalty towards him. He was the people's candidate, and they would not have any other candidate; this present state of popular feeling, which soon became plain as the sun in heaven, settled the matter.

Thereupon, however, the malcontents, unwilling to accept defeat, broached a new scheme. The Republican nominating convention had been summoned to meet on June 7, 1864; the opponents of Mr. Lincoln now sought to have it postponed until September. William Cullen Bryant favored this. Mr. Greeley also artfully said that a nomination made so early would expose the Union party to a dangerous and possibly a successful flank movement. But deception was impossible; all knew that the postponement itself was a flank movement, and that it was desired for the chance of some advantage turning up for those who now had absolutely nothing to lose.

Mr. Lincoln all the while preserved the same attitude which he had held from the beginning. He had too much honesty and good sense to commit the vulgar folly of pretending not to want what every one knew perfectly well that he did want very much. Yet no fair enemy could charge him with doing any objectionable act to advance his own interests. He declined to give General Schurz leave of absence to make speeches in his behalf. "Speaking in the North," he said, "and fighting in the South at the same time are not possible; nor could I be justified to detail any officer to the political campaign during its continuance, and then return him to the army." When the renomination came to him, he took it with clean hands and a clear conscience; and it did come surely and promptly. The postponers were quenched by general disapproval; and promptly on the appointed day, June 7, the Republican Convention met at Baltimore. As Mr. Forney well said: the body had not to originate, but simply to republish, a policy; not to choose a candidate, but only to adopt the previous choice of the people. Very wisely the "Radical-union," or anti-Lincoln, delegation from Missouri was admitted, as against the contesting pro-Lincoln delegates. The delegations from Tennessee, Arkansas and Louisiana were also admitted. The President had desired this. Perhaps, as some people charged, he thought that it would be a useful precedent for counting the votes of these States in the election itself, should the Republican party have need to do so. The platform, besides many other things, declared against compromise with the rebels; advocated a constitutional amendment to abolish slavery; and praised the President and his policy. The first ballot showed 484 for Lincoln, 22 for Grant. The Missouri radicals had cast the vote for Grant; they rose and transferred it to Lincoln, and thus upon the first ballot he was nominated unanimously.

There was some conflict over the second place. A numerous body felt, and very properly, that Mr. Hamlin deserved the approval of renomination. But others said that policy required the selection of a war Democrat. The President's advice was eagerly and persistently sought. Messrs. Nicolay and Hay allege that he not only ostensibly refused any response, but that he would give no private hint; and they say that therefore it was "with minds absolutely untrammeled by even any knowledge of the President's wishes, that the convention went about its work of selecting his associate on the ticket." Others assert, and, as it seems to me, strongly sustain their assertion, that the President had a distinct and strong purpose in favor of Andrew Johnson,—not on personal, but on political grounds,—and that it was due to his skillful but occult interference that the choice ultimately fell upon the energetic and aggressive war Democrat of Tennessee. [71] The first ballot showed for Mr. Johnson 200, for Mr. Hamlin 150, and for Daniel S. Dickinson, a war Democrat of New York, 108. The nomination of Mr. Johnson was at once made unanimous.

To the committee who waited upon Mr. Lincoln to notify him formally of his nomination, he replied briefly. His only noteworthy remark was made concerning that clause in the platform which proposed the constitutional abolition of slavery; of which he said, that it was "a fitting and necessary conclusion to the final success of the Union cause."

During the ensuing summer of 1864 the strain to which the nation was subjected was excessive. The political campaign produced intense excitement, and the military situation caused profound anxiety. The Democrats worked as men work when they anticipate glorious triumph; and even the Republicans conceded that the chance of their opponents was alarmingly good. The frightful conflict which had devoured men and money without stint was entering upon its fourth year, and the weary people had not that vision which enabled the leaders from their watch-tower to see the end. Wherefore the Democrats, stigmatizing the war policy as a failure, and crying for peace and a settlement, held out an alluring purpose, although they certainly failed to explain distinctly their plan for achieving this consummation without sacrificing the Union. Skillfully devoting the summer to assaults on the Republicans, they awaited the guidance of the latest phase of the political situation before making their own choice. Then, at the end of August, their convention nominated General George B. McClellan. At the time it seemed probable that the nomination was also the gift of the office. So unpromising was the outlook for the Republicans during these summer months that many leaders, and even the President himself, felt that their only chance of winning in November lay in the occurrence before that time of some military success great enough to convince the people that it was not yet time to despair of the war.

It was especially hard for the Republicans to make head against their natural enemies, because they were so severely handicapped by the bad feeling and division among themselves. Mr. Wade, Henry Winter Davis, Thaddeus Stevens, and a host more, could not do otherwise than accept the party nominee; yet with what zeal could they work for the candidate when they felt that they, the leaders of the party, had been something worse than ignored in the selection of him? And what was their influence worth, when all who could be reached by it knew well their extreme hostility and distrust towards Mr. Lincoln? Stevens grudgingly admitted that Lincoln would not be quite so bad a choice as McClellan, yet let no chance go by to assail the opinions, measures, and policy of the Republican President. In this he was imitated by others, and their reluctant adhesion in the mere matter of voting the party ticket was much more than offset by this vehemence in condemning the man in whose behalf they felt it necessary to go to the polls. In a word the situation was, that the common soldiers of the party were to go into the fight under officers who did not expect, and scarcely desired, to win. Victory is rare under such circumstances.

The opposition of the Democratic party was open and legitimate; the unfriendliness of the Republican politicians was more unfortunate than unfair, because it was the mistake of sincere and earnest men. But in the way of Mr. Lincoln's success there stood still other opponents whose antagonism was mischievous, insidious, and unfair both in principle and in detail. Chief in this band appeared Horace Greeley, with a following and an influence fluctuating and difficult to estimate, but considerable. His present political creed was a strange jumble of Democratic and Republican doctrines. No Democrat abused the administration or cried for "peace on almost any terms" louder than he did; yet he still declaimed against slavery, and proposed to buy from the South all its slaves for four hundred millions of dollars. Unfortunately those of his notions which were of importance in the pending campaign were the Democratic ones. If he had come out openly as a free lance, which was his true character, he would have less seriously injured the President's cause. This, however, he would not do, but preferred to fight against the Republicans in their own camp and wearing their own uniform, and in this guise to devote all his capacity to embarrassing the man who was the chosen president and the candidate of that party. Multitudes in the country had been wont to accept the editorials of the "Tribune" as sound political gospels, and the present disaffected attitude of the variable man who inspired those vehement writings was a national disaster. He created and led the party of peace Republicans. Peace Democracy was a legitimate political doctrine; but peace Republicanism was an illogical monstrosity. It lay, with the mortal threat of a cancer, in the political body of the party. It was especially unfortunate just at this juncture that clear thinking was not among Mr. Greeley's gifts. In single-minded pursuit of his purpose to destroy Mr. Lincoln by any possible means, he had at first encouraged the movement for Fremont, though it was based on views directly contrary to his own. But soon losing interest in that, he thereafter gave himself wholly to the business of crying aloud for immediate peace, which he continued to do throughout the presidential campaign, always unreasonably, sometimes disingenuously, but without rest, and with injurious effect. The vivid picture which he loved to draw of "our bleeding, bankrupt, and almost dying country," longing for peace and shuddering at the "prospect of new rivers of human blood," scared many an honest and anxious patriot.

In July and August Mr. Greeley was misled into lending himself to the schemes of some Southerners at Niagara Falls, who threw out intimations that they were emissaries from the Confederacy and authorized to treat for peace. He believed these men, and urged that negotiations should be prosecuted with them. By the publicity which he gave to the matter he caused much embarrassment to Mr. Lincoln, who saw at once that the whole business was certainly absurd and probably treacherous. The real purpose of these envoys, he afterwards said, was undoubtedly "to assist in selecting and arranging a candidate and a platform for the Chicago Convention." Yet clearly as he understood this false and hollow scheme, he could not altogether ignore Greeley's demands for attention to it without giving too much color to those statements which the editor was assiduously scattering abroad, to the effect that the administration did not desire peace, and would not take it when proffered. So there were reasons why this sham offer must be treated as if it were an honest one, vexatious as the necessity appeared to the President. Perhaps he was cheered by the faith which he had in the wisdom of proverbs, for now, very fortunately, he permitted himself to be guided by a familiar one; and he decided to give to his annoyer liberal rope. Accordingly he authorized Mr. Greeley himself to visit in person these emissaries, to confer with them, and even to bring them to Washington in case they should prove really to have from Jefferson Davis any written proposition "for peace, embracing the restoration of the Union and abandonment of slavery." It was an exceedingly shrewd move, and it seriously discomposed Mr. Greeley, who had not counted upon being so frankly met, and whose disquietude was amusingly evident as he reluctantly fluttered forth to Niagara upon his mission of peace, less wise than a serpent and unfortunately much less harmless than a dove.

There is no room here to follow all the intricacies of the ensuing "negotiations." The result was an utter fiasco, fully justifying the President's opinion of the fatuity of the whole business. The so-called Southern envoys had no credentials at all; they appeared to be mere adventurers, and members of that Southern colony in Canada which became even more infamous by what it desired to do than mischievous by what it actually did during the war. If they had any distinct purpose on this occasion, it was to injure the Republican party by discrediting its candidate in precisely the way in which Mr. Greeley was aiding them to do these things. But he never got his head sufficiently clear to appreciate this, and he faithfully continued to play the part for which he had been cast by them, but without understanding it. He persistently charged the responsibility for his bootless return and ignominious situation upon Mr. Lincoln; and though his errand proved conclusively that the South was making no advances, [72] and though no man in the country was more strictly affected with personal knowledge of this fact than he was, yet he continued to tell the people, with all the weight of his personal authority, that the President was obstinately set against any and all proffers of peace. Mr. Lincoln, betwixt mercy and policy, refrained from crushing his antagonist by an ungarbled publication of all the facts and documents; and in return for his forbearance he long continued to receive from Mr. Greeley vehement assurances that every direful disaster awaited the Republican party. The cause suffered much from these relentless diatribes of the "Tribune's" influential manager, for nothing else could make the administration so unpopular as the belief that it was backward in any possible exertion to secure an honorable peace.

If by sound logic the Greeley faction should have voted with the Democrats, — since in the chief point in issue, the prosecution of the war, they agreed with the Democracy, — so the war Democrats, being in accord with the Republicans, upon this same overshadowing issue should, at the coming election at least, have voted with that party. Many of them undoubtedly did finally prefer Lincoln, coupled with Andrew Johnson, to McClellan. But they also had anxieties, newly stirred, and entirely reasonable in men of their political faith. It was plain to them that Mr. Lincoln had been finding his way to the distinct position that the abolition of slavery was an essential condition of peace. Now this was undeniably a very serious and alterative graft upon the original doctrine that the war was solely for the restoration of the Union. The editor of a war-Democratic newspaper in Wisconsin sought information upon this point. In the course of Mr. Greeley's negotiatory business Mr. Lincoln had offered to welcome "any proposition which embraces the restoration of peace, the integrity of the whole Union, and the abandonment of slavery." Now this, said the interrogating editor, implies "that no steps can be taken towards peace ... unless accompanied with an abandonment of slavery. This puts the whole war question on a new basis and takes us war Democrats clear off our feet, leaving us no ground to stand upon. If we sustain the war and war policy, does it not demand the changing of our party politics?" Nicolay and Hay print the draft of a reply by Mr. Lincoln which, they say, was "apparently unfinished and probably never sent." In this he referred to his past utterances as being still valid. But he said that no Southerner had "intimated a willingness for a restoration of the Union in any event or on any condition whatever.... If Jefferson Davis wishes for himself, or for the benefit of his friends at the North, to know what I would do if he were to offer peace and reunion, saying nothing about slavery, let him try me." It must be admitted that this was not an answer, but was a clear waiver of an answer. The President could not or would not reply categorically to the queries of the editor. Perhaps the impossibility of doing so both satisfactorily and honestly may explain why the paper was left unfinished and unsent. It was not an easy letter to write; its composition must have puzzled one who was always clear both in thought and in expression. Probably Mr. Lincoln no longer expected that the end of the war would leave slavery in existence, nor intended that it should do so; and doubtless he anticipated that the course of events would involve the destruction of that now rotten and undermined institution, without serious difficulty at the opportune moment. The speeches made at the Republican nominating convention had been very outspoken, to the effect that slavery must be made to "cease forever," as a result of the war. Yet a blunt statement that abolition would be a *sine qua non* in any arrangements for peace, emanating directly from the President, as a declaration of his policy, would be very costly in the pending campaign, and would imperil rather than advance the fortunes of him who had this consummation at heart, and would thereby also diminish the chance for the consummation itself. So at last he seems to have left the war Democrats to puzzle over the conundrum, and decide as best they could. Of course the doubt affected unfavorably the votes of some of them.

A measure of the mischief which was done by these suspicions and by Greeley's assertions that the administration did not desire peace, may be taken from a letter, written to Mr. Lincoln on August 22 by Mr. Henry J. Raymond, chairman of the National Executive Committee of the Republican party. From all sides, Mr. Raymond says, "I hear but one report. The tide is setting strongly against us." Mr. Washburne, he writes, despairs of Illinois, and Mr. Cameron of Pennsylvania, and he himself is not hopeful of New

York, and Governor Morton is doubtful of Indiana; "and so of the rest." For this melancholy condition he assigns two causes: the want of military successes, and the belief "that we are not to have peace in any event under this administration until slavery is abandoned. In some way or other the suspicion is widely diffused that we can have peace with union, if we would." Then even this stanch Republican leader suggests that it might be good policy to sound Jefferson Davis on the feasibility of peace "on the sole condition of acknowledging the supremacy of the Constitution,—all other questions to be settled in a convention of the people of all the States." The President might well have been thrown into inextricable confusion of mind, betwixt the assaults of avowed enemies, the denunciations and predictions of inimical friends, the foolish advice of genuine supporters. It is now plain that all the counsel which was given to him was bad, from whatsoever quarter it came. It shows the powerfulness of his nature that he retained his cool and accurate judgment, although the crisis was such that even he also had to admit that the danger of defeat was imminent. To Mr. Raymond's panic-stricken suggestions he made a very shrewd response by drafting some instructions for the purpose of sending that gentleman himself on the mission to Mr. Davis. It was the same tactics which he had pursued in dispatching Mr. Greeley to meet the Southerners in Canada. The result was that the fruitlessness of the suggestion was admitted by its author.

As if all hurtful influences were to be concentrated against the President, it became necessary just at this inopportune time to make good the terrible waste in the armies caused by expiration of terms of service and by the bloody campaigns of Grant and Sherman. Volunteering was substantially at an end, and a call for troops would have to be enforced by a draft. Inevitably this would stir afresh the hostility of those who dreaded that the conscription might sweep into military service themselves or those dear to them. It was Mr. Lincoln's duty, however, to make the demand, and to make it at once. He did so; regardless of personal consequences, he called for 500,000 more men.

Thus in July and August the surface was covered with straws, and every one of them indicated a current setting strongly against Mr. Lincoln. Unexpectedly the Democratic Convention made a small counter-eddy; for the peace Democrats, led by Vallandigham, were ill advised enough to force a peace plank into the platform. This was at once repudiated by McClellan in his letter of acceptance, and then again was reiterated by Vallandigham as the true policy of the party. Thus war Democrats were alarmed, and a split was opened. Yet it was by no means such a chasm as that which, upon the opposite side, divided the radicals and politicians from the mass of their Republican comrades. It might affect ratios, but did not seem likely to change results. In a word, all political observers now believed that military success was the only medicine which could help the Republican prostration, and whether this medicine could be procured was very doubtful.

[64] Arnold, *Lincoln*, 384, 385. Nicolay and Hay seem to me to go too far in belittling the opposition to Mr. Lincoln within the Republican party.

[65] See Arnold, *Lincoln*, 385. But the fact is notorious among all who remember those times.

[66] *Polit. Recoll. 243 et seq.* Mr. Julian here gives a vivid sketch of the opposition to Mr. Lincoln.

[67] In the *National Intelligencer*, February 22, 1864.

[68] Lovejoy had generally stood faithfully by the President.

[69] N. and H. ix. 40.

[70] I Samuel xxii. 2.

[71] See, more especially, McClure, *Lincoln and Men of War-Times*, chapter on "Lincoln and Hamlin," 104-118. This writer says (p. 196) that Lincoln's first selection was General Butler.

[72] Further illustration of this unquestionable fact was furnished by the volunteer mission of Colonel Jaquess and Mr. Gilmore to Richmond in July. N. and H. vol. ix. ch. ix.

# CHAPTER X
# MILITARY SUCCESSES, AND THE
# REËLECTION OF THE PRESIDENT

It is necessary now to return to military matters, and briefly to set forth the situation. No especial fault was found with General Meade's operations in Virginia; yet it was obvious that a system quite different from that which had hitherto prevailed must be introduced there. To fight a great battle, then await entire recuperation of losses, then fight again and wait again, was a process of lingering exhaustion which might be prolonged indefinitely. In February, 1864, Congress passed, though with some reluctance, and the President much more readily signed, a bill for the appointment of a lieutenant-general, "authorized, under the direction and during the pleasure of the President, to command the armies of the United States." [73] All understood that the place was made for General Grant, and it was at once given to him by Mr. Lincoln. On March 3 the appointment was confirmed by the Senate. By this Halleck was substantially laid aside; his uselessness had long since become so apparent, that though still holding his dignified position, he seemed almost forgotten by every one.

Grant came to Washington, [74] arriving on March 8, and there was induced by what he heard and saw to lay aside his own previous purpose and the strenuous advice of Sherman, and to fall in with Mr. Lincoln's wishes; that is to say, to take personal control of the campaign in Virginia. He did this with his usual promptness, and set Sherman in command in the middle of the country, the only other important theatre of operations. It is said that Grant, before accepting the new rank and taking Virginia as his special province, stipulated that he was to be absolutely free from all interference, especially on the part of Stanton. Whether this agreement was formulated or not, it was put into practical effect. No man hereafter interfered with General Grant. Mr. Lincoln occasionally made suggestions, but strictly and merely as suggestions. He distinctly and pointedly said that he did not know, and did not wish to know, the general's plans of campaign. [75] When the new commander had duly considered the situation, he adopted precisely the same broad scheme which had been previously devised by Mr. Lincoln and General McClellan; that is to say, he arranged a simultaneous vigorous advance all along the line. It was the way to make weight and numbers tell; and Grant had great faith in weight and numbers; like Napoleon, he believed that Providence has a shrewd way of siding with the heaviest battalions.

On April 30, all being ready for the advance, the President sent a note of God-speed to the general. "I wish to express," he said, "my entire satisfaction with what you have done up to this time, so far as I understand it. The particulars of your plan I neither know, nor seek to know.... If there is anything wanting which is within my power to give, do not fail to let me know it." The general replied in a pleasant tone: "I have been astonished at the readiness with which everything asked for has been yielded, without even an explanation being asked. Should my success be less than I desire and expect, the least I can say is, the fault is not with you." When the President read these strange words his astonishment must have far exceeded that expressed by the general. Never before had he been thus addressed by any commander in Virginia! Generally he had been told that a magnificent success was about to be achieved, which he had done nothing to promote and perhaps much to retard, but which would nevertheless be secured by the ability of a general in spite of unfriendly neglect by a president.

On May 4 General Grant's army started upon its way, with 122,146 men present for duty. Against them General Lee had 61,953. The odds seemed excessive; but Lee had inside lines, the defensive, and intrenchments, to equalize the disparity of numbers. At once began those bloody and incessant campaigns by which General Grant intended to end, and finally did end, the war. The North could afford to lose three men where the South lost two, and would still have a balance left after the South had spent all. The expenditure in this proportion would be disagreeable; but if this was the inevitable and only price, Grant was willing to pay it, justly regarding it as cheaper than a continuation of the process of purchase by piecemeal. In a few hours the frightful struggle in the Wilderness was in progress. All day on the 5th, all day on the 6th, the terrible slaughter continued in those darksome woods and swamps. "More desperate fighting has not been witnessed on this continent," said Grant. The Union troops could not force their way through those tangled forests. Thereupon, accepting the situation in his imperturbable way, he arranged to move, on May 7, by the left flank southerly towards Spottsylvania. Lee, disappointed and surprised that Grant was advancing instead of falling back, could not do otherwise than move in the same course; for, in fact, the combatants were locked together in a grappling campaign. Then took place more bloody and determined fighting. The Union losses were appalling, since the troops were attacking an army in position. Yet Grant was sanguine; it was in a dispatch of May 11 that he said that he had been getting the better in the struggle, and that he proposed to fight it out on that line if it took all summer. The result of the further slaughter at Spottsylvania was not a victory for either leader, but was more hurtful to Lee because he could less well afford to have his men killed and wounded. Grant, again finding that he could not force Lee out of his position, also again moved by the left flank, steadily approaching Richmond and dragging Lee with him. The Northern loss had already reached the frightful total of 37,335 men; the Confederate loss was less, but enormous. Amid the bloodshed, however, Grant scented success. On May 26 he wrote: "Lee's army is really whipped.... Our men feel that they have gained the morale over the enemy.... I may be mistaken, but I feel that our success over Lee's army is already assured." He even gratified the President by again disregarding all precedent in Virginian campaigns, and saying that the promptness with which reinforcements had been forwarded had contributed largely to the promising situation! But almost immediately after this the North shuddered at the enormous and profitless carnage at Cold Harbor. Concurrently with all this bloodshed, there also took place the famous and ill-starred movement of General Butler upon Richmond, which ended in securely shutting up him and his forces at Bermuda Hundred, "as in a bottle strongly corked."

Such was the Virginian situation early in June. By a series of most bloody battles, no one of which had been a real victory, Grant had come before the defenses of Richmond, nearly where McClellan had already been. And now, like McClellan, he proposed to move around to the southward and invest the city. It must be confessed that in all this there was nothing visible to the inexperienced vision of the citizens at home which made much brighter in their eyes the prestige of Mr. Lincoln's war policy. Nor could they see, as that summer of the presidential campaign came and went, that any really great change or improvement was effected.

On the other hand, there took place in July what is sometimes lightly called General Early's raid against Washington. In fact, it was a genuine and very serious campaign, wherein that general was within a few hours of capturing the city. Issuing out of that Shenandoah Valley whence, as from a cave of horrors rather than one of the loveliest valleys in the world, so much of terror and mischief had so often burst out against the North, Early, with 17,000 veteran troops, moved straight and fast upon the national capital. On the evening of July 10 Mr. Lincoln rode out to his summer quarters at the Soldiers' Home. But the Confederate troops were within a few miles, and Mr. Stanton insisted that he should come back. The next day the Confederates advanced along the Seventh Street road, in full expectation of marching into the city with little opposition. There was brisk artillery firing, and Mr. Lincoln, who had driven out to the scene of action, actually came under fire; an officer was struck down within a few feet of him.

The anticipation of General Early was sanguine, yet by no means ill founded. The veterans in Washington were a mere handful, and though the green troops might have held the strong defenses for a little while, yet the Southern veterans would have been pretty sure to make their way. It was, in fact, a very close question of time. Grant had been at first incredulous of the reports of Early's movements; but when he could no longer doubt, he sent reinforcements with the utmost dispatch. They arrived none too soon. It was while General Early was making his final arrangements for an attack, which he meant should be irresistible, that General Wright, with two divisions from the army of the Potomac, landed at the river wharves and marched through the city to the threatened points. With this the critical hours passed away. It had really been a crisis of hours, and might have been one of minutes. Now Early saw that the prize had slipped through his fingers actually as they closed upon it, and so bitter was his disappointment that—since he was disappointed—even a Northerner can almost afford him sympathy. So, his chance being gone, he must go too, and that speedily; for it was he who was in danger now. Moving rapidly, he saved himself, and returned up the Shenandoah Valley. He had accomplished no real harm; but that the war had been going on for three years, and that Washington was still hardly a safe place for the President to live in, was another point against the war policy.

Sherman had moved out against Johnston, at Dalton, at the same time that Grant had moved out against Lee, and during the summer he made a record very similar to that of his chief. He pressed the enemy without rest, fought constantly, suffered and inflicted terrible losses, won no signal victory, yet constantly got farther to the southward. Fortunately, however, he was nearer to a specific success than Grant was, and at last he was able to administer the sorely needed tonic to the political situation. Jefferson Davis, who hated Johnston, made the steady retreat of that general before Sherman an excuse for removing him and putting General Hood in his place. The army was then at Atlanta. Hood was a fighting man, and immediately he brought on a great battle, which happily proved to be also a great mistake; for the result was a brilliant and decisive victory for Sherman and involved the fall of Atlanta. This was one of the important achievements of the war; and when, on September 3, Sherman telegraphed, "Atlanta is ours, and fairly won," the news came to the President like wine to the weary. He hastened to tender the "national thanks" to the general and his gallant soldiers, with words of gratitude which must have come straight and warm from his heart. There was a chance now for the Union cause in November.

About ten days before this event Farragut, in spite of forts and batteries, iron-clads and torpedoes, had possessed himself of Mobile Bay and closed that Gulf port which had been so useful a mouth to the hungry stomach of the Confederacy. No efficient blockade of it had ever been possible. Through it military, industrial, and domestic supplies had been brought in, and invaluable cotton had gone out to pay for them. Now, however, the sealing of the South was all but hermetical. As a naval success the feat was entitled to high admiration, and as a practical injury to the Confederacy it could not be overestimated.

Achievements equally brilliant, if not quite so important, were quickly contributed by Sheridan. In spite of objections on the part of Stanton, Grant had put this enterprising fighter in command of a strong force of cavalry in the Shenandoah Valley, where Lee was keeping Early as a constant menace upon Maryland, Pennsylvania, and Washington. Three hard-fought battles followed, during September and October. In each the Federals were thoroughly victorious. The last of the three was that which was made famous by "Sheridan's ride." He had been to Washington and was returning on horseback, when to his surprise he encountered squads of his own troops hurrying back in disorderly flight from a battle which, during his brief absence, had unexpectedly been delivered by Early. Halting them and carrying them back with him, he was relieved, as he came upon the field, to find a part of his army still standing firm and even pressing the Confederates hard. He communicated his own spirit to his troops, and turned partial defeat into brilliant victory. By this gallant deed was shattered forever the Confederate Army of the Valley; and from that time forth there issued out of that fair concealment no more gray-uniformed troopers to foray Northern fields or to threaten Northern towns. For these achievements Lincoln made Sheridan a major-general, dictating the appointment in words of unusual compliment.

Late as the Democrats were in holding their nominating convention, they would have done well to hold it a little later. They might then have derived wisdom from these military and naval events, and not improbably they would have been less audacious in staking their success upon the issue that the war was a failure, and would have so modified that craven proposition as to make it accord with the more patriotic sentiment of their soldier candidate. But the fortunes alike of the real war and of the political war were decidedly and happily against them. Even while they were in session the details of Farragut's daring and victorious battle in Mobile Bay were coming to hand. Scarcely had they adjourned when the roar of thunderous salvos in every navy yard, fort, and arsenal of the North hailed the triumph of Sherman at Atlanta. Before these echoes had died away the people were electrified by the three battles in Virginia which Sheridan fought and won in style so brilliant as to seem almost theatrical. Thus from the South, from the West, and from the East came simultaneously the fierce contradiction of this insulting Copperhead notion, that the North had failed in the war. The political blunder of the party was now much more patent than was any alleged military failure on the part of its opponents. In fact the Northerners were beholding the sudden turning over of a great page in the book of the national history, and upon the newly exposed side of it, amid the telegrams announcing triumphs of arms, they read in great plain letters the reëlection of Mr. Lincoln. Before long most persons conceded this. He himself had said, a few months earlier, that the probabilities indicated that the presidential campaign would be a struggle between a Union candidate and a Disunion candidate. McClellan had sought to give to it a complexion safer for his party and more honorable for himself, but the platform and events combined to defeat his wise purpose. In addition to these difficulties the South also burdened him with an untimely and compromising friendship. The Charleston "Courier," with reckless frankness, declared that the armies of the Confederacy and the peace-men at the North were working together for the procurement of peace; and said: "Our success in battle insures the success of McClellan. Our failure will inevitably lead to his defeat." No words could have been more imprudent; the loud proclamation of such an alliance was the madness of self-destruction. In the face of such talk the Northerners could not but believe that the issue was truly made up between war and Union on the one side, peace and disunion on the other. If between the two, when distinctly formulated, there could under any circumstances have been doubt, the successes by sea and land turned the scale for the Republicans.

During the spring and summer many prominent Republicans strenuously urged Mr. Lincoln to remove the postmaster-general, Montgomery Blair, from the cabinet. The political purpose was to placate the Radicals, whose unnatural hostility within the party greatly disturbed the President's friends. Many followers of Fremont might be conciliated by the elimination of the bitter and triumphant opponent of their beloved chieftain; and besides this leader, the portentous list of those with whom the postmaster was on ill terms included many magnates,—Chase, Seward, Stanton, Halleck, and abundance of politicians. Henry Wilson wrote to the President: "Blair every one hates. Tens of thousands of men will be lost to you, or will give a reluctant vote, on account of the Blairs." Even the Republican National Convention had covertly assailed him; for a plank in the platform, declaring it "essential to the general welfare that harmony should prevail in the national councils," was known to mean that he should no longer remain in the cabinet. Yet to force him out was most distasteful to the President, who was always slow to turn against any man. Replying to a denunciatory letter from Halleck he said: "I propose continuing to be myself the judge as to when a member of the cabinet shall be dismissed." He made a like statement, curtly and decisively, in a cabinet meeting. Messrs. Nicolay and Hay say that he did not yield to the pressure until he was assured of his reëlection, and that then he yielded only because he felt that he ought not obstinately to retain an adviser in whom the party had lost confidence. On September 23 he wrote to Mr. Blair a kindly note: "You have generously said to me more than once that whenever your resignation could be a relief to me, it was at my disposal. The time has come. You very well know that this proceeds from no dissatisfaction of mine with you, personally or officially. Your uniform kindness has been unsurpassed by that of any friend." Mr. Blair immediately relieved the President from the embarrassing situation, and he and his family behaved afterward with honorable spirit, giving loyal support to Mr. Lincoln during the rest of the campaign. Ex-Governor Dennison of Ohio was appointed to the vacant office.

Many and various were the other opportunities which the President was urged to seize for helping both himself and other Republican candidates. But he steadfastly declined to get into the mud of the struggle. It was a jest of the campaign that Senator King was sent by some New York men to ask whether Lincoln meant to support the Republican ticket. He did: he openly admitted that he believed his reëlection to be for the best interest of the country. As an honest man he could not think otherwise. "I am for the regular nominee in all cases," he bluntly said, in reply to a request for his interference concerning a member of Congress; and the general principle covered, of course, his own case. To the postmaster of Philadelphia, however, whose employees displayed suspicious Republican unanimity, he administered a sharp and imperious warning. He even would not extend to his close and valued friend, Mr. Arnold, assistance which that gentleman too sorely needed. More commendable still was his behavior as to the draft. On July 18, as has been said, he issued a call for 500,000 men, though at that time he might well have believed that by so doing he was burying beyond resurrection all chance of reëlection. Later the Republican leaders entreated him, with earnest eloquence and every melancholy presage, to suspend the drafting under this call for a few weeks only. It seemed to him, however, that the army could not wait a few weeks. "What is the presidency worth to me, if I have no country?" he said; and the storm of persuasion could not induce him to issue the postponing order.

Campaign slanders were rife as usual. One of them Mr. Lincoln cared to contradict. Some remarks made by Mr. Seward in a speech at Auburn had been absurdly construed by Democratic orators and editors to indicate that Mr. Lincoln, if defeated at the polls, would use the remainder of his term for doing what he could to ruin the government. This vile charge, silly as it was, yet touched a very sensitive spot. On October 19, in a speech to some serenaders, and evidently having this in mind, he said:—

"I am struggling to maintain the government, not to overthrow it. I am struggling especially to prevent others from overthrowing it.... Whoever shall be constitutionally elected in November shall be duly installed as President on the fourth of March.... In the interval I shall do my utmost that whoever is to hold the helm for the next voyage shall start with the best possible chance to save the ship. This is due to the people both on principle and under the Constitution.... If they should deliberately resolve to have immediate peace, even at the loss of their country and their liberty, I know [have?] not the power or the right to resist them. It is their business, and they must do as they please with their own."

In this connection it is worth while to recall an incident which occurred on August 26, amid the dark days. Anticipating at that time that he might soon be compelled to encounter the sore trial of administering the government during four months in face of its near transmission to a successor all whose views and purposes would be diametrically opposite to his own, and desiring beforehand clearly to mark out his duty in this stress, Mr. Lincoln one day wrote these words:—

"This morning, as for some days past, it seems exceedingly probable that this administration will not be reëlected. Then it will be my duty to so cooperate with the President-elect as to save the Union between the election and the inauguration, as he will have secured his election on such ground that he cannot possibly save it afterwards."

He then closed the paper so that it could not be read, and requested each member of the cabinet to sign his name on the reverse side.

In the end, honesty was vindicated as the best policy, and courage as the soundest judgment. The preliminary elections in Vermont and Maine in September, the important elections in Pennsylvania, Ohio, and Indiana in October, showed that a Republican wave was sweeping across the North. It swept on and gathered overwhelming volume in the brief succeeding interval before November 8. On that momentous day, the voting in the States showed 2,213,665 Republican votes, to which were added 116,887 votes of soldiers in the field, electing 212 presidential electors; 1,802,237 Democratic votes, to which were added 33,748 votes of soldiers in the field, electing

21 presidential electors. Mr. Lincoln's plurality was therefore 494,567; and it would have been swelled to over half a million had not the votes of the soldiers of Vermont, Kansas, and Minnesota arrived too late to be counted, and had not those of Wisconsin been rejected for an informality. Thus were the dreary predictions of the midsummer so handsomely confuted that men refused to believe that they had ever been deceived by them.

On the evening of election day Mr. Lincoln went to the War Department, and there stayed until two o'clock at night, noting the returns as they came assuring his triumph and steadily swelling its magnitude. Amid the good news his feelings took on no personal complexion. A crowd of serenaders, meeting him on his return to the White House, demanded a speech. He told them that he believed that the day's work would be the lasting advantage, if not the very salvation, of the country, and that he was grateful for the people's confidence; but, he said, "if I know my heart, my gratitude is free from any taint of personal triumph. I do not impugn the motives of any one opposed to me. It is no pleasure to me to triumph over any one; but I give thanks to the Almighty for this evidence of the people's resolution to stand by free government and the rights of humanity." A hypocrite would, probably enough, have said much the same thing; but when Mr. Lincoln spoke in this way, men who were themselves honest never charged him with hypocrisy. On November 10 a serenade by the Republican clubs of the District called forth this: —

"It has long been a grave question whether any government, not too strong for the liberties of its people, can be strong enough to maintain its own existence in great emergencies. On this point the present rebellion brought our republic to a severe test, and a presidential election occurring in regular course during the rebellion added not a little to the strain. If the loyal people united were put to the utmost of their strength by the rebellion, must they not fail when divided and partially paralyzed by a political war among themselves? But the election was a necessity. We cannot have free government without elections; and if the rebellion could force us to forego or postpone a national election, it might fairly claim to have already conquered and ruined us. The strife of the election is but human nature practically applied to the facts of the case. What has occurred in this case must ever recur in similar cases. Human nature will not change. In any future great national trial, compared with the men of this, we shall have as weak and as strong, as silly and as wise, as bad and as good. Let us, therefore, study the incidents of this, as philosophy to learn wisdom from, and none of them as wrongs to be revenged. But the election, along with its incidental and undesirable strife, has done good, too. It has demonstrated that a people's government can sustain a national election in the midst of a great civil war. Until now, it has not been known to the world that this was a possibility. It shows, also, how sound and how strong we still are. It shows that, even among candidates of the same party, he who is most devoted to the Union and most opposed to treason can receive most of the people's votes. It shows, also, to the extent yet known, that we have more men now than we had when the war began. Gold is good in its place; but living, brave, patriotic men are better than gold.

"But the rebellion continues; and, now that the election is over, may not all having a common interest reunite in a common effort to save our common country? For my own part, I have striven and shall strive to avoid placing any obstacle in the way. So long as I have been here, I have not willingly planted a thorn in any man's bosom. While I am deeply sensible to the high compliment of a reëlection, and duly grateful, as I trust, to Almighty God for having directed my countrymen to a right conclusion, as I think, for their own good, it adds nothing to my satisfaction that any other man may be disappointed or pained by the result.

"May I ask those who have not differed with me to join with me in this same spirit towards those who have? And now let me close by asking three hearty cheers for our brave soldiers and seamen, and their gallant and skillful commanders."

The unfortunate disputes about reconstruction threatened to cause trouble at the counting of the votes in Congress. Of the States which had seceded, two, Arkansas and Tennessee, had endeavored to reconstruct themselves as members of the Union; and their renewed statehood had received some recognition from the President. He, however, firmly refused to listen to demands, which were urgently pushed, to obtain his interference in the arrangements made for choosing presidential electors. To certain Tennesseeans, who sent him a protest against the action of Governor Johnson, he replied that, "by the Constitution and the laws, the President is charged with no duty in the conduct of a presidential election in any State; nor do I in this case perceive any military reason for his interference in the matter.... It is scarcely necessary to add that if any election shall be held, and any votes shall be cast, in the State of Tennessee, ... it will belong not to the military agents, nor yet to the executive department, but exclusively to another department of the government, to determine whether they are entitled to be counted, in conformity with the Constitution and laws of the United States." His prudent abstention from stretching his official authority afterward saved him from much embarrassment in the turn which this troublesome business soon took. In both Arkansas and Tennessee Republican presidential electors were chosen, who voted, and sent on to Washington the certificates of their votes to be counted in due course with the rest. But Congress jealously guarded its position on reconstruction against this possible flank movement, and in January, 1865, passed a joint resolution declaring that Virginia, North and South Carolina, Georgia, Florida, Alabama, Mississippi, Louisiana, Texas, Arkansas, and Tennessee were in such a condition on November 8 that no valid election of presidential electors was held in any of them, and that therefore no electoral votes should be received or counted from any of them. When this resolution came before Mr. Lincoln for his signature it placed him in an embarrassing position, because his approval might seem to be an implied contradiction of the position which he had taken concerning the present status of Tennessee and Arkansas. It was not until February 8, the very day of the count, that he conquered his reluctance, and when at last he did so and decided to sign the resolution, he at the same time carefully made his position plain by a brief message. He said that he conceived that Congress had lawful power to exclude from the count any votes which it deemed illegal, and that therefore he could not properly veto a joint resolution upon the subject; he disclaimed "all right of the executive to interfere in any way in the matter of canvassing or counting electoral votes;" and he also disclaimed that, by signing the resolution, he had "expressed any opinion on the recitals of the preamble, or any judgment of his own upon the subject of the resolution." That is to say, the especial matter dealt with in this proceeding was *ultra vires* of the executive, and the formal signature of the President was affixed by him without prejudice to his official authority in any other business which might arise concerning the restored condition of statehood.

When the counting of the votes began, the members of the Senate and House did not know whether Mr. Lincoln had signed the resolution or not; and therefore, in the doubt as to what his action would be, the famous twenty-second joint rule, regulating the counting of electoral votes, was drawn in haste and passed with precipitation. [76] It was an instance of angry partisan legislation, which threatened trouble afterward and was useless at the time. No attempt was made to present or count the votes of Arkansas and Tennessee, and the president of the Senate acted under the joint resolution and not under the joint rule. Yet the vote of West Virginia was counted, and it was not easy to show that her title was not under a legal cloud fully as dark as that which shadowed Arkansas and Tennessee.

When Mr. Lincoln said concerning his reëlection, that the element of personal triumph gave him no gratification, he spoke far within the truth. He was not boasting of, but only in an unintentional way displaying, his dispassionate and impersonal habit in all political relationships,—a distinguishing trait, of which history is so chary of parallels that perhaps no reader will recall even one. A striking instance of it occurred in this same autumn. On October 12, 1864, the venerable Chief Justice Taney died, and at once the friends of Mr. Chase named him for the succession. There were few men whom Mr. Lincoln had less reason to favor than this gentleman, who had only condescended to mitigate severe condemnation of his capacity by mild praise of his character, who had hoped to displace him from the presidency, and who, in the effort to do so, had engaged in what might have been stigmatized even as a cabal. Plenty of people were ready to tell him stories innumerable of Chase's hostility to him, and contemptuous remarks about him; but to all such communications he quietly refused to give ear. What Mr. Chase thought or felt concerning him was not pertinent to the question whether or no Chase would make a good chief justice. Yet it was true that Montgomery Blair would have liked the place, and the President had many personal reasons for wishing to do a favor to Blair. It was also true that the opposition to Mr. Chase was so bitter and came from so many quarters, and was based on so many alleged reasons, that had the President chosen to prefer another to him, it would have been impossible to attribute the preference to personal prejudice. In his own mind, however, Mr. Lincoln really believed that, in spite of all the objections which could be made, Mr. Chase was the best man for the position; and his only anxiety was that one so restless and ambitious might still scheme for the presidency to the inevitable prejudice of his judicial duties. He had some thought of speaking frankly with Chase on this subject, perhaps seeking something like a pledge from him; but he was deterred from this by fear of misconstruction. Finally having, after his usual fashion, reached his own conclusion, and communicated it to no one, he sent the nomination to the Senate, and it received the honor of immediate confirmation without reference to a committee.

[73] The rank had been held by Washington; also, but by brevet only, by Scott.

[74] For curious account of his interview with Mr. Lincoln, see N. and H. viii. 340-342.

[75] In this connection, see story of General Richard Taylor, and contradiction thereof, concerning choice of route to Richmond, N. and H. viii. 343.

[76] This was the rule which provided that if, at the count, any question should arise as to counting any vote offered, the Senate and House should separate, and each should vote on the question of receiving or not receiving the vote; and it should not be received and counted except by concurrent assent.

# CHAPTER XI
# THE END COMES INTO SIGHT: THE SECOND INAUGURATION

When Congress came together in December, 1864, the doom of the Confederacy was in plain view of all men, at the North and at the South. If General Grant had sustained frightful losses without having won any signal victory, yet the losses could be afforded; and the nature of the man and his methods in warfare were now understood. It was seen that, with or without victory, and at whatever cost, he had moved relentlessly forward. His grim, irresistible persistence oppressed, as with a sense of destiny, those who tried to confront it; every one felt that he was going to "end the job." He was now beleaguering Petersburg, and few Southerners doubted that he was sure of taking it and Richmond. In the middle country Sherman, after taking Atlanta, had soon thereafter marched cheerily forth on his imposing, theatrical, holiday excursion to the sea, leaving General Thomas behind him to do the hard fighting with General Hood. The grave doubt as to whether too severe a task had not been placed upon Thomas was dispelled by the middle of the month, when his brilliant victory at Nashville so shattered the Southern army that it never again attained important proportions. In June preceding, the notorious destroyer, the Alabama, had been sunk by the Kearsarge. In November the Shenandoah, the last of the rebel privateers, came into Liverpool, and was immediately handed over by the British authorities to Federal officials; for the Englishmen had at last found out who was going to win in the struggle. In October, the rebel ram Albemarle was destroyed by the superb gallantry of Lieutenant Cushing. Thus the rebel flag ceased to fly above any deck. Along the coast very few penetrable crevices could still be found even by the most enterprising blockade-runners; and already the arrangements were making which brought about, a month later, the capture of Fort Fisher and Wilmington.

Under these circumstances the desire to precipitate the pace and to reach the end with a rush possessed many persons of the nervous and eager type. They could not spur General Grant, so they gave their vexatious attention to the President, and endeavored to compel him to open with the Confederate government negotiations for a settlement, which they believed, or pretended to believe, might thus be attained. But Mr. Lincoln was neither to be urged nor wheedled out of his simple position. In his message to Congress he referred to the number of votes cast at the recent election as indicating that, in spite of the drain of war, the population of the North had actually increased during the preceding four years. This fact shows, he said, "that we are not exhausted nor in process of exhaustion; that we are *gaining* strength, and may, if need be, maintain the contest indefinitely. This as to men. Material resources are now more complete and abundant than ever. The natural resources, then, are unexhausted, and, as we believe, inexhaustible. The public purpose to reëstablish and maintain the national authority is unchanged, and, as we believe, unchangeable. The manner of continuing the effort remains to choose. On careful consideration of all the evidence accessible, it seems to me that no attempt at negotiation with the insurgent leader could result in any good. He would accept nothing short of severance of the Union,—precisely what we will not and cannot give. His declarations to this effect are explicit and oft-repeated. He does not attempt to deceive us. He affords us no excuse to deceive ourselves. He cannot voluntarily re-accept the Union; we cannot voluntarily yield it. Between him and us the issue is distinct, simple, and inflexible. It is an issue which can only be tried by war, and decided by victory. If we yield, we are beaten; if the Southern people fail him, he is beaten. Either way, it would be the victory and defeat following war.

"What is true, however, of him who heads the insurgent cause is not necessarily true of those who follow. Although he cannot re-accept the Union, they can; some of them, we know, already desire peace and reunion. The number of such may increase. They can at any moment have peace simply by laying down their arms and submitting to the national authority under the Constitution.

"After so much, the government could not, if it would, maintain war against them. The loyal people would not sustain or allow it. If questions should remain, we would adjust them by the peaceful means of legislation, conference, courts, and votes, operating only in constitutional and lawful channels. Some certain, and other possible, questions are, and would be, beyond the executive power to adjust,—as, for instance, the admission of members into Congress, and whatever might require the appropriation of money.

"The executive power itself would be greatly diminished by the cessation of actual war. Pardons and remissions of forfeitures, however, would still be within executive control. In what spirit and temper this control would be exercised can be fairly judged of by the past."

If rebels wished to receive, or any Northerners wished to extend, a kindlier invitation homeward than this, then such rebels and such Northerners were unreasonable. Very soon the correctness of Mr. Lincoln's opinion was made so distinct, and his view of the situation was so thoroughly corroborated, that all men saw clearly that no reluctance or unreasonable demands upon his part contributed to delay peace. Mr. Francis P. Blair, senior, though in pursuit of a quite different object, did the service of setting the President in the true and satisfactory light before the people. This restless politician was anxious for leave to seek a conference with Jefferson Davis, but could not induce Mr. Lincoln to hear a word as to his project. On December 8, however, by personal insistence, he extorted a simple permit "to pass our lines, go South, and return." He immediately set out on his journey, and on January 12 he had an interview with Mr. Davis at Richmond and made to him a most extraordinary proposition, temptingly decorated with abundant flowers of rhetoric. Without the rhetoric, the proposition was: that the pending war should be dropped by both parties for the purpose of an expedition to expel Maximilian from Mexico, of which tropical crusade Mr. Davis should be in charge and reap the glory! So ardent and so sanguine was Mr. Blair in his absurd project, that he fancied that he had impressed Mr. Davis favorably. But in this undoubtedly he deceived himself, for in point of fact he succeeded in bringing back nothing more than a short letter, addressed to himself, in which Mr. Davis expressed willingness to appoint and send, or to receive, agents "with a view to secure peace to the two countries." The last two words lay in this rebel communication like the twin venom fangs in the mouth of a serpent, and made of it a proposition which could not safely be touched. It served only as distinct proof that the President had correctly stated the fixedness of Mr. Davis.

Of more consequence, however, than this useless letter was the news which Mr. Blair brought: that other high officials in Richmond—"those who follow," as Mr. Lincoln had hopefully said—were in a temper far more despondent and yielding than was that of their chief. These men might be reached. So on January 18, 1865, Mr. Lincoln wrote a few lines, also addressed to Mr. Blair, saying that he was ready to receive any Southern agent who should be informally sent to him, "with the view of securing peace to the people of our one common country." The two letters, by their closing words, locked horns. Yet Mr. Davis nominated Alexander H. Stephens, R.M.T. Hunter, and John A. Campbell, as informal commissioners, and directed them, "in conformity with the letter of Mr. Lincoln," to go to Washington and informally confer "for the purpose of securing peace to the two countries." This was disingenuous, and so obviously so that it was also foolish; for no conference about "two countries" was "in conformity" with the letter of Mr. Lincoln. By reason of the difficulty created by this silly trick the commissioners were delayed at General Grant's headquarters until they succeeded in concocting a note, which eliminated the obstacle by the simple process of omitting the objectionable words. Then, on January 31, the President sent Mr. Seward to meet them, stating to him in writing "that three things are indispensable, to wit: 1. The restoration of the national authority throughout all the States. 2. No receding by the executive of the United States on the slavery question from the position assumed thereon in the late annual message to Congress, and in preceding documents. 3. No cessation of hostilities short of an end of the war and the disbanding of all forces hostile to the government. You will inform them that all propositions of theirs, not inconsistent with the above, will be considered and passed upon in a spirit of sincere liberality. You will hear all they may choose to say, and report it to me. You will not assume to definitely consummate anything."

The following day Mr. Lincoln seemed to become uneasy at being represented by any other person whomsoever in so important a business; for he decided to go himself and confer personally with the Southerners. Then ensued, and continued during four hours, on board a steamer in Hampton Roads, the famous conference between the President and his secretary of state on the one side and the three Confederate commissioners on the other. It came to absolutely nothing; nor was there at any time pending its continuance any chance that it would come to anything. Mr. Lincoln could neither be led forward nor cajoled sideways, directly or indirectly, one step from the primal condition of the restoration of the Union. On the other hand, this was the one impossible thing for the Confederates. The occasion was historic, and yet, in fact, it amounted to nothing more than cumulative evidence of a familiar fact, and really its most interesting feature is that it gave rise to one of the best of the "Lincoln stories." The President was persisting that he could not enter into any agreement with "parties in arms against the government;" Mr. Hunter tried to persuade him to the contrary, and by way of doing so, cited precedents "of this character between Charles I. of England and the people in arms against him." Mr. Lincoln could not lose such an opportunity! "I do not profess," he said, "to be posted in history. On all such matters I will turn you over to Seward. All I distinctly recollect about the case of Charles I. is, *that he lost his head!*" Then silence fell for a time upon Mr. Hunter.

Across the wide chasm of the main question the gentlemen discussed the smaller topics: reconstruction, concerning which Mr. Lincoln expressed his well-known, most generous sentiments; confiscation acts, as to which also he desired to be, and believed that Congress would be, liberal; the

Emancipation Proclamation, and the Thirteenth Amendment, concerning which he said, that the courts of law must construe the proclamation, and that he personally should be in favor of appropriating even so much as four hundred millions of dollars to extinguish slavery, and that he believed such a measure might be carried through. West Virginia, in his opinion, must continue to be a separate State. Yet there was little practical use in discussing, and either agreeing or disagreeing, about all these dependent parts; they were but limbs which it was useless to set in shape while the body was lacking. Accordingly the party broke up, not having found, nor having ever had any prospect of finding, any common standing-ground. The case was simple; the North was fighting for Union, the South for disunion, and neither side was yet ready to give up the struggle. Nevertheless, it is not improbable that Mr. Lincoln, so far as he personally was concerned, brought back from Hampton Roads all that he had expected and precisely what he had hoped to bring. For in the talk of those four hours he had recognized the note of despair, and had seen that Mr. Davis, though posing still in an imperious and monumental attitude, was, in fact, standing upon a disintegrated and crumbling pedestal. It seemed not improbable that the disappointed supporters of the rebel chief would gladly come back to the old Union if they could be fairly received, although at this conference they had felt compelled by the exigencies of an official situation and their representative character to say that they would not. Accordingly Mr. Lincoln, having no idea that a road to hearty national re-integration either should or could be overshadowed by Caudine forks, endeavored to make as easy as possible the return of discouraged rebels, whether penitent or impenitent. If they were truly penitent, all was as it should be. If they were impenitent, he was willing to trust to time to effect a change of heart. Accordingly he worked out a scheme whereby Congress should empower him to distribute between the slave States $400,000,000, in proportion to their respective slave populations, on condition that "all resistance to the national authority [should] be abandoned and cease on or before the first day of April next;" one half the sum to be paid when such resistance should so cease; the other half whenever, on or before July 1 next, the Thirteenth Amendment should become valid law. So soon as he should be clothed with authority, he proposed to issue "a proclamation looking to peace and reunion," in which he would declare that, upon the conditions stated, he would exercise this power; that thereupon war should cease and armies be reduced to a peace basis; that all political offenses should be pardoned; that all property, except slaves, liable to confiscation or forfeiture, should be released therefrom (except in cases of intervening interests of third parties); and that liberality should be recommended to Congress upon all points not lying within executive control. On the evening of February 5 he submitted to his cabinet a draft covering these points. His disappointment may be imagined when he found that not one of his advisers agreed with him; that his proposition was "unanimously disapproved." "There may be such a thing," remarked Secretary Welles, "as so overdoing as to cause a distrust or adverse feeling." It was also said that the measure probably could not pass Congress; that to attempt to carry it, without success, would do harm; while if the offer should really be made, it would be misconstrued by the rebels. In fact scarcely any Republican was ready to meet the rebels with the free and ample forgiveness which Lincoln desired to offer; and later opinion seems to be that his schemes were impracticable.

The fourth of March was close at hand, when Mr. Lincoln was a second time to address the people who had chosen him to be their ruler. That black and appalling cloud, which four years ago hung oppressively over the country, had poured forth its fury and was now passing away. His anxiety then had been lest the South, making itself deaf to reason and to right, should force upon the North a civil war; his anxiety now was lest the North, hardening itself in a severe if not vindictive temper, should deal so harshly with a conquered South as to perpetuate a sectional antagonism. To those who had lately come, bearing to him the formal notification of his election, he had remarked: "Having served four years in the depths of a great and yet unended national peril, I can view this call to a second term in no wise more flattering to myself than as an expression of the public judgment that I may better finish a difficult work, in which I have labored from the first, than could any one less severely schooled to the task." Now, mere conquest was not, in his opinion, a finishing of the difficult work of restoring a Union.

The second inaugural was delivered from the eastern portico of the Capitol, as follows:—

"FELLOW COUNTRYMEN,—At this second appearing to take the oath of the presidential office, there is less occasion for an extended address than there was at the first. Then, a statement, somewhat in detail, of a course to be pursued, seemed fitting and proper. Now, at the expiration of four years, during which public declarations have been constantly called forth on every point and phase of the great contest which still absorbs the attention and engrosses the energies of the nation, little that is new could be presented. The progress of our arms, upon which all else chiefly depends, is as well known to the public as to myself; and it is, I trust, reasonably satisfactory and encouraging to all. With high hope for the future, no prediction in regard to it is ventured.

"On the occasion corresponding to this four years ago, all thoughts were anxiously directed to an impending civil war. All dreaded it,—all sought to avert it. While the inaugural address was being delivered from this place, devoted altogether to saving the Union without war, insurgent agents were in the city seeking to destroy it without war—seeking to dissolve the Union, and divide effects, by negotiation. Both parties deprecated war; but one of them would make war rather than let the nation survive; and the other would accept war rather than let it perish. And the war came.

"One eighth of the whole population were colored slaves, not distributed generally over the Union, but localized in the southern part of it. These slaves constituted a peculiar and powerful interest. All knew that this interest was, somehow, the cause of the war. To strengthen, perpetuate, and extend this interest was the object for which the insurgents would rend the Union, even by war; while the government claimed no right to do more than to restrict the territorial enlargement of it. Neither party expected for the war the magnitude or the duration which it has already attained. Neither anticipated that the cause of the conflict might cease with, or even before, the conflict itself should cease. Each looked for an easier triumph, and a result less fundamental and astounding. Both read the same Bible, and pray to the same God; and each invokes his aid against the other. It may seem strange that any men should dare to ask a just God's assistance in wringing their bread from the sweat of other men's faces; but let us judge not, that we be not judged. The prayers of both could not be answered,—that of neither has been answered fully. The Almighty has his own purposes. 'Woe unto the world because of offenses! for it must needs be that offenses come; but woe to that man by whom the offense cometh.' If we shall suppose that American slavery is one of those offenses which, in the providence of God, must needs come, but which, having continued through his appointed time, He now wills to remove, and that He gives to both North and South this terrible war, as the woe due to those by whom the offense came, shall we discern therein any departure from those divine attributes which the believers in a living God always ascribe to Him? Fondly do we hope, fervently do we pray, that this mighty scourge of war may speedily pass away. Yet, if God wills that it continue until all the wealth piled by the bondman's two hundred and fifty years of unrequited toil shall be sunk, and until every drop of blood drawn with the lash shall be paid by another drawn with the sword, as was said three thousand years ago, so still it must be said, 'The judgments of the Lord are true and righteous altogether.'

"With malice toward none, with charity for all, with firmness in the right, as God gives us to see the right, let us strive on to finish the work we are in; to bind up the nation's wounds; to care for him who shall have borne the battle, and for his widow, and his orphan,—to do all which may achieve and cherish a just and lasting peace among ourselves, and with all nations."

This speech has taken its place among the most famous of all the written or spoken compositions in the English language. In parts it has often been compared with the lofty portions of the Old Testament. Mr. Lincoln's own contemporaneous criticism is interesting. "I expect it," he said, "to wear as well as, perhaps better than, anything I have produced; but I believe it is not immediately popular. Men are not flattered by being shown that there has been a difference of purpose between the Almighty and them. To deny it, however, in this case is to deny that there is a God governing the world. It is a truth which I thought needed to be told; and as whatever of humiliation there is in it falls most directly on myself, I thought others might afford for me to tell it."

# CHAPTER XII
# EMANCIPATION COMPLETED

On January 1, 1863, when the President issued the Proclamation of Emancipation, he stepped to the uttermost boundary of his authority in the direction of the abolition of slavery. Indeed a large proportion of the people believed that he had trespassed beyond that boundary; and among the defenders of the measure there were many who felt bound to maintain it as a legitimate exercise of the war power, while in their inmost souls they thought that its real basis of justification lay in its intrinsic righteousness. Perhaps the President himself was somewhat of this way of thinking. He once said: "I felt that measure, otherwise unconstitutional, might become lawful by becoming indispensable to the preservation of the Constitution through the preservation of the Union.... I was, in my best judgment, driven to the alternative of either surrendering the Union, and with it the Constitution, or of laying strong hand upon the colored element." Time, however, proved that the act had in fact the character which Mr. Lincoln attributed to it as properly a war measure. It attracted the enlistment of negroes, chiefly Southern negroes, in the army; and though to the end of the war the fighting value of negro troops was regarded as questionable, yet they were certainly available for garrisons and for many duties which would otherwise have absorbed great numbers of white soldiers. Thus, as the President said, the question became calculable mathematically, like horse-power in a mechanical problem. The force of able-bodied Southern negroes soon reached 200,000, of whom most were in the regular military service, and the rest were laborers with the armies. "We have the men," said Mr. Lincoln, "and we could not have had them without the measure." Take these men from us, "and put them in the battlefield or cornfield against us, and we should be compelled to abandon the war in three weeks."

But the proclamation was operative only upon certain individuals. The President's emancipatory power covered only those persons (with, perhaps, their families) whose freedom would be a military loss to the South and a military gain to the North in the pending war. He had no power to touch the *institution of slavery*. That survived, for the future, and must survive in spite of anything that he alone, as President, could do. Nevertheless, in designing movements for its permanent destruction he was not less earnest than were the radicals and extremists, though he was unable to share their contempt for legalities and for public opinion. It has been shown how strong was his desire that legislative action for abolition should be voluntarily initiated among the border slave States themselves. This would save their pride, and also would put a decisive end to all chance of their ever allying themselves with the Confederacy. He was alert to promote this purpose whenever and wherever he conceived that any opportunity offered for giving the first impulse. In time rehabilitated governments of some States managed with more or less show of regularity to accomplish the reform. But it was rather a forced transaction, having behind it an uncomfortably small proportion of the adult male population of the several States; and by and by the work, thus done, might be undone; for such action was lawfully revocable by subsequent legislatures or conventions, which bodies would be just as potent at any future time to reëstablish slavery as the present bodies were now potent to disestablish it. It was entirely possible that reconstruction would leave the right of suffrage in such shape that in some States pro-slavery men might in time regain control.

In short, the only absolute eradicating cure was a constitutional amendment; [77] and, therefore, it was towards securing this that the President bent all his energies. He could use, of course, only personal influence, not official authority; for the business, as such, lay with Congress. In December, 1863, motions for such an amendment were introduced in the House; and in January, 1864, like resolutions were offered in the Senate. The debate in the Senate was short; it opened on March 28, and the vote was taken April 8; it stood 38 ayes, 6 noes. This was gratifying; but unfortunately the party of amendment had to face a very different condition of feeling in the House. The President, says Mr. Arnold, "very often, with the friends of the measure, canvassed the House to see if the requisite number could be obtained, but we could never count a two-thirds vote." The debate began on March 19; not until June 15 was the vote taken, and then it showed 93 ayes, 65 noes, being a discouraging deficiency of 27 beneath the requisite two thirds. Thereupon Ashley of Ohio changed his vote to the negative, and then moved a reconsideration, which left the question to come up again in the next session. Practically, therefore, at the adjournment of Congress, the amendment was left as an issue before the people in the political campaign of the summer of 1864; and in that campaign it was second only to the controlling question of peace or war.

Mr. Lincoln, taking care to omit no effort in this business, sent for Senator Morgan, the chairman of the Republican National Committee, which was to make the Republican nomination for the presidency and to frame the Republican platform, and said to him: "I want you to mention in your speech, when you call the convention to order, as its keynote, and to put into the platform, as the keystone, the amendment of the Constitution abolishing and prohibiting slavery forever." Accordingly the third plank in that platform declared that slavery was the cause and the strength of the rebellion, that it was "hostile to the principle of republican government," and that the "national safety demanded its utter and complete extirpation from the soil of the Republic," and that to this end the Constitution ought to be so amended as to "terminate and forever prohibit the existence of slavery within the limits or the jurisdiction of the United States." Thus at the special request of the President the issue was distinctly presented to the voters of the country. The Copperheads, the conservatives, and reactionaries, and many of the war Democrats, promptly opened their batteries against both the man and the measure.

The Copperhead Democracy, as usual, went so far as to lose force; they insisted that the Emancipation Proclamation should be rescinded, and all ex-slaves restored to their former masters. This, in their opinion, would touch, a conciliatory chord in Southern breasts, and might lead to pacification. That even pro-slavery Northerners should urgently advocate a proposition at once so cruel and so disgraceful is hardly credible. Yet it was reiterated strenuously, and again and again Mr. Lincoln had to repeat his decisive and indignant repudiation of it. In the message to Congress, December, 1863, he said that to abandon the freedmen now would be "a cruel and astounding breach of faith.... I shall not attempt to retract or modify the Emancipation Proclamation, nor shall I return to slavery any person who is free by the terms of that proclamation, or by any of the acts of Congress." In May, 1864, he spurned the absurdity of depending "upon coaxing, flattery, and concession to get them [the Secessionists] back into the Union." He said: "There have been men base enough to propose to me to return to slavery our black warriors of Port Hudson and Olustee, and thus win the respect of the masters they fought. Should I do so, I should deserve to be damned in time and eternity. Come what will, I will keep my faith with friend and foe." He meant never to be misunderstood on this point. Recurring to it after the election, in his message to Congress in December, 1864, he quoted his language of the year before and added: "If the people should, by whatever mode or means, make it an executive duty to reinslave such persons, another, and not I, must be their instrument to perform it." All this was plain and spirited. But it is impossible to praise Mr. Lincoln for contemning a course which it is surprising to find any person sufficiently ignoble to recommend. It was, nevertheless, recommended by many, and thus we may partly see what extremities of feeling were produced by this most debasing question which has ever entered into the politics of a civilized nation.

The anxieties of the war Democrats, who feared that Mr. Lincoln was making abolition an essential purpose of the war, have already been set forth. In truth he was not making it so, but by the drifting of events and the ensnarlment of facts it had practically become so without his responsibility. His many utterances which survive seem to indicate that, having from the beginning hoped that the war would put an end to slavery, he now knew that it must do so. He saw that this conclusion lay at the end of the natural course of events, also that it was not a goal which was set there by those to whom it was welcome, or which could be taken away by those to whom it was unwelcome. It was there by the absolute and uncontrollable logic of facts. His function was only to take care that this natural course should not be obstructed, and this established goal should not be maliciously removed away out of reach. When he was asked why his expressions of willingness to negotiate with the Confederate leaders stipulated not only for the restoration of the Union but also for the enfranchisement of all slaves, he could only reply by intimating that the yoking of the two requirements was unobjectionable from any point of view, because he was entirely assured that Mr. Davis would never agree to reunion, either with or without slavery. Since, therefore, Union could not be had until after the South had been whipped, it would be just as well to demand abolition also; for the rebels would not then be in a position to refuse it, and we should practically buy both in one transaction. To him it seemed an appalling blunder to pay the price of this great war simply in order to cure this especial outbreak of the great national malady, and still to leave existing in the body politic that which had induced this dissension and would inevitably afterward induce others like unto it. The excision of the cause was the only intelligent action. Yet when pushed to the point of declaring what he would do in the supposed case of an opportunity to restore the Union, with slavery, he said: "My enemies pretend I am now carrying on the war for the sole purpose of abolition. So long as I am President, it shall be carried on for the sole purpose of restoring the Union." The duty of his official oath compelled him to say this, but he often and plainly acknowledged that he had no fear of ever being brought face to face with the painful necessity of saving both the Union and slavery.

It is worth noticing that the persons who charged upon the President that he would never assent to a peace which was not founded upon the abolition of slavery as one of its conditions or stipulations, never distinctly stated by what right he could insist upon such a condition or stipulation, or by what process he could establish it or introduce it into a settlement. Mr. Lincoln certainly never had any thought of negotiating with the seceded States as an independent country, and making with them a treaty which could embody an article establishing emancipation and permanent abolition. He had not power to enter with them into an agreement of an international character, nor, if they should offer to return to the Union, retaining their slave institutions, could he lawfully reject them. The endeavor would be an act of usurpation, if it was true that no State could go out. The plain truth was that, from any save a revolutionary point of view, the constitutional amendment was the only method of effecting the consummation permanently. When, in June, 1864, Mr. Lincoln said that abolition of slavery was "a fitting and necessary condition to the final success of the Union cause," he was obviously speaking of what was logically "fitting and necessary," and in the same sentence he clearly specified a constitutional amendment as the practical process. There is no indication that he ever had any other scheme.

In effect, in electing members of Congress in the autumn of 1864, the people passed upon the amendment. Votes for Republicans were votes for the amendment, and the great Republican gain was fairly construed as an expression of the popular favor towards the measure. But though the elections thus made the permanent abolition of slavery a reasonably sure event in the future, yet delay always has dangers. The new Congress would not meet for over a year. In the interval the Confederacy might collapse, and abolition become ensnarled with considerations of reconciliation, of reconstruction, of politics generally. All friends of the measure, therefore, agreed on the desirability of disposing of the matter while the present Congress was in the way with it, if this could possibly be compassed. That it could be carried only by the aid of a contingent of Democratic votes did not so much discourage them as stimulate their zeal; for such votes would prevent the mischief of a partisan or sectional aspect. In his message to Congress, December 6, 1864, the President referred to the measure which, after its failure in the preceding session, was now to come up again, by virtue of that shrewd motion for reconsideration. Intelligibly, though not in terms, he appealed for Democratic help. He said: —

"Although the present is the same Congress and nearly the same members, and without questioning the wisdom or patriotism of those who stood in opposition, I venture to recommend the reconsideration and passage of the measure at the present session. Of course the abstract question is not changed; but an intervening election shows, almost certainly, that the next Congress will pass the measure if this does not. Hence there is only a question of *time* as to when the proposed amendment will go to the States for their action; and as it is so to go, at all events, may we not agree that the sooner the better. It is not claimed that the election has imposed a duty on members to change their views or their votes, any further than, as an additional element to be considered, their judgment may be affected by it. It is the voice of the people now for the first time heard upon the question. In a great national crisis like ours unanimity of action among those seeking a common end is very desirable, — almost indispensable. And yet no approach to such unanimity is attainable unless some deference shall be paid to the will of the majority. In this case the common end is the maintenance of the Union, and among the means to secure that end, such will, through the election, is more clearly declared in favor of such a constitutional amendment."

In the closing sentence the word "maintenance" is significant. So far as the *restoration* of Union went, the proclamation had done nearly all that could be done. This amendment was to insure the future *maintenance* of the Union by cutting out the cause of disunion.

The President did not rest content with merely reiterating sentiments which every man had long known that he held. Of such influence as he could properly exert among members of the House he was not chary. The debate began on January 6, 1865, and he followed it closely and eagerly. On the 27th it was agreed that the voting should take place on the following day. No one yet felt sure of the comparative strength of the friends and opponents of the measure, and up to the actual taking of the vote the result was uncertain. We knew, says Arnold, "we should get some Democratic votes; but whether enough, none could tell." Ex-Governor English of Connecticut, a Democrat, gave the first Aye from his party; whereupon loud cheers burst forth; then ten others followed his example. Eight more Democrats gave their indirect aid by being absent when their names were called. Thus both the great parties united to establish the freedom of all men in the United States. As the roll-call drew to the end, those who had been anxiously keeping tally saw that the measure had been carried. The speaker, Mr. Colfax, announced the result; ayes 119, noes 56, and declared that "the joint resolution is passed." At once there arose from the distinguished crowd an irrepressible outburst of triumphant applause; there was no use in rapping to order, or trying to turn to other business, and a motion to adjourn, "in honor of this immortal and sublime event," was promptly made and carried. At the same moment, on Capitol Hill, artillery roared loud salutation to the edict of freedom.

The crowds poured to the White House, and Mr. Lincoln, in a few words, of which the simplicity fitted well with the grandness of the occasion, congratulated them, in homely phrase, that "the great job is ended." Yet, though this was substantially true, he did not live to see the strictly legal completion. Ratification by the States was still necessary, and though this began at once, and proceeded in due course as their legislatures came into session, yet the full three quarters of the whole number had not passed the requisite resolutions at the time of his death. This, however, was mere matter of form. The question was really settled when Mr. Colfax announced the vote of the representatives. [78]

[77] A constitutional amendment requires for its passage a two thirds vote in the Senate and the House of Representatives, and ratification by three fourths of the States.

[78] Thirteenth Amendment. *First*: Neither slavery nor involuntary servitude, except as a punishment for crime whereof the party shall have been duly convicted, shall exist within the United States, or any place subject to their jurisdiction. *Second*: Congress shall have power to enforce this article by appropriate legislation.

# CHAPTER XIII
# THE FALL OF RICHMOND, AND THE
# ASSASSINATION OF PRESIDENT LINCOLN

From the Capitol, where he had spoken his inaugural on March 4, 1865, Mr. Lincoln came back to the White House with less than five weeks of life before him; yet for those scant weeks most men would have gladly exchanged their full lifetimes. To the nation they came fraught with all the intoxicating triumph of victory; but upon the President they laid the vast responsibility of rightly shaping and using success; and it was far less easy to end the war wisely than it had been to conduct it vigorously. Two populations, with numbers and resources amply enough for two powerful nations, after four years of sanguinary, relentless conflict, in which each side had been inspired and upheld by a faith like that of the first crusaders, were now to be reunited as fellow citizens, and to be fused into a homogeneous body politic based upon universal suffrage. As if this did not verge closely enough on the impossible, millions of people of a hitherto servile race were suddenly established in the new status of freedom. It was very plain that the problems which were advancing with approaching peace were more perplexing than those which were disappearing with departing war. Much would depend upon the spirit and terms of the closing of hostilities.

If the limits of the President's authority were vague, they might for that very reason be all the more extensive; and, wherever they might be set, he soon made it certain that he designed to part with no power which he possessed. On the evening of March 3 he went up, as usual, to the Capitol, to sign bills during the closing hours of the last session of the Thirty-eighth Congress. To him thus engaged was handed a telegram from General Grant, saying that General Lee had suggested an interview between himself and Grant in the hope that, upon an interchange of views, they might reach a satisfactory adjustment of the present unhappy difficulties through a military convention. Immediately, exchanging no word with any one, he wrote:—

"The President directs me to say that he wishes you to have no conference with General Lee, unless it be for the capitulation of General Lee's army, or on some minor or purely military matter. He instructs me to say that you are not to decide, discuss, or confer upon any political questions. Such questions the President holds in his own hands, and will submit them to no military conferences or conventions. Meanwhile, you are to press to the utmost your military advantages."

This reply he showed to Seward, then handed it to Stanton and ordered him to sign and dispatch it at once.

About this same time General Lee notified Mr. Davis that Petersburg and Richmond could not be held many more days. Indeed, they would probably have been evacuated at once, had not the capital carried so costly a freight of prestige as well as of pride. It was no surprising secret which was thus communicated to the chief rebel; all the common soldiers in the Confederate army had for a long while known it just as well as the general-in-chief did; and they had been showing their appreciation of the situation by deserting and coming within the Union lines in such increasing numbers that soon General Grant estimated that the Confederate forces were being depleted by the equivalent of nearly a regiment every day. The civilian leaders had already suggested the last expedients of despair,—the enrolling of boys of fourteen years and old men of sixty-five, nay, even the enlistment of slaves. But there was no cure for the mortal dwindling. The Confederacy was dying of anaemia.

Grant understood the situation precisely as his opponents did. That Petersburg and Richmond were about to be his was settled. But he was reaching out for more than only these strongholds, and that he could get Lee's army also was by no means settled. As March opened he lay down every night in the fear that, while he was sleeping, the evacuation might be furtively, rapidly, in progress, and the garrison escaping. He dreaded that, any morning, he might awake to find delusive picket lines, guarding nothing, while Lee and his soldiers were already well in the lead, marching for the South. For him, especially, it was a period of extreme tension. Since the capture of Savannah and the evacuation of Charleston several weeks ago, Sherman with his fine army had been moving steadily northward. In front of Sherman was Johnston, with a considerable force which had been got together from the remnants of Hood's army and other sources. At Bentonsville a battle took place, which resulted in Johnston's falling back, but left him still formidable. General Grant had not yet been able to break the Richmond and Danville Railroad, which ran out from Richmond in a southwesterly direction; and the danger was that by this and the "South Side" railroad, Lee might slip out, join Johnston, and overwhelm Sherman before Grant could reach him. In time, this peril was removed by the junction of Schofield's army, coming from Wilmington, with that of Sherman at Goldsboro. Yet, even after this relief, there remained a possibility that Lee, uniting with Johnston, and thus leading a still powerful army of the more determined and constant veterans, might prolong the war indefinitely.

Not without good reason was Grant harassed by this thought, for in fact it was precisely this thing that the good soldier in Petersburg was scheming to do. The closing days of the month brought the endeavor and the crisis. To improve his chances Lee made a desperate effort to demoralize, at least temporarily, the left or western wing of the Union army, around which he must pass in order to get away, when he should actually make his start. March 25, therefore, he made so fierce an assault, that he succeeded in piercing the Union lines and capturing a fort. But it was a transitory gleam of success; the Federals promptly closed in upon the Confederates, and drove them back, capturing and killing 4000 of them. In a few hours the affair was all over; the Northern army showed the dint no more than a rubber ball; but the Confederates had lost brave men whom they could not spare.

On March 22 Mr. Lincoln went to City Point; no one could say just how soon important propositions might require prompt answering, and it was his purpose to be ready to have any such business transacted as closely as possible in accordance with his own ideas. On March 27 or 28, the famous conference [79] was held on board the River Queen, on James River, hard by Grant's headquarters, between the President, General Grant, General Sherman, who had come up hastily from Goldsboro, and Admiral Porter. Not far away Sheridan's fine body of 13,000 seasoned cavalrymen, fresh from their triumphs in the Shenandoah Valley, was even now crossing the James River, on their way into the neighborhood of Dinwiddie Court House, which lies southwest of Richmond, and where they could threaten that remaining railroad which was Lee's best chance of escape. General Sherman reported that on April 10 he should be ready to move to a junction with Grant. But Grant, though he did not then proclaim it, did not mean to wait so long; in fact he had the secret wish and purpose that the Eastern army, which had fought so long and so bloodily in Virginia, should have all to itself the well-deserved glory of capturing Richmond and conquering Lee, a purpose which Mr. Lincoln, upon suggestion of it, accepted. [80] The President then returned to City Point, there to stay for the present, awaiting developments.

On April 1 General Sheridan fought and won the important battle at Five Forks. Throughout that night, to prevent a too vigorous return-assault upon Sheridan, the Federal batteries thundered all along the line; and at daybreak on the morning of April 2 the rebel intrenchments were fiercely assaulted. After hard fighting the Confederates were forced back upon their inner lines. Then General Grant sent a note to City Point, saying: "I think the President might come out and pay us a visit to morrow;" and then also

General Lee, upon his part, sent word to Jefferson Davis that the end had come, that Petersburg and Richmond must be abandoned immediately.

The news had been expected at any moment by the Confederate leaders, but none the less it produced intense excitement. Away went Mr. Davis, in hot haste, also the members of his cabinet and of his congress, and the officials of the rebel State of Virginia, and, in short, every one who felt himself of consequence enough to make it worth his while to run away. The night was theirs, and beneath its friendly shade they escaped, with archives and documents which had suddenly become valuable chiefly for historical purposes. Grant had ordered that on the morning of April 3 a bombardment should begin at five o'clock, which was to be followed by an assault at six o'clock. But there was no occasion for either; even at the earlier hour Petersburg was empty, and General Grant and General Meade soon entered it undisturbed. A little later Mr. Lincoln joined them, and they walked through streets in which neither man nor animal, save only this little knot, was to be seen. [81]

At quarter after eight o'clock, that same morning, General Weitzel, with a few attendants, rode into the streets of Richmond. That place, however, was by no means deserted, but, on the contrary, it seemed Pandemonium. The rebels had been blowing up and burning warships and stores; they had also gathered great quantities of cotton and tobacco into the public storehouses and had then set them on fire. More than 700 buildings were feeding a conflagration at once terrible and magnificent to behold, and no one was endeavoring to stay its advance. The negroes were intoxicated with joy, and the whites with whiskey; the convicts from the penitentiary had broken loose; a mob was breaking into houses and stores and was pillaging madly. Erelong the Fifth Massachusetts Cavalry, a negro regiment under Colonel C.F. Adams, Jr., paraded through the streets, and then the Southern whites hid themselves within doors to shun the repulsive spectacle. It may be that armed and hostile negroes brought to them the dread terror of retaliation and massacre in the wild hour of triumph. But if so, their fear was groundless; the errand of the Northern troops was, in fact, one of safety and charity; they began at once to extinguish the fires, to suppress the riot, and to feed the starving people.

On the following day President Lincoln started on his way up the river from City Point, upon an excursion to the rebel capital. Obstructions which had been placed in the stream stopped the progress of his steamer; whereupon he got into a barge and was rowed to one of the city wharves. He had not been expected, and with a guard of ten sailors, and with four gentlemen as comrades, he walked through the streets, under the guidance of a "contraband," to the quarters of General Weitzel. This has been spoken of as an evidence of bravery; but, regarded in this light, it was only superfluous evidence of a fact which no one ever doubted; it really deserves better to be called foolhardiness, as Captain Penrose, who was one of the party, frankly described it in his Diary. The walk was a mile and a half long, and this gentleman says: "I never passed a more anxious time than in this walk. In going up [the river] ... we ran the risk of torpedoes and the obstructions; but I think the risk the President ran in going through the streets of Richmond was even greater, and shows him to have great courage. The streets of the city were filled with drunken rebels, both officers and men, and all was confusion.... A large portion of the city was still on fire." Probably enough the impunity with which this great risk was run was due to the dazing and bewildering effect of an occasion so confused and exciting. Meantime, Lee, abandoning Petersburg, but by no means abandoning "the Cause," pushed his troops with the utmost expedition to gain that southwestern route which was the slender thread whence all Confederate hope now depended. His men traveled light and fast; for, poor fellows, they had little enough to carry! But Grant was an eager pursuer. Until the sixth day that desperate flight and chase continued. Lee soon saw that he could not get to Danville, as he had hoped to do, and thereupon changed his plan and struck nearly westward, for open country, via Appomattox Court House. All the way, as he marched, Federal horsemen worried the left flank of his columns, while the infantry came ever closer upon the rear, and kept up a ceaseless skirmishing. It had become "a life and death struggle with Lee to get south to his provisions;" and Grant was struggling with not less stern zeal, along a southerly line, to get ahead of him in this racing journey. The Federal troops, sanguine and excited, did their part finely, even marching a whole day and night without rations. On April 6 there was an engagement, in which about 7000 Southerners, with six general officers, surrendered; and perhaps the captives were not deeply sorry for their fate. Sheridan telegraphed: "If the thing is pressed, I think that Lee will surrender." Grant repeated this to the President, who replied: "Let the thing be pressed," —not that there was any doubt about it! Yet, April 7, General Lee was cheered by an evanescent success in an engagement. It was trifling, however, and did not suffice to prevent many of his generals from uniting to advise him to capitulate. Grant also sent to him a note saying that resistance was useless, and that he desired to shift from himself the responsibility of further bloodshed by asking for a surrender. Lee denied the hopelessness, but asked what terms would be offered. At the same time he continued his rapid retreat. On April 8, about sunset, near Appomattox Station, his advance encountered Sheridan's cavalry directly across the road. The corral was complete. Nevertheless, there ensued a few critical hours; for Sheridan could by no means stand against Lee's army. Fortunately, however, these hours of crisis were also the hours of darkness, in which troops could march but could not fight, and at dawn, on April 9, the Southerners saw before them a great force of Federal soldiery abundantly able to hold them in check until Grant's whole army could come up. "A sharp engagement ensued," says General Grant, "but Lee quickly set up a white flag." He then notified Sheridan, in his front, and Meade, in his rear, that he had sent a note to General Grant with a view to surrender, and he asked a suspension of hostilities. These commanders doubted a ruse, and reluctantly consented to hold their troops back for two hours. That was just enough; pending the recess Grant was reached by the bearer of the dispatch, and at once rode in search of Lee.

The two met at the house of a villager and easily came to terms, for Grant's offer transcended in liberality anything which Lee could fairly have expected. General Grant hastily wrote it out in the form of a letter to Lee: The Confederates, officers and men, were to be paroled, "not to take up arms against the government of the United States until properly exchanged;" arms, artillery, and public property were to be turned over to the Federals except the side-arms of the officers, their private horses, and baggage. "This done, each officer and man will be allowed to return to their homes, not to be disturbed by United States authority so long as they observe their parole and the laws in force where they may reside." This closing sentence practically granted amnesty to all persons then surrendering, not excluding even the rebel general-in-chief. It was afterward severely criticised as trenching upon the domain of the President, and perhaps, also, on that of Congress. For it was practically an exercise of the pardoning power; and it was, or might be, an element in reconstruction. Not improbably the full force of the language was not appreciated when it was written; but whether this was so or not, and whether authority had been unduly assumed or not, an engagement of General Grant was sure to be respected, especially when it was entirely in harmony with the spirit of the President's policy, though it happened to be contrary to the letter of his order.

General Lee had no sooner surrendered than he asked for food for his starving troops; and stated, by way of estimate, that about twenty-five thousand rations would be needed. The paroles, as signed, showed a total of 28,231. To so trifling a force had his once fine army been reduced by the steady drain of battles and desertions. [82] The veterans had long since understood that their lives were a price which could buy nothing, and which therefore might as well be saved.

The fall of Richmond and the surrender of Lee were practically the end of the war. Remnants of secession indeed remained, of which Mr. Lincoln did not live to see the disposition. Johnston's army was still in the field; but on learning that there really was no longer either a Confederacy or a cause to fight for, it surrendered on April 26. Jefferson Davis also arranged for himself [83] the most effectual of all amnesties by making himself ridiculous; for though some persons had designed a serious punishment for this dethroned ruler, they recognized that this became impossible after he had put himself into petticoats. It was hardly fair that Mr. Lincoln was robbed of the amusement which he would have gathered from this exploit.

On April 11, in the evening, a multitude gathered before the White House, bringing loud congratulations, and not to be satisfied without a speech from the President. Accordingly he came out and spoke to the cheering crowd, and by a few simple, generous words, turned over the enthusiastic acclamation, which seemed to honor him, to those "whose harder part" had given the cause of rejoicing. "Their honors," he said, "must not be parceled out with others. I myself was near the front, and had the high pleasure of transmitting much of the good news to you; but no part of the honor, for plan or execution, is mine. To General Grant, his skillful officers and brave men, all belongs. The gallant navy stood ready, but was not in reach to take an active part." He then at once turned to the subject of reconstruction, and the last words which he addressed to the people were mingled of argument and appeal in behalf of the humane and liberal policy which he had inaugurated in Louisiana, which was still in the experimental stage, yet which had already excited the bitter denunciations of the politicians.

So soon as it was known in the autumn of 1860 that Abraham Lincoln was to be the next president of the United States, he was at once beset by two pests: the office-seekers, and the men who either warned him to fear assassination or anonymously threatened him with it. Of the two, the office-seekers annoyed him by far the more; they came like the plague of locusts, and devoured his time and his patience. His contempt and disgust towards them were unutterable; he said that the one purpose in life with at least one half of the nation seemed to be that they should live comfortably at the expense of the other half. But it was the fashion of the people, and he was obliged to endure the affliction, however it might stir his indignation and contempt. The matter of assassination he was more free to treat as he chose. A curious incident, strangely illustrating the superstitious element in his nature, was narrated by him as follows:—

"It was just after my election in 1860, when the news had been coming in thick and fast all day, and there had been a great 'hurrah boys!' so that I was well tired out and went home to rest, throwing myself upon a lounge in my chamber. Opposite to where I lay was a bureau with a swinging glass upon it; and, in looking in that glass, I saw myself reflected nearly at full length; but my face, I noticed, had two separate and distinct images, the tip of the nose of one being about three inches from the tip of the other. I was a little bothered, perhaps startled, and got up and looked in the glass; but the illusion vanished. On lying down again I saw it a second time, plainer, if possible, than before; and then I noticed that one of the faces was a little paler—say five shades—than the other. I got up and the thing melted away; and I went off, and in the excitement of the hour forgot all about it,—nearly, but not quite, for the thing would once in a while come up, and give me a little pang, as though something uncomfortable had happened. When I went home, I told my wife about it; and a few days after I tried the experiment again, when, sure enough, the thing came back again; but I never succeeded in bringing the ghost back after that, though I once tried very industriously to show it to my wife, who was worried about it somewhat. She thought it was 'a sign' that I was to be elected to a second term of office, and that the paleness of one of the faces was an omen that I should not see life through the last term."

From this time forth anonymous threats and friendly warnings came thick and fast up to the fatal day when the real event befell. Some of these he kept, and after his death they were found in his desk, labeled "Assassination Letters." Before he left Springfield for his journey to Washington, many ingenious fears were suggested to him; but, except for his change of route toward the close of his journey, none of these presagings visibly influenced him, and his change of purpose concerning the passage through Baltimore was never afterward recalled by him without vexation. From that time forth he resolutely ignored all danger of this kind. During most of the time that he was in office any one could easily call upon him, unguarded, at the White House; he moved through the streets of Washington like any private citizen; and he drove about the environs, and habitually in the warm season took the long drive to and from the Soldiers' Home, with substantially no protection. When, at last, a guard at the White House and an escort upon his drives were fairly forced upon him by Mr. Stanton (who was declared by the gossip of the unfriendly to be somewhat troubled with physical timidity), he rebelled against these incumbrances upon his freedom, and submitted, when he had to do so, with an ill grace. To those who remonstrated with him upon his carelessness he made various replies. Sometimes, half jocosely, he said that it was hardly likely that any intelligent Southerner would care to get rid of him in order to set either Vice-President Hamlin or, later, Vice-President Johnson, in his place. At other times he said: "What is the use of setting up the *gap*, when the fence is down all round?" or, "I do not see that I can make myself secure except by shutting myself up in an iron box, and in that condition I think I could hardly satisfactorily transact the business of the presidency." Again he said: "If I am killed, I can die but once; but to live in constant dread of it, is to die over and over again." This was an obvious reflection, easy enough of suggestion for any one who was not within the danger line; but to live every day in accordance with it, when the danger was never absent, called for a singular tranquillity of temperament, and a kind of courage in which brave men are notoriously apt to be deficient.

On April 9 the President was coming up the Potomac in a steamer from City Point; the Comte de Chambrun was of the party and relates that, as they were nearing Washington, Mrs. Lincoln, who had been silently gazing toward the town, said: "That city is filled with our enemies;" whereupon Mr. Lincoln "somewhat impatiently retorted: 'Enemies! we must never speak of that!'" For he was resolutely cherishing the impossible idea that Northerners and Southerners were to be enemies no longer, but that a pacification of the spirit was coming throughout the warring land contemporaneously with the cessation of hostilities,—a dream romantic and hopelessly incapable of realization, but humane and beautiful. Since he did not live to endeavor to transform it into a fact, and thereby perhaps to have his efforts cause even seriously injurious results, it is open to us to forget the impracticability of the fancy and to revere the nature which in such an hour could give birth to such a purpose.

The fourteenth day of April was Friday,—Good Friday. Many religious persons afterward ventured to say that if the President had not been at the theatre upon that sacred day, the awful tragedy might never have occurred at all. Others, however, not less religiously disposed, were impressed by the coincidence that the fatal shot was fired upon that day which the Christian world had agreed to adopt as the anniversary of the crucifixion of the Saviour of mankind. General Grant and his wife were in Washington on that day and the President invited them to go with him to see the play at Ford's theatre in the evening, but personal engagements called them northward. In the afternoon the President drove out with his wife, and again the superstitious element comes in; for he appeared in such good spirits, as he chatted cheerfully of the past and the future, that she uneasily remarked to him: "I have seen you thus only once before; it was just before our dear Willie died." Such a frame of mind, however, under the circumstances at that time must be regarded as entirely natural rather than as ominous.

About nine o'clock in the evening the President entered his box at the theatre; with him were his wife, Major Rathbone, and a lady; the box had been decorated with an American flag, of which the folds swept down to the stage. Unfortunately it had also been tampered with, in preparation for the plans of the conspirators. Between it and the corridor was a small vestibule; and a stout stick of wood had been so arranged that it could in an instant be made to fasten securely, on the inside, the door which opened from the corridor into this vestibule. Also in the door which led from the vestibule into the box itself a hole had been cut, through which the situation of the different persons in the box could be clearly seen. Soon after the party had entered, when the cheering had subsided and the play was going forward, just after ten o'clock, a man approached through the corridor, pushed his visiting card into the hands of the attendant who sat there, hastily entered the vestibule, and closed and fastened the door behind him. A moment later the noise of a pistol shot astounded every one, and instantly a man was seen at the front of the President's box; Major Rathbone sprang to grapple with him, but was severely slashed in the arm and failed to retard his progress; he vaulted over the rail to the stage, but caught his spur in the folds of the flag, so that he did not alight fairly upon his feet; but he instantly recovered himself, and with a visible limp in his gait hastened across the stage; as he went, he turned towards the audience, brandished the bloody dagger with which he had just struck Rathbone, and cried *"Sic semper tyrannis!"* Some one recognized John Wilkes Booth, an actor of melodramatic characters. The door at the back of the theatre was held open for him by Edward Spangler, an employee, and in the alley hard by a boy, also employed about the theatre, was holding the assassin's horse, saddled and bridled. Booth kicked the boy aside, with a curse, climbed into the saddle with difficulty, — for the small bone of his leg between the knee and ankle had been broken in his fall upon the stage, — and rode rapidly away into the night. Amid the confusion, no efficient pursuit was made.

The President had been shot at the back of the head, on the left side; the bullet passed through the brain, and stopped just short of the left eye. Unconsciousness of course came instantaneously. He was carried to a room in a house opposite the theatre, and there he continued to breathe until twenty-two minutes after seven o'clock in the morning, at which moment he died.

The man Booth, who had done this deed of blood and madness, was an unworthy member of the family of distinguished actors of that name. He was young, handsome, given to hard drinking, of inordinate vanity, and of small capacity in his profession; altogether, he was a disreputable fellow, though fitted to seem a hero in the eyes of the ignorant and dissipated classes. Betwixt the fumes of the brandy which he so freely drank and the folly of the melodramatic parts which he was wont to act, his brain became saturated with a passion for notoriety, which grew into the very mania of egotism. His crime was as stupid as it was barbarous; and even from his own point of view his achievement was actually worse than a failure. As an act of revenge against a man whom he hated, he accomplished nothing, for he did not inflict upon Mr. Lincoln so much as one minute of mental distress or physical suffering. To the South he brought no good, and at least ran the risk of inflicting upon it much evil, since he aroused a vindictive temper among persons who had the power to carry vindictiveness into effect; and he slew the only sincere and powerful friend whom the Southerners had among their conquerors. He passed a miserable existence for eleven days after the assassination, moving from one hiding-place to another, crippled and suffering, finding concealment difficult and escape impossible. Moreover, he had the intense mortification to find himself regarded with execration rather than admiration, loathed as a murderer instead of admired as a hero, and charged with having wrought irreparable hurt to those whom he had foolishly fancied that he was going to serve conspicuously. It was a curious and significant fact that there was among the people of the North a considerable body of persons who, though undoubtedly as shocked as was every one else at the method by which the President had been eliminated from the political situation, were yet well pleased to see Andrew Johnson come into power; [84] and these persons were the very ones who had been heretofore most extreme in their hostility to slavery, most implacable towards the people of the Confederacy. There were no persons living to whom Booth would have been less willing to minister gratification than to these men. Their new President, it is true, soon disappointed them bitterly, but for the moment his accession was generally regarded as a gain for their party.

Late on April 25 a squad of cavalry traced Booth to a barn in Virginia; they surrounded it, but he refused to come out; thereupon they set fire to it, and then one of them, Boston Corbett, contrary to orders, thrust his musket through a crevice and fired at Booth. Probably he hit his mark, though some think that the hunted wretch at this last desperate moment shot himself with his own revolver. Be this as it may, the assassin was brought forth having a bullet in the base of his brain, and with his body below the wound paralyzed. He died on the morning of April 26.

While the result of Booth's shot secured for him that notoriety which he loved, the enterprise was in fact by no means wholly his own. A conspiracy involving many active members, and known also to others, had been long in existence. For months plans had been laid and changed, and opportunities had been awaited and lost. Had the plot not been thus delayed, its success might have done more practical mischief. Now, in addition to what the plotters lost by reason of this delay, only a part of their whole great scheme was carried out. At the same time that the tragedy was enacting at Ford's Theatre an assault was perpetrated upon Mr. Seward, who was then confined to his bed by hurts lately received in an accident. The assassin gained admission into the house under pretense of bringing medicine; thus he reached the bedroom, and at once threw himself upon the secretary, whom he stabbed about the face and neck; then encountering in turn two sons of Mr. Seward and two men nurses, he wounded them all more or less seriously, and escaped. But much as had been done, as much or more was left undone; for there can be little doubt that the plot also included the murder of the Vice-President, General Grant, and Secretary Stanton; the idea being, so far as there was any idea or any sense at all in the villainy, that the sudden destruction of all these men would leave the government with no lawful head, and that anarchy would ensue.

Not many days elapsed before the government had in custody seven men, Herold, Spangler, Payne, O'Laughlin, Arnold, Atzerodt, and Mudd, and one woman, Mary E. Surratt, all charged with being concerned in the conspiracy. But though they had been so happily caught, there was much difficulty in determining just how to deal with them. Such was the force of secession feeling in the District of Columbia that no jury there could be expected to find them guilty, unless the panel should be packed in a manner which would be equally against honesty and good policy. After some deliberation, therefore, the government decided to have recourse to a military commission, provided this were possible under the law, and the attorney-general, under guise of advising the administration, understood distinctly that he must find that it was possible. Accordingly he wrote a long, sophistical, absurd opinion, in which he mixed up the law of nations and the "laws of war," and emerged out of the fog very accurately at the precise point at which he was expected to arrive. Not that fault should be found with him for performing this feat; it was simply one of many instances, furnished by the war, of the homage which necessity pays to law and which law repays to necessity. That which must be done must also be stoutly and ingeniously declared to be legal. It was intolerable that the men should escape, yet their condemnation must be accomplished in a respectable way. So the Military Commission was promptly convened, heard the evidence which could be got together at such short notice, and found all the accused guilty, as undoubtedly they were. The men were a miserable parcel of fellows, belonging in that class of the community called "roughs," except only Mudd, who was a country doctor. Mrs. Surratt was a fit companion for such company. Herold, Atzerodt and Payne were hanged on July 7; O'Laughlin, Spangler, Arnold, and Mudd were sent to the Dry Tortugas, there to be kept at hard labor in the military prison for life, save Spangler, whose term was six years. Mrs. Surratt was also found guilty and condemned to be hanged. Five members of the commission signed a petition to President Johnson to commute this sentence, but he refused, and on July 7 she also met the fate which no one could deny that she deserved.

John H. Surratt escaped for the time, but was apprehended and tried in the District of Columbia, in 1867; he had then the advantage of process under the regular criminal law, and the result was that on September 22, 1868, a *nolle prosequi* was entered, and he was set free, to swell the multitude of villains whose impunity reflects no great credit upon our system of dealing with crime.

Besides those who have been named, the government also charged several other persons with complicity in the plot. Among these were Jefferson Davis and some members of that notorious colony of Confederates who, in the wholesome and congenial safety of Canada, had been plotting mean crimes during the war. Of course, since these men could not be captured and actually placed upon trial, there was little object in seeking evidence against them, and only so much was produced as came to the possession of the government incidentally in the way of its endeavor to convict those prisoners who were in its possession. Under these circumstances there was not sufficient evidence to prove that any one of them aided or abetted, or had a guilty knowledge of, the conspiracy; yet certainly there was evidence enough to place them under such suspicion, that, if they were really innocent, they deserve commiseration for their unfortunate situation.

It is startling to contemplate the responsibility so lightly taken by the mad wretch who shortly and sharply severed the most important life which any man was living on the fourteenth day of April, 1865. Very rarely, in the course of the ages, have circumstances so converged upon a single person and a special crisis as to invest them with the importance which rested upon this great leader at this difficult time. Yet, in the briefest instant that can be measured, an ignoble tippler had dared to cut the life-thread from which depended no small portion of the destinies of millions of people. How the history of this nation might have been changed, had Mr. Lincoln survived to bear his influential part in reconstructing and reuniting the shattered country, no man can tell. Many have indulged in the idle speculation, though to do so is but to waste time. The life which he had already lived gives food enough for reflection and for study without trying to evolve out of arbitrary fancy the further things which might have been attempted by him, which might have been of wise or of visionary conception, might have brilliantly succeeded or sadly failed.

It is only forty years since Abraham Lincoln became of much note in the world, yet in that brief time he has been the subject of more varied discussion than has been expended upon any other historical character, save, perhaps, Napoleon; and the kind of discussion which has been called forth by Lincoln is not really to be likened to that which has taken place concerning Napoleon or concerning any other person whomsoever. The great men of the various eras and nations are comprehensible, at least upon broad lines. The traits to which each owes his peculiar power can be pretty well agreed upon; the capacity of each can be tolerably well expressed in a formula; each can be intelligibly described in fairly distinct phrases; and whether this be in the spirit of admiration or of condemnation will, in all cases which admit of doubt, be largely a question of the personal sympathies of the observer. But Lincoln stands apart in striking solitude, — an enigma to all men. The world eagerly asks of each person who endeavors to write or speak of him: What illumination have you for us? Have you solved the mystery? Can you explain this man? The task has been essayed many times; it will be essayed many times more; it never has been, and probably it never will be entirely achieved. Each biographer, each writer or speaker, makes his little contribution to the study, and must be content to regard it merely as a contribution. For myself, having drawn the picture of the man as I see him, though knowing well that I am far from seeing him all, and still farther from seeing inwardly through him, yet I know that I cannot help it by additional comments. Very much more than is the case with other men, Lincoln means different things to different persons, and the aspect which he presents depends to an unusual degree upon the moral and mental individuality of the observer. Perhaps this is due to the breadth and variety of his own nature. As a friend once said to me: Lincoln was like Shakespeare, in that he seemed to run through the whole gamut of human nature. It was true. From the superstition of the ignorant backwoodsman to that profoundest faith which is the surest measure of man's greatness, Lincoln passed along the whole distance. In his early days he struck his roots deep down into the common soil of the earth, and in his latest years his head towered and shone among the stars. Yet his greatest, his most distinctive, and most abiding trait was his humanness of nature; he was the expression of his people; at some periods of his life and in some ways it may be that he expressed them in their uglier forms, but generally he displayed them in their noblest and most beautiful developments; yet, for worse or for better, one is always conscious of being in close touch with him as a fellow man. People often call him the greatest man who ever lived; but, in fact, he was not properly to be compared with any other. One may set up a pole and mark notches upon it, and label them with the names of Julius Caesar, William of Orange, Cromwell, Napoleon, even Washington, and may measure these men against each other, and dispute and discuss their respective places. But Lincoln cannot be brought to this pole, he cannot be entered in any such competition. This is not necessarily because he was greater than any of these men; for, before this could be asserted, the question would have to be settled: How is greatness to be estimated? One can hardly conceive that in any age of the world or any combination of circumstances a capacity and temperament like that of Caesar or Napoleon would not force itself into prominence and control. On the other hand, it is easy to suppose that, if precisely such a great moral question and peculiar crisis as gave to Lincoln his opportunity had not arisen contemporaneously with his years of vigor, he might never have got farther away from obscurity than does the ordinary member of Congress. Does this statement limit his greatness, by requiring a rare condition to give it play? The question is of no serious consequence, since the condition existed; and the discussion which calls it forth is also of no great consequence. For what is gained by trying to award him a number in a rank-list of heroes? It is enough to believe that probably Lincoln alone among historical characters could have done that especial task which he had to do. It was a task of supreme difficulty, and like none which any other man ever had to undertake; and he who was charged with it was even more distantly unlike any other man in both moral and mental equipment. We cannot force lines to be parallel, for our own convenience or curiosity, when in fact they are not parallel. Let us not then try to compare and to measure him with others, and let us not quarrel as to whether he was greater or less than Washington, as to whether either of them, set to perform the other's task, would have succeeded with it, or, perchance, would have failed. Not only is the competition itself an ungracious one, but to make Lincoln a competitor is foolish and useless. He was the most individual man who ever lived; let us be content with this fact. Let us take him simply as Abraham Lincoln, singular and solitary, as we all see that he was; let us be thankful if we can make a niche big enough for him among the world's heroes, without worrying ourselves about the proportion which it may bear to other niches; and there let him remain forever, lonely, as in his strange lifetime, impressive, mysterious, unmeasured, and unsolved.

FOOTNOTES:

[79] See *ante*, pp. 237-241 (chapter on Reconstruction).

[80] Grant, *Memoirs*, ii. 460.

[81] Grant, *Memoirs*, ii. 459. This differs from the statement of N. and H. x. 216, that "amid the wildest enthusiasm, the President again reviewed the victorious regiments of Grant, marching through Petersburg in pursuit of Lee." Either

picture is good; perhaps that of the silent, deserted city is not the less effective.

[82] Between March 29 and the date of surrender, 19,132 Confederates had been captured, a fate to which it was shrewdly suspected that many were not averse.

[83] May 11, 1865.

[84] Hon. George W. Julian says: "I spent most of the afternoon in a political caucus, held for the purpose of considering the necessity for a new cabinet and a line of policy less conciliatory than that of Mr. Lincoln; and while everybody was shocked at his murder, the feeling was nearly universal that the accession of Johnson to the presidency would prove a godsend to the country." *Polit. Recoll.* 255.

# INDEX

## Alabama

not ready to secede, but opposed to coercion

wishes Southern convention

secedes

## Alabama

Confederate privateer

sunk by Kearsarge

## Albert, Prince

revises Palmerston's dispatch on Trent affair

## Anderson, Robert

signs Lincoln's certificate of discharge in Black Hawk war

commands at Fort Moultrie in 1860

moves forces to Sumter

asks instructions in vain

appeals to Lincoln

refuses to surrender Sumter

## Andrew, Governor John A.

prepares Massachusetts militia

asks United States for muskets

sends on troops

## Anthony, Henry B

in Senate in 1861

## Antietam

battle of

## Arkansas

refuses to furnish Lincoln troops

at first Unionist, finally secedes

campaign of Curtis in

reconstructed

chooses electors

## Armstrong, Jack

his wrestling match with Lincoln

his later friendship with Lincoln

aids him in politics

## Arnold, Isaac N

in House in 1861

describes drilling of Army of Potomac

on importance of Lincoln's action in Trent case

introduces bill abolishing slavery under federal jurisdiction

on composition of Gettysburg address

dreads danger in election of 1864

Lincoln's only supporter in Congress

refusal of Lincoln to help in campaign

on Lincoln's attempt to push thirteenth amendment through Congress

on second vote on thirteenth amendment

## Arnold, Samuel

accomplice of Booth, tried and condemned

## Ashley, James M

in House in 1861

moves to reconsider thirteenth amendment

## Ashmun, George

presides over Republican Convention of 1860

## Assassination of Lincoln

plot of 1861

threats during term of office-

successful plot of 1865-

death of Booth

trial and punishment of other persons concerned-

**Atlanta**

battle of

**Atzerodt, Geo. A**

accomplice of Booth, tried and condemned-

**Baker, Edward D**

in Illinois campaign of 1838

at Illinois bar

candidate for Congress

elected

his agreement with Lincoln and others

introduces Lincoln at inauguration

killed at Ball's Bluff

responsible for disaster

**Ball's Bluff**

battle of

**Banks, Nathaniel P**

in Federal army

his corps in 1862

defeated by Jackson

takes Port Hudson

**Barnard, General John G**

opposes McClellan's plan of campaign

on impossibility of taking Yorktown

**Bates, Edward**

candidate for Republican nomination

favored by Greeley

his chances as a moderate candidate

vote for

attorney-general

opposes reinforcing Sumter

**Bayard, James A**

in Senate in 1861

**Beauregard, General P.G.T**

commands at Charleston

notified by Lincoln of purpose to reinforce Sumter

requests surrender of Sumter

commands bombardment

commands Confederate army at Manassas

at battle of Bull Run

at battle of Shiloh

evacuates Corinth

**Bell, John**

candidate of Constitutional Union party

vote for

**Benjamin, Judah P**

denounces Buchanan

in Confederate cabinet

**Bentonsville**

battle of

**Berry, Wm. F**

his partnership with Lincoln, and failure

**Big Bethel**

battle of

**Black, Jeremiah S**

in Buchanan's cabinet

succeeds Cass in State Department

after vacillation turns toward coercion

forces Buchanan to alter reply to South Carolina commissioners

his character

his end

## Border States

necessity of retaining in Union

dealings of Lincoln with, in 1861

their neutrality policy explained in annual message

both pro-slavery and Unionist

desire to conciliate controls Lincoln's policy

with their slave property guaranteed by North

oppose bill freeing slaves used in war

oppose other anti-slavery bills-

irritated by congressional policy

urged by Lincoln to agree to emancipation-

refuse to approve

Lincoln's policy toward, denounced by Abolitionists

their support in 1862 saves Lincoln

## Boutwell, George S

urges emancipation upon Lincoln

## Bragg, General Braxton

invades Kentucky

outmarched by Buell

at battle of Stone's River

retreats

reinforced

at battle of Chickamauga

besieges Chattanooga

defeated by Grant

## Breckenridge, John C

elected Vice-President

nominated by South for President

carries Southern States

distracted in body and mind

receives secession commissioners of South Carolina

a Unionist in feeling

his message on secession

wishes to shirk responsibility

declares coercion unconstitutional

ridiculed by Republicans

excuse for his position

declines to receive Southern commissioners

virtually abdicates power to cabinet

denounced by South

forced to appoint Dix to Treasury Department

calls extra session of Senate to aid Lincoln

his futile policy towards Fort Sumter

## Buckner, General Simon B

surrenders Fort Donelson

## Buell, General D.C

his resemblance in character to McClellan

refuses to seize East Tennessee

snubbed by McClellan

recommended by Halleck for promotion

takes Nashville

saves battle of Shiloh

allows slave-owners to reclaim fugitives

seizes Louisville before Bragg

opposes Halleck's plan to invade Tennessee

resigns

## Bull Run

first battle of

second battle of

## Burlingame, Anson D

hopes that Douglas will join Republicans

**Calhoun, John**

appoints Lincoln deputy surveyor

**Calhoun, John C**

his speech on Compromise of 1850

**California**

annexed

gold fever in

asks admission as State

prohibits slavery

refusal of South to admit

admitted

**Cameron, Simon**

candidate for Republican presidential nomination in 1860

sells his vote for promise of a place in cabinet

willing to sacrifice anything to save Union

secretary of war

difficulty over his appointment

opposes relieving Fort Sumter

refuses muskets to Massachusetts militia

wishes to leave War Department

appointed minister to Russia

instructs Butler not to return slaves

authorizes Sherman to use negroes

suggests arming slaves in annual report

his report suppressed by Lincoln

supports Lincoln for reëlection

**Campbell, Judge John A**

acts as intermediary between Seward and Confederate commissioners

on Confederate Peace Commission

**Cartwright, Peter**

defeated by Lincoln for Congress

his character as itinerant preacher

## Cass, Lewis

attacked by Lincoln in Congress

in Buchanan's cabinet

wishes to coerce South

resigns when Buchanan refuses to garrison Southern forts

## Caucus

denounced by Whigs in Illinois

## Cedar Mountain

battle of

## Chambrun, Comte de

on Lincoln's magnanimity

## Chancellorsville

battle of

## Chandler, Zachariah

in Senate in 1861

denounces conservatives

threatens Lincoln

## Chase, Salmon P

in debate on Compromise

candidate for Republican nomination in 1860

secretary of treasury

objected to by Pennsylvania protectionists

wishes to reinforce Sumter

dislikes subordination to Lincoln

wishes McClellan to advance

asks him his plans and is snubbed

favors Lincoln's plan of campaign

on ease of a victory

less admired after his visit at Ashland

offers Compromise of 1850

## Clinton, George

denounced in New York for calling secession "rebellion,"

## Cobb, Howell

in Congress with Lincoln

on "making better terms out of the Union than in it,"

in Buchanan's cabinet

candidate for presidency of South

resigns from cabinet

## Cochrane, General John

nominated for Vice-President

## Cold Harbor

battle of

## Colfax, Schuyler

expects Douglas to join Republicans

in House in 1861

on Lincoln's tenacity

announces passage of thirteenth amendment

## Collamer, Jacob

in Congress with Lincoln

vote for, in Republican Convention of 1860

in Senate in 1861

## Colonization

favored by Lincoln

## Compromise of 1850

history of

## Confederate States

formed by convention

organization of

sends commissioners to United States

its envoys rejected by Lincoln

prepares to seize Fort Sumter

amused at Lincoln's call for volunteers

receives Virginia

belligerency of, recognized by England and France

refusal of Lincoln to receive Stephens embassy from

sells bonds in England

dealings of supposed emissaries from, with Greeley-

refusal of Lincoln to negotiate with

dealings of Blair with

sends commissioners

conference of Lincoln and Seward with commissioners of

government of, collapses

## Congress

proposes amendment to Constitution to protect slavery

counts electoral votes

extra session called

votes to support Lincoln

creates Committee on Conduct of War

discusses battle of Shiloh

passes Crittenden resolution disavowing slavery as cause of war

passes bill freeing slaves used in war

refuses to reaffirm Crittenden resolution

passes bill for emancipation in District

prohibits officers to return fugitive slaves

abolishes slavery in Territories, etc.

passes act freeing slaves of rebels

passes act to arm negroes-

fails to provide equal pay

ignores Lincoln's wishes to conciliate Border States

passes resolution to cooperate with States adopting emancipation

unpopularity of Lincoln with

continues in 1862 to oppose Lincoln

fails to pass bill offering compensated emancipation to Missouri

character of, in 1863

accepts Representatives from reconstructed Louisiana

jealous of Lincoln's plan of reconstruction

desires to control matter itself

passes reconstruction bill-

wishes to supplant Lincoln by Chase-

creates lieutenant-general

refuses to recognize electors from Southern reconstructed States

fails to adopt thirteenth amendment

after election of 1864, passes amendment-

## Conkling, James C

letter of Lincoln to-

## Conkling, Roscoe

in House in 1861

## Constitution

slavery compromises in

in relation to doctrine of non-intervention

in relation to slavery in States

in relation to emancipation

in relation to popular sovereignty and Dred Scott decision

attitude of Abolitionists and Republicans toward

its relation to secession, Buchanan's view

proposal to amend, in 1861

its relation to secession, Lincoln's view

in relation to blockade

strained by civil war

kills Booth

**Covode, John**

in House in 1861

**Cox, Samuel S**

in House in 1861

**Crittenden, John J**

offers compromise in 1861

in House in 1861

offers resolution that war is not against slavery

opposes Lincoln's plan of emancipation in Kentucky

**Curtin, Governor Andrew G**

invites governors to meet at Altoona

on connection of conference with emancipation proclamation

reflected

**Curtis, Benjamin R**

his opinion in Dred Scott case

**Curtis, General Samuel R**

his campaign in Missouri and Arkansas

**Cushing, Lieutenant William B**

destroys the Albemarle

**Davis, David**

at Illinois bar

disgusted at election of Trumbull in 1855

Lincoln's manager in convention of 1860

**Davis, Garrett**

succeeds Breckenridge in Senate

his plea against arming negroes

**Davis, Henry Winter**

introduces reconstruction bill

issues address denouncing Lincoln for vetoing bill

obliged to support Lincoln rather than McClellan

## Davis, Jefferson

advocates extension of Missouri Compromise in 1850

sneers at attempted compromise in 1861

elected President of Confederate States

defies North

hopes to entrap Seward into debate with commissioners

urged by South to do something

prefers to make North aggressor

tries to win over Kentucky

offers to issue "letters of marque and reprisal,"

when secretary of war, sent McClellan to Europe

sends troops to seize East Tennessee

wishes to free Kentucky

his escape wished by Lincoln

replaces Johnston by Hood

proposition of Blair to

expresses willingness to treat for peace

nominates commissioners to treat for peace with independence

notified by Lee of approaching fall of Richmond

escapes from city

makes himself ridiculous and escapes punishment

suspected of complicity in Booth's plot

## Dawson

leads Lincoln in vote for legislature in 1834

## Dayton, William L

nominated by Republicans in 1856

candidate for nomination in 1860

## Democratic party

controls Illinois

wins in 1852

factions in

elects Buchanan in 1856

in. Illinois, nominates Douglas for Senate

torn with factions

breaks up in 1860 into Northern and Southern wings

nominates two sets of candidates

campaign of, in 1860

attempts to reunite

in North, members of, become Union men

effort of Lincoln to placate, by giving recognition in cabinet

Copperhead and other factions of

"War Democrats,"

makes campaign in 1862 on opposition to anti-slavery legislation

gains in Congressional elections

wishes Lincoln to compromise

denounces seizure of Vallandigham

agitates against military tyranny

commits error in opposing war

loses ground in 1863

applauds Fremont's candidacy

hopes for success in 1864

denounces war as failure and nominates McClellan

war faction of, hesitates to vote for Lincoln, on slavery grounds

divided over peace plank

damaged by Federal military successes

hurt by Southern approval

defeated in election

members of, in Congress, aid in passage of thirteenth amendment

**Dennison, William**

succeeds Blair as postmaster-general

## Dickinson, Daniel S

candidate for vice-presidential nomination

## Diplomatic history

Seward's proposed foreign wars to prevent disunion

recognition of Southern belligerency by England and France

instructions of Seward to Adams

difficulties over English privateers

message of Lincoln on foreign relations

the Trent affair

the Oreto affair

the Alabama affair

## District of Columbia

bill to emancipate slaves in, advocated by Lincoln

slave trade in, abolished

abolition in, favored by Lincoln

emancipation in, carried

## Dix, John A

on possible secession of New York

appointed to Treasury Department

his order to protect American flag

## Dixon, Archibald

offers amendment repealing Missouri Compromise

## Donelson, Andrew J

nominated for presidency by Whigs and Know-Nothings

## Donelson, Fort

battle of

## Doolittle, James R

in Senate in 1861

## Doubleday, General Abner

on Hooker's plan in Chancellorsville campaign

## Douglas, Stephen A

meets Lincoln in 1835

encounters him in campaign of 1840

Lincoln's rival in love affair

his position at Illinois bar

charges Lincoln with lacking patriotism in opposing Mexican war

introduces Kansas-Nebraska Bill

mobbed in Chicago

debates with Lincoln in campaign of 1854

proposes a truce

candidate for Democratic nomination in 1856

opposes Lecompton Constitution

leading figure in public life

his character and ability

his doctrine of "popular sovereignty,"

avoids consequences of Dred Scott decision

defies Buchanan

his conduct in Lecompton case dictated by desire to secure reëlection

to Senate

attacks "English Bill" as unfair

his candidacy for reëlection gives Lincoln opportunity

renominated by Democrats

denounced by South

opposed by administration

accepts Lincoln's challenge to joint debates

his attacks upon Lincoln

accused by Lincoln of a plot to make slavery national

denies any plot

on status of negro under Declaration of Independence

acquiesces in blockade

enraged at Trent affair

demands reparation

admitted by Lincoln to be in the right

reply of Seward

Northern hatred of

wisdom of Lincoln's attitude toward

people of, gratified by emancipation proclamation

fails to detain Oreto and Alabama

subscribes to Confederate loan

### English, James E

in House in 1861

votes for thirteenth amendment

### Ericsson, John

designs the Monitor

### Evarts, William M

moves to make Lincoln's nomination unanimous

### Everett, Edward

nominated for Vice-President by Constitutional Union party

delivers oration at Gettysburg

### Ewell, General R.S

enters Shenandoah Valley

enters Pennsylvania

### Ewing

defeats Lincoln for speakership in Illinois legislature

### Farragut, Captain D.G

takes New Orleans

his campaign on Mississippi

takes Mobile

quarrels on question of reinforcing Sumter and resigns

runs away from Fort Donelson

## Foote, Admiral Andrew H

his operations in 1862

captures Fort Henry

## Ford, Governor

remark on Lincoln's political luck

## Forney, John W

on Republican Convention of 1864

## Forquer, George

taunts Lincoln with youth

retort of Lincoln to

## Fox, G.V

his plan to relieve Fort Sumter

## Franklin, General William B

summoned by Lincoln to consultation

does not tell McClellan

favors McClellan's plan of attack

his division sent to McClellan, but not used

his force occupies West Point

## Fremont, Mrs. Jessie Benton

her interview with Lincoln

## Fremont, John C

nominated for presidency by Republicans

appointed to command in Missouri

his quarrelsomeness and inefficiency

arrests Blair

the idol of Abolitionists

removed

wishes a Southern convention

how led to secede

Union minority in

## Gettysburg

battle of

Lincoln's address at-

## Giddings, Joshua R

favors Lincoln's emancipation bill in 1849

member of Republican Convention of 1860

## Gilmer, John A

refuses to enter Lincoln's cabinet

## Gist

governor of South Carolina, sends circular letter asking about secession

feeling in South

## Grant, Ulysses S

his operations in 1862

captures Forts Henry and Donelson

recommended by Halleck for promotion

condemned by Halleck and relieved from command

reinstated

advances to Pittsburg Landing

attacked by Johnston

does not admit defeat at Shiloh

on severity of battle

his conduct of battle criticised

harassed by Halleck, asks to be relieved

on Halleck's mistakes

on Copperheads

forms plan to take Vicksburg

tries to approach city from south

besieges and takes Vicksburg

his credit for campaign

his relations with Lincoln

accused of drunkenness

congratulated by Lincoln

given command of the West

orders Thomas to hold Chattanooga

relieves siege

wins battle of Chattanooga

sends Sherman to relieve Burnside

on reconstruction

his conference with Lincoln

movement to nominate for President in 1864

appointed lieutenant-general

given free control

prepares plan of campaign

correspondence with Lincoln

his campaigns in Virginia

sends force to hold Washington against Early

sends Sheridan against Early

character of his military methods

reports proposal of Lee for a conference

ordered by Lincoln to refuse

on desertions from Lee's army

his plan to entrap Lee's army

wishes to capture Lee without Sherman's aid

enters Petersburg

pursues Lee

urges Lee to surrender

his liberal terms to Lee

praised by Lincoln

unable to accept Lincoln's invitation to theatre the evening of his assassination

## Greeley, Horace

    prefers Douglas to Lincoln in 1858

    in convention of 1860, works against Seward

    his influence used against Lincoln

    willing to admit peaceable secession

    on comparative strength of North and South

    suddenly denounces compromise

    a secessionist in 1861

    publishes address to President

    his influence

    answered by Lincoln

    his abusive retort

    suggests French mediation

    condemns Lincoln in 1864

    on movement to delay nomination

    his political creed

    claims to be a Republican while denouncing Lincoln

    favors Fremont

    wishes peace at any price

    wishes to treat with Confederates

    authorized to do so by Lincoln

    conditions named by Lincoln

    abuses Lincoln for causing failure of negotiations

## Green, Duff

    tries to induce Lincoln to support Buchanan

## Greene, Bolin

    lends Lincoln money

## Grimes, James W

    in Senate in 1861

## Grow, Galusha A

speaker of House in 1861

## Habeas Corpus

suspension of, by Lincoln

## Hale, John P

sums up Buchanan's secession doctrine

in Senate in 1861

denounces administration in Trent affair

## Halleck, General Henry W

letter of Lincoln to, on plan of war

commands in Missouri

sends news of capture of Fort Donelson and asks for command in West

assumes command

complains of Grant

drives Grant to request to be relieved

his slow advance upon Corinth

refuses to fight

enters Corinth unopposed

fails to use powerful army

appointed general-in-chief,

compared with McClellan

gains advancement because unopposed and unnoticed by politicians

expels slaves from camp

favors recall of McClellan from Peninsula

allowed free hand by Lincoln

inferior to McClellan

his telegraphic dispute with McClellan

begs McClellan's assistance after Pope's defeat

instructs McClellan to command defences of Washington

alarmed over safety of capital

has friction with Hooker

refuses to give Hooker garrison of Harper's Ferry

urges Meade to attack after Gettysburg

wishes Buell and Rosecrans

to invade Tennessee

superseded by Grant

on bad terms with Blair

## Hamlin, Hannibal

nominated for Vice-President

reasons why not renominated

## Hanks, John

aids Lincoln to split rails

on Lincoln's first sight of slavery

brings rails split by Lincoln into Republican Convention

## Hanks, Nancy

mother of Lincoln, 2

descends from a "poor white" family, 7

her character, 7, 8, 9

marries Thomas Lincoln, 8

her death

## Hardin, Colonel John J

defeats Lincoln and Baker for Congress

defeated by Lincoln

## Harlan, James

in Senate in 1861

## Harrison, W.H

campaign for, in 1840

## Hawkins, George S

opposes compromise in 1861 as futile

## Hayti

recognized

**Heintzelman, General Samuel P**

opposes McClellan's plan of campaign

appointed corps commander

on force necessary to protect Washington

**Henderson, John B**

approves Lincoln's emancipation scheme

**Henry, Fort**

captured

**Herndon, William H**

law partner of Lincoln

prevents Lincoln from association with Abolitionists

aids Lincoln in organizing Republican party

visits East to counteract Greeley's influence against Lincoln

**Herold, David E**

tried for assassination of Lincoln

hanged

**Hickman, John**

calls Lincoln's emancipation scheme unmanly

**Hicks, Governor Thomas H**

opposed to secession

suggests referring troubles to Lord Lyons as arbitrator

**"Higher Law,"**

Seward's doctrine of

**Hitchcock, General Ethan A**

considers Washington insufficiently protected

**Holt, Joseph**

succeeds Floyd in Buchanan's cabinet

joins Black and Stanton in coercing Buchanan

fears attempt of South to seize Washington

## Hood, General John Bell

succeeds Johnston

defeated by Sherman

## Hooker, General Joseph

allows slave owners to reclaim fugitives

replaces Burnside in command

letter of Lincoln to

his abilities

in Chancellorsville campaign

throws away chance of success

fails to use all of troops

orders retreat

wishes to resume attack

first prevented, then urged by Lincoln

wishes to capture Richmond

follows Lee to North

instructed by Lincoln to obey Halleck

irritated by Halleck, resigns

sent to aid Rosecrans

storms Lookout Mountain

## House of Representatives

election of Lincoln to, and career in

members of

debates Mexican war

struggles in, over Wilmot proviso

refuses to pass Lincoln's emancipation bill of 1849

settles question of admission of Kansas

proposes Constitutional amendment in 1861

rejects plan of Peace Congress

leaders of, in 1861

thanks Captain Wilkes

approves emancipation proclamation

fails to pass thirteenth amendment

later passes amendment-

## Houston, Samuel

opposes secession in Texas

## Hunter, General David

asked by Lincoln to aid Fremont

succeeds Fremont

proclaims martial law and abolishes slavery in Georgia, Florida, and

South Carolina

his order revoked

organizes a negro regiment

## Hunter, R.M.T

on Confederate peace commission

retort of Lincoln to

## Hyer, Tom

hired by Seward's supporters in Republican Convention

## Illinois

early settlers and society of

in Black Hawk war

early politics in

land speculation in

career of Lincoln in legislature of

the career of "Long Nine" in

internal improvement craze in

adopts resolutions condemning Abolitionists and emancipation in the

District

suffers from financial collapse

joins Johnston and attacks McClellan

compels McClellan to retreat to James River

defeats Banks

reinforced

marches around Pope

on too good condition of Federal armies

breaks Federal right at Chancellorsville

accidentally shot by his own soldiers

### Johnson, Andrew

in Congress with Lincoln

in Senate in 1861

instructed by Lincoln to reorganize government in Tennessee

stern opinion of treason

repudiates Sherman's terms with Johnston

his nomination for vice-presidency aided by Lincoln

protested against, by Tennesseeans

his accession to presidency welcomed by radicals

refuses to commute Mrs. Surratt's sentence

### Johnson, Bushrod R

captured at Fort Donelson

### Johnson, Herschel V

nominated for Vice-President in 1860

votes against secession in 1860

### Johnson, Oliver

supports Lincoln in 1864

### Johnston, General A.S

plans to crush Grant and Buell in detail

commands at battle of Shiloh

killed

### Johnston, Joseph

succeeds Jackson at Harper's Ferry

aids Beauregard at Bull Run

on condition of Confederate army

evacuates Manassas

fears that McClellan will storm Yorktown

begins attack on McClellan

retreats from Sherman after Vicksburg

terms of Sherman with, in 1865

campaign against Sherman in 1864

removed by Davis

campaign against Sherman in Carolinas

plan of Lee to join

surrenders

## Johnston, Sally

marries Thomas Lincoln

her character

## Jones, Abraham

ancestor of Lincoln, 4

## Judd, N.B

asked by Lincoln to help his canvass in 1860

urges Lincoln to avoid danger of assassination

## Julian, George W

in House in 1861

on Republican dissatisfaction with Lincoln

## Kane, Marshal Geo. P

telegraphs for Southern aid to oppose passage of troops through

Baltimore

## Kansas

struggle in, between free and slave-state men

rival constitutions of

admission of, under Lecompton Constitution, urged by Buchanan

opposed by Douglas

attempt of Congress to bribe into acceptance of Lecompton Constitution

rejects offer

speeches of Lincoln in

## Kansas-Nebraska bill

introduced

repeals Missouri Compromise

## Keitt, Lawrence M

his fight with Grow

## Kellogg, Win. Pitt

letter of Lincoln to, on extension of slavery

## Kentucky

desire of Lincoln to retain in Union

refuses to furnish troops

attempt of Secessionists to carry

wishes to be neutral

thereby intends to aid South

skillful dealings of Lincoln with

remains in Union

saved by State loyalty

its neutrality violated by South, joins North

campaign of Grant in

invaded by Bragg

## Keyes, General Erasmus D

favors McClellan's plan of campaign

appointed corps commander

on force necessary to protect Washington

on impossibility of taking Yorktown

## Know-Nothings

their career in 1854-1856

attempt to draw out Lincoln in 1860

## Lamon, Colonel Ward H

connection with assassination story

## Lane, James H

senator from Kansas

## Lane, Joseph

nominated for Vice-President on Breckinridge ticket in 1860

## Lee, Robert E

offered command of Union army

opposes secession

resigns from army and accepts command of State troops

becomes Confederate general

commands against Pope

prepares to invade Maryland

his contempt for McClellan

at Antietam

at Fredericksburg

outmanoeuvred by Hooker

at Chancellorsville

hopes to conquer a peace

enters Pennsylvania

retreats after Gettysburg

sends reinforcements to Bragg

campaign in Virginia against Meade

his campaign against Grant

suggests a conference with Grant

notifies Davis that Richmond must fall

his chance of escape

attacks Federal lines

tries to escape

surrenders at Appomattox

asks for food

## Liberia

recognized

## Lincoln, Abraham

his ignorance concerning his ancestry

sensitive regarding it

his own statements

anxious to appear of respectable stock,

his genealogy as established later,

his reputed illegitimacy

his birth

his references to his mother,

his childhood

befriended by his step-mother

his education

early reading

early attempts at humorous writing

storytelling

youthful exploits

let out by his father

helps his father settle in Sangamon County, Ill

works for himself

his trip to New Orleans for Offut

impressed with slavery

in Offut's store

fights Armstrong

later friendship with Armstrong

borrows a grammar

his honesty

loses situation

involved in border quarrels

his temperance considered eccentric

careless habits of dress

in the country groceries

coarseness of speech

his sympathetic understanding of the people

his standards dependent on surroundings

enlists in Black Hawk war

chosen captain

his services

### Frontier Politician

Announces himself a candidate for the legislature

a "Clay man,"

his campaign and defeat

enters grocery store, fails

pays off debt

studies law

postmaster at New Salem

settles account with government

surveyor

elected to legislature

borrows money to ride to capital

his career in legislature

love affair with Ann Rutledge

his gloom

its inexplicable character

affair with Mary Owens, 48 and n

again a candidate, his platform

calms excitement in campaign

his fairness

his retort to Forquer

elected as one of "Long Nine,"

favors unlimited internal improvements

acknowledges his blunder

his skill as log-roller

gains popularity in county

protests against anti-abolition resolutions

admitted to bar, settles in Springfield

partnership with Stuart

studies debating

political ambitions

shows evidences of high ideals

incidents of his canvass in 1838

opposes repudiation, in legislature

reflected in 1840, unsuccessful candidate for speaker

jumps out of window to break a quorum

in campaign of 1840

his courtship of Mary Todd

fails to appear on wedding day

married

character of his married life

quarrels with Shields

later ashamed of it

improves prospects by a partnership with Logan

later joins with Herndon

his competitors at the bar

considers law secondary to politics

his legal ability

a "case lawyer,"

his ability as jury lawyer

refuses to conduct a bad case

on Whig electoral ticket in 1844

later disillusioned with Clay

fails to get nomination to Congress

alleged understanding with Baker and others

renews candidacy in 1846

disappointed at defeat by Douglas

exhausted by his efforts

asked to contribute to campaign fund

### *Candidate for Presidency*

Makes speeches in Ohio

calls Douglas pro-slavery

invited to speak in New York, prepares address

journey through Kansas

his New York address

states the situation

praised by newspapers

tour in New England

comprehensive nature of his speeches

ignores disunion

by dwelling on wrong of slavery, makes disunion wrong

slow to admit publicly a desire for presidency

enters field in 1859

nominated as candidate by Illinois Republican Convention

his managers at National Convention

yelled for by hired shouters

supposed to be more moderate than Seward

his own statement of principles

votes secured for, by bargains

nominated on third ballot

accepts nomination in dejection

his nomination a result of "availability,"

little known in country at large

anxious to avoid discussion of side issues

opposed by Abolitionists

supported by Giddings

elected

the choice of a minority

*President-elect.*

his cabinet

seeks representatives of all views

prefers individual strength to unity in cabinet

criticised by radical Republicans

has difficulties in satisfying Cameron

dissuades Seward from refusing to join cabinet

his statement of purpose to Virginia commissioners

annoys South by failing to notice it

irritates Northern extremists

asks opinion of Scott as to relieving Sumter

asks advice of cabinet

promises South to take no action without warning

again asks cabinet

forms plan to relieve Fort Pickens

spoils plan to relieve Sumter by sending Powhatan to Pensacola

announces intention to provision Sumter

admits blame for failure

question of his fault in delaying to relieve fort

issues proclamation calling for volunteers for three months

his purpose

expects Northerners to equal Southerners as fighters

calls Congress for special session

wishes to gain Kentucky

dreads effect of Baltimore riot on Border States

offers to send troops around Baltimore

soothes Maryland

cut off from North for a week

tries in vain to prevent Virginia from seceding

tries to secure Lee

successful in his policy for retaining Kentucky in Union

unable to reach North Carolina, Tennessee, or Arkansas

tries to aid Missouri loyalists

confident in efficiency of North

his capacities unknown to people

question of his "inspiration,"

his masterfulness not realized

question as to his relations with advisers

obliged to restrain Chase and Seward

his relations with Chase

receives Seward's "Thoughts,"

his reply to Seward

realizes his own responsibility and accepts it

receives absurd advice

proclaims blockade of Southern ports

advised to "close" ports

sees necessity of admitting war

decides to act efficiently without regard to Constitution

instructs Scott to watch Maryland legislature

issues order to arrest Maryland secessionists

orders Scott to suspend writ of habeas corpus

denounced by Taney

issues proclamation authorizing further suspension

states his argument to Congress

calls for more volunteers

takes pains with message which he sends to Congress

on neutrality of Kentucky

on blockade

on secession

appeals for ample means to end war

appoints McClellan to command Army of Potomac

avoids connection with Ball's Bluff affair

appoints McClellan to succeed Scott

sees that popular demand for action must be followed

puzzled by McClellan's refusal to move

forced to bear military responsibility

his freedom from self-seeking

urges McClellan to advance

discouraged by McClellan's illness, consults McDowell and Franklin

consults McClellan

exasperates McClellan by his action

appoints Stanton to succeed Cameron

his lack of personal feeling against Stanton

his patience toward Stanton

his letter to Halleck

wishes a direct attack

accused by McClellan's friends of meddling

decides to force action

issues General War Order No. 1

its purpose political rather than military

orders McClellan to move South

asks McClellan to justify his plan

calls council of generals

accepts McClellan's plan

insists on preservation of capital

political reasons for his anxiety to hold Washington

reasons why his plan should have been adopted

never convinced of superiority of McClellan's scheme

issues General War Order to secure Washington

unmoved by abuse of McClellan's enemies

relieves McClellan of general command

forced by Congress to divide Army of Potomac into corps

appreciates importance of Western operations

urges on Western generals

unable to supply troops

appoints Fremont to command Department of West

tries to guide Fremont

appealed to by Mrs. Fremont

removes Fremont, his reasons

sees military importance of Cumberland Gap

urges construction of a railroad there

urges Buell on

annoyed by Buell's refusal to move

death of his son

discusses plan to capture New Orleans

suddenly obliged to consider foreign affairs

his corrections on Seward's instructions to Adams

his statement of foreign relations in message of December, 1861

avoids either timidity or defiance

objects from beginning to seizure of Mason and Slidell

proposes to arbitrate the matter

thinks England's claim just

wisdom of his course in surrendering the envoys

unable to prevent slavery from entering into war

disapproves of Fremont's order freeing slaves of rebels

by rescinding it, makes an enemy of Fremont

revokes order of Hunter freeing slaves

takes responsibility of matter upon himself

prevents Cameron from urging arming of negroes

advises recognition of Hayti and Liberia

in message suggests compensated emancipation and colonization

approves bill abolishing slavery, with compensation, in District

signs bill prohibiting return of fugitive slaves

signs bill abolishing slavery in United States Territories

signs bill to emancipate slaves of rebels

slow to execute bill to enlist slaves

finally recognizes value of black troops

his conciliatory policy not followed by Congress

his reasons for advocating compensated emancipation

hopes to induce Border States to emancipate voluntarily

sends special message urging gradual emancipation

practically warns Border State men

denounced by both sides

tries in vain to persuade Border State representatives

his plans repudiated

repeats appeal in proclamation

his scheme impracticable, but magnanimous

sees future better than others

refrains from filling vacancies on Supreme Bench with Northern men

agrees to McClellan's peninsular campaign

still worried over safety of capital

neglects to demand any specific force to protect it

forced to detach troops from McClellan to reinforce Fremont

nearly orders McClellan to attack

his plan better than McClellan's

orders McDowell to return to Washington

alarmed at condition of defenses of capital

question of his error in retaining McDowell

shows apparent vacillation

explains situation in letter to McClellan

urges him to strike

annoyed by politicians

tries to forward troops

orders McDowell to join McClellan without uncovering capital

criticised by McClellan

refuses to let McDowell move in time

sends McDowell to rescue Banks

loses his head

insists on McDowell's movement

his blunder a fatal one

not a quick thinker

ruins McClellan's campaign

begins to lose patience with McClellan's inaction

appoints Halleck commander-in-chief

his constancy in support of McClellan

does not sacrifice McClellan as scapegoat

visits Harrison's Landing

avoids any partisanship in whole affair

appears better than McClellan in campaign

yet makes bad blunders

stands alone in failure

remains silent

allows Halleck a free hand

his reasons for appointing Halleck and Pope

decides to reappoint McClellan

shows sound judgment

places everything in McClellan's hands

indignant at slight results from Antietam

urges McClellan to pursue

his order ignored by McClellan

writes McClellan a blunt letter insinuating sluggishness or cowardice

replaces McClellan by Burnside

his extreme reticence as to his motives

attacked by Copperheads

criticised by defenders of the Constitution

harassed by extreme Abolitionists

denounced for not issuing a proclamation of emancipation

his reasons for refusing

explains his attitude as President toward slavery

struggles to hold Border States

general dissatisfaction with, in 1862

held inefficient by Chase

and by Congressmen

but believed in by people

addressed by Greeley with "Prayer of 20,000,000"

his reply to Greeley

his reply to Abolitionist clergymen

points out folly of a mere proclamation

thinks silently for himself under floods of advice

writes draft of Emancipation Proclamation

questions expediency of issuing

reads proclamation to cabinet

adopts Seward's suggestion to postpone until a victory

issues preliminary proclamation after Antietam

takes entire responsibility

not influenced by meeting of governors

fails to appease extremists

supported by party

thinks an earlier proclamation would not have been sustained

warned that he will cause loss of fall elections

always willing to trust people on a moral question

supported by Border States in election

renews proposals for compensated emancipation

favors it as a peaceful measure

his argument

fails to persuade Missouri to accept plan

issues definite proclamation

his remark on signing

tries to stimulate enlistment of blacks

threatens retaliation for Southern excesses

shows signs of care and fatigue

never asks for sympathy

slow to displace McClellan until sure of a better man

doubtful as to Burnside's plan of attack

refuses to accept Burnside's resignation after Fredericksburg

sends Vallandigham within Confederate lines

replies to addresses condemning martial law

obliged to begin draft

insists upon its execution

his letter to Illinois Union Convention

shows necessity of war

impossibility of compromise

justifies emancipation

points to successes

really controls government autocratically

able to, because supported by people

gains military experience

has measure of generals

henceforward supervises rather than specifically orders

begged by Chandler to disregard conservatives

prepares address for Gettysburg

the address

his theory of "reconstruction,"

recognizes a state government of Virginia

appoints military governors for conquered States

urges them to organize state governments

wishes only Union men to act

wishes bona fide elections

instructs new State organizers to recognize emancipation

fails to prevent quarrels

issues amnesty proclamation

proposes reconstruction by one tenth of voters

at first generally applauded

later opposed by Congress

on negro suffrage

doubts power of Congress over slavery in States

refuses to sign reconstruction bill

denounced by radicals

assailed by Greeley

embarrassed by Greeley's dealings with Confederate emissaries

authorizes Greeley to confer

charged by Greeley with failure

asked if he intends to insist on abolition

for political reasons, does not reply

renews call for soldiers

waits for military success

appoints Grant lieutenant-general

agrees not to interfere with Grant

wishes Grant success

astonished by a civil reply

under fire during Early's attack on Washington

discredited by fact of Washington's being still in danger

thanks Sherman for victory of Atlanta

rewards Sheridan for defeating Early

his election secured by these successes

urged by radicals to remove Blair

refuses at first, later does so

refuses to interfere in campaign

refuses to postpone call for more troops

refutes campaign slanders

prepares for defeat

re-elected easily

his remarks on election

refuses to intervene to secure counting of electoral votes of Border States

signs bill rejecting elections in Southern States, his reasons

shows magnanimity in appointing Chase chief justice

refuses to try to hasten matters

refuses to negotiate with Davis

marries Nancy Hanks

his children

moves from Kentucky to Indiana

marries again

moves to Illinois

later relations with Abraham

his manner of fighting

## Logan, Stephen T

partnership with, and influence upon, Lincoln

leader of Illinois bar

agrees with Lincoln to receive election to House in turn

defeated for Congress

manages Lincoln's candidacy in Republican Convention of 1860

## Longstreet, General James

sent to reinforce Jackson

enters Pennsylvania

sent to reinforce Bragg

at battle of Chickamauga

sent to crush Burnside

retreats from Sherman

## Louisiana

not ready for secession

but prepared to resist coercion

plan of Lincoln to reconstruct

## Lovejoy, Elijah P

killed at Alton

## Lovejoy, Owen

tries to commit Lincoln to joining Abolitionists

prevents Lincoln's election as senator

in House in 1861

his rage after Trent affair

supports Lincoln in 1864

## Lyons, Lord

suggested by Hicks as arbitrator between North and South

instructed to insist on instant reply in Trent affair

confers with Seward

## McCall, General George A

favors McClellan's plan of campaign

his division sent to aid McClellan

## McClellan, George B

given command of Army of Potomac

his record prior to 1861

his organizing ability

promoted to succeed Scott

his arrogance and contempt for civilians

causes discontent by inactivity

considers army unfit to move

unwilling from temperament to take any risks

fails to appreciate political situation

overestimates preparations of Confederates

overestimates Confederate numbers

wishes to end war by a crushing campaign

ignores Lincoln's suggestion to move

falls ill

hearing of conferences, becomes well and makes appearance

snubs McDowell and Chase

objects to a direct attack on Confederates

his plan

his opponents become a recognized faction

his scheme repudiated by Lincoln

protests and explains views

liberality of Lincoln towards

continues advance

forbidden to use McDowell so as to uncover Washington

protests

follows Lincoln's plan and extends right wing to meet McDowell

informed by Lincoln of withdrawal of McDowell to pursue Jackson

attacked by Johnston and Jackson

refuses to move for two weeks

wears out Lincoln's patience by delay

retorts sharply to suggestions

retreats to James River

writes bitter letter to Stanton

proves his incapacity to attack

wishes to resume offensive by James River

his prestige ruined at Washington

his recall demanded by Pope and Halleck

supported by Lincoln in spite of attacks

finally ordered to retreat

discussion of his conduct

beloved by army

predicts defeat of Pope

accused of failing to support Pope

exchanges telegrams with Halleck

his aid asked by Halleck after Pope's defeat

kept inactive during Pope's campaign

appointed by Lincoln, in spite of protests, to command in Washington

his fitness to reorganize army

describes steps taken to put him in command

cautious attitude toward Lee

at Antietam

welcomed by troops

fails to use advantages

urged by Lincoln to pursue

disappoints country by inaction

ordered by Lincoln to advance

letter of Lincoln to

fails to move

relieved from command

conduct of Lincoln towards

praised by conservative Democrats

endangers of emancipation

nominated for President

repudiates peace plank

his election hoped for by South

## McClernand, General John A

letter of Lincoln to, on difficulties of equipping armies

## McClure, A.K

on influence of New York "Tribune,"

## McDougall, James A

in Congress in 1861

## McDowell, General Irwin

commands Federal army

obliged to attack

at battle of Bull Run

summoned by Lincoln to consultation

does not tell McClellan

describes McClellan's appearance at conference

favors Lincoln's plan of campaign

appointed to command a corps

on force necessary to defend Washington

his corps retained at Washington

reasons of Lincoln for retaining

again ordered to support McClellan

ordered not to uncover Washington

prevented from advancing by Lincoln's superstition

ordered to turn and pursue Jackson

protests vigorously

obliged to abandon McClellan

foretells that Jackson will escape

## McLean, John

candidate for Republican nomination in 1860

## Magruder, General J.B

confronts McClellan at Yorktown

evacuates Yorktown

## Maine

Democratic gains in, during 1862

## Mallory, S.R

in Confederate cabinet

## Malvern Hill

battle of

## Maryland

passage of troops through

effect of Baltimore conflict upon

danger of its secession

determines to stand neutral

importance of its action

furnishes South with troops

military arrests in, to prevent secession

Lee's invasion of-

## Mason, James M

captured by Wilkes

imprisoned in Port Warren

surrendered

arrested in Maryland

attempt of Taney to liberate

## Mexican war

denounced by Whigs

character of

## Mexico

driven into war

abolishes slavery

## Michigan

Republican losses in election of 1862

## Miles, Colonel Dixon S

at Harper's Ferry

## Miller, Mrs. Nancy

bargains with Lincoln to make a pair of trousers

## Mississippi

not ready to secede

secedes

sends commissioner to persuade North Carolina

## Missouri

refuses to furnish Lincoln with troops

Unionist and Southern elements in

civil war in

refuses to secede

Fremont's career in

saved from South by General Curtis

refuses compensated emancipation

factional quarrels in

declares for Fremont against Lincoln

delegates from, in Republican Convention

carried by Democrats in 1862

## New Mexico

plan of South to occupy as slave territory

urged by Taylor to ask for admission as a State

organized as a Territory

## New York

Lincoln's speech in

secession threatened in

carried by Democrats in 1862

tries to evade draft

draft riots in

## North

surpasses South in development

begins to oppose spread of slavery

denounces Kansas-Nebraska Act

anti-Southern feeling in

enraged at Dred Scott decision

annoyed at both Secessionists and Abolitionists

effect of Lincoln's "House divided" speech upon

effect of Lincoln's speeches in

its attitude toward slavery the real cause of secession

carried by Republicans in 1860

its condition between Lincoln's election and his inauguration

panic in, during 1860

urged to let South secede in peace

proposals in, to compromise with South

led by Lincoln to oppose South on grounds of union, not slavery

irritated at inaction of Lincoln

effect of capture of Fort Sumter upon

rushes to arms

compared with South infighting qualities

responds to Lincoln's call for troops

military enthusiasm

doubtful as to Lincoln's ability

wishes to crush South without delay

forces McDowell to advance

enlightened by Bull Run

impatient with slowness of McClellan to advance

expects sympathy of England

annoyed at recognition of Southern belligerency by England

rejoices at capture of Mason and Slidell

its hatred of England

unity of, in 1861

inevitably led to break on slavery question

depressed by Peninsular campaign

opponents of the war in

public men of, condemn Lincoln

popular opinion supports him

effect of Emancipation Proclamation upon

forced by Lincoln to choose between emancipation and failure of war

depressed after Chancellorsville

discouraged by European offers of mediation

adjusts itself to war

waning patriotism in

tries to evade draft

draft riots in

bounty-jumping in

Republican gains in

really under Lincoln's dictatorship

relieved from gloom by successes of 1864

rejoicings in 1865

## North Carolina

not at first in favor of secession

ready to oppose coercion

urged by Mississippi to secede

refuses to furnish Lincoln troops

finally secedes

**Offut, Denton, sends Lincoln to New Orleans with a cargo,**

makes Lincoln manager of a store

brags of Lincoln's abilities

fails and moves away

**Oglesby, Governor R.J**

presides over Illinois Republican Convention

**Ohio**

campaign of 1858 in

carried by Democrats in 1862

career of Vallandigham in

reply of Lincoln to Democrats of

election of 1863 in

renominates Lincoln in 1864

**O'Laughlin, Michael**

accomplice of Booth, tried and condemned-

**Ordinance of 1787**

its adoption and effect

**Owens, Mary**

rejects Lincoln

**Pain, John**

Lincoln's only hearer at "mass meeting" to organize Republican party

**Palmerston, Lord**

drafts British ultimatum in Mason and Slidell case

shows it to Queen

asks for two millions to buy territory

## Pomeroy, Samuel C

senator from Kansas

an enemy of Lincoln

urges Chase's friends to organize to oppose Lincoln's renomination

## Pope, General John

recommended by Halleck for promotion

prevented by Halleck from fighting

urges recall of McClellan from Peninsula

his military abilities

commands Army of Virginia

shows arrogance and lack of tact

fails to cut off Jackson from Lee

insists on fighting

beaten at Bull Run

discredited

## Popular sovereignty

doctrine of, in Compromise of 1850

used by Douglas to justify repeal of Missouri Compromise

theory of, destroyed by Dred Scott decision

attempt of Douglas to reconcile, with Dred Scott case

## Porter, General Andrew

favors McClellan's

plan of campaign

## Porter, David D

takes Powhatan under Lincoln's orders

refuses to obey Seward's order

aids Grant at Vicksburg

confers with Lincoln

upholds Sherman in referring to Lincoln as authorizing Johnston's

terms of surrender

## Porter, General Fitz-John

favors McClellan's plan of campaign

sent to meet McDowell

## Powell, L.W

denounces Lincoln's emancipation scheme

## Rathbone, Major Henry R

at Lincoln's assassination

## Raymond, Henry J

warns Lincoln of danger done to Republican party by emancipation

policy

reply of Lincoln to

## Reagan, J.H

in Confederate cabinet

## Reconstruction

constitutional theory of

begun by appointment of military governors

Lincoln's plan for

blocked by refusal of Congress to receive representatives

usually associated with new constitutions

method laid down in amnesty proclamation

difficulties in way of

extremist proposals concerning

Reconstruction bill passed

bill for, vetoed by Lincoln

later statements of Lincoln concerning

involved in Sherman's terms of surrender given to Johnston

Lincoln's scheme discussed

members of, denounce Lincoln for vetoing reconstruction bill

movement in, to nominate Chase

movement in, to nominate Fremont

masses of, adhere to Lincoln

fails to postpone nominating convention

nominates Lincoln

nominates Johnson for Vice-President

receives reluctant support of radicals

damaged by Greeley's denunciations of Lincoln

dreads defeat in summer of 1864

damaged by draft

radical element of, forces dismissal of Blair

conduct of campaign by

gains election in 1864

makes thirteenth amendment a plank in platform

radical members of, rejoice at accession of Johnson after murder of

Lincoln

## Reynolds, Governor

calls for volunteers in Black Hawk war

## Rhode Island

renominates Lincoln

## Richardson, W.A

remark on congressional interference with armies

## Rives, W.C

remark of Lincoln to, on coercion

## Rosecrans, General William S

succeeds Buell

disapproves Halleck's plan to invade East Tennessee

fights battle of Stone's River

reluctant to advance

drives Bragg out of Tennessee

refuses to move

finally advances to Chattanooga

defeated at Chickamauga

unnerved after Chickamauga

cheered by Lincoln

besieged in Chattanooga

relieved by Grant

**Russell, Earl**

his prejudices in favor of South

recognizes belligerency of South

revises Palmerston's dispatch in Trent affair

condemns Emancipation Proclamation

calls Alabama affair a scandal

**Rutledge, Ann**

love affair of Lincoln with

**Saulsbury, Willard**

in Senate in 1861

**Saxton, General Rufus**

permitted to raise negro troops

**Schofield, General John M**

treats with Johnston

his removal from Missouri refused by Lincoln

**Schurz, General Carl**

refused permission by Lincoln

to leave army to support his canvass

**Scott, Winfield**

in Mexican war

supported by Lincoln for President

suggests division of country into four parts

his help expected by Secessionists

advises reinforcement of Southern garrisons

threatens Southerners with violence

warns Lincoln of plot to murder

his military preparations

thinks Sumter must be abandoned

assembles troops at Washington

wishes to induce Lee to command Northern army

instructed to watch Maryland legislature

authorized to suspend writ of habeas corpus

has difficulties with McClellan

retires

## Seaton, William W

promises to help Lincoln's emancipation bill

## Secession

mention of, avoided by Douglas and Lincoln

question of its justification in 1860

process of, in 1860

discussed by Buchanan

admitted by Northern leaders

threatened by New York Democrats

Lincoln's view of

Southern theory of

its success makes union, not slavery, the issue at stake

renewed by Border States

recognized as not the ultimate cause of war

again asserted by Lincoln to be cause of war

## Sedgwick, General John

beaten at Chancellorsville

## Semmes, Captain Raphael

his career with the Alabama

warning

makes mistake in order concerning Powhatan

said to have led Lincoln to sign papers without understanding contents

made to feel subordination by Lincoln

submits thoughts for President's consideration

wishes foreign war

offers to direct the government

reasons for his actions

repressed by Lincoln

advises against a paper blockade

wishes to maintain friendly relations with England

angered at Russell's conduct

writes menacing instructions to Adams

his attitude in Mason and Slidell affair

drafts reply to England's ultimatum

disavows Wilkes's act and surrenders envoys

advises Lincoln to withhold Emancipation Proclamation until after a

victory

suggests promise to maintain freedom of slaves

dealings with England

rejects offer of French mediation

denounced by radicals

plan to force his resignation

offers resignation

withdraws it at Lincoln's request

on Copperhead societies

denounced by Chandler

on bad terms with Blair

his remarks used against Lincoln

sent by Lincoln to confer with Confederate peace commission, his

instructions

shown Lincoln's dispatch to Grant

attempt to assassinate

**Seymour, Horatio**

elected governor of New York

denounces tyranny of Lincoln

tries to prevent draft

asks Lincoln to delay enforcement until Supreme Court gives judgment

inefficient at time of draft riots

**Shackford, Samuel**

investigates Lincoln's ancestry, 3

**Shellabarger, Samuel**

in House in 1861

**Shepley, Governor G.F**

remark of Lincoln to

**Sheridan, General Philip H**

at battle of Chattanooga

his campaign against Early

plans to cut off Lee

wins Five Forks

at Appomattox

**Sherman, John**

in Senate in 1861

**Sherman, General W.T**

unappreciated by Halleck

authorized by Cameron to use slaves

assaults Vicksburg

pursues Johnston

sent to reinforce Rosecrans

storms Missionary Ridge

relieves Burnside

confers with Lincoln

his terms to Johnston in 1865 involve political reconstruction

his terms annulled by Stanton

shows resentment toward Stanton

makes terms with Johnston

refers to Lincoln as authority

his terms disapproved by Grant

appointed to command in West

drives Johnston southward

defeats Hood at Atlanta

thanked by Lincoln

marches to the sea

marches north through Carolinas

ready to join Grant

## Shields, General James A

paper duel of Lincoln with

loses reëlection to Senate

his force joined to McDowell's

## Shipley, Mary

ancestor of Lincoln

## Short, James

lends Lincoln money

## Sickles, Daniel E

threatens secession of New York city

## Sigel, General Franz

replaces Fremont

## Slavery

its entrance into politics described

compromises concerning, in Constitution

settled by Missouri Compromise

attitude of South toward

necessity of extending area of, in order to preserve

Lincoln's description of struggle over

attitude of Lincoln toward

moral condemnation of, by North, the real cause of secession

wisdom of Lincoln in passing over, as cause of war

forced to front as real cause of war

comes into question through action of Federal generals

attempts of Fremont and Hunter to abolish, revoked by Lincoln

acts of Congress affecting

Emancipation Proclamation against

regard for, hinders War Democrats from supporting Lincoln

not touched as an institution by Emancipation Proclamation

necessity of a constitutional amendment to abolish

desire of Copperheads to reëstablish

## Slaves

during Civil War, called "contraband" by Butler

escape to Northern armies

declared free by Fremont

this declaration revoked by Lincoln

declared free by Hunter

inconsistent attitude of generals toward

proposal of Cameron to arm, cancelled by Lincoln

protected from return to owners by Congress

armed

not paid equally with whites until 1864

armed in 1863

threatened with death by South

## Slidell, John

seized by Wilkes

imprisoned in Fort Warren

released

## Smith, Caleb B

delivers votes to Lincoln in convention of 1860

secretary of interior

opposes relieving Sumter

## Smith, General C.W

praised by Halleck

## Smith, General W.F

favors McClellan's plan of campaign

## Smoot, Coleman

lends Lincoln money

## South

its early sectionalism

demands political equality with North

its inferior development

gains by annexation of Texas

enraged at organization of California as a free State

threatens disunion

demands Fugitive Slave Law

asserts doctrine of non-intervention in Territories

not satisfied with Compromise of 1850

fails to secure Kansas

applauds Brooks for his assault on Sunnier

enraged at Douglas's opposition to Lecompton Constitution.

reads Douglas out of party

its policy described by Lincoln

fairness of Lincoln toward

demands that North cease to call slavery wrong

question of its justification in seceding

its delegates disrupt Democratic party

scatters vote in 1860

process of secession in

agitation of dis-unionists in

State loyalty in

justified by Greeley and others

threatens North

repudiates Peace Congress

its leaders in Congress remain to hamper government

forms Confederacy

expects Scott to aid

wishes to seize Washington

impressed by Lincoln's inaugural

its real grievance the refusal of North to admit validity of slavery

its doctrine of secession

"Union men" in

makes secession, not slavery, the ground of war

irritated at failure of secession to affect North

purpose of Lincoln to put in the wrong

rejoices over capture of Sumter

compared with North in fighting qualities

elated over Bull Bun

its strength overestimated by McClellan

expects aid from Northern sympathizers

hopes of aid from England disappointed

after Chancellorsville, wishes to invade North and conquer a peace

welcomes Vallandigham

economically exhausted in 1863

reconstruction in

applauds McClellan

evidently exhausted in 1864

hopes of Lincoln to make its surrender easy

## South Carolina

desires secession

suggests it to other States

secedes

sends commissioners to treat for division of property with United States

refusal of Buchanan to receive

refuses to participate in Peace Congress

besieges Fort Sumter

## Spangler, Edward

aids Booth to escape

tried by court martial

condemned

## Speed, Joshua

letter of Lincoln to, on slavery

goes with Lincoln to Kentucky

## Spottsylvania

battle of

## Sprague, Governor William

of Rhode Island

## Stanton, Edwin M

attorney-general under Buchanan

joins Black in forcing Buchanan to alter reply to South Carolina

Commissioners

share in Stone's punishment

appointed secretary of war

his previous insulting attitude toward Lincoln

discussion of his qualities, good and bad

an efficient secretary

sneers at generals who favor McClellan's plans

shows incompetence in organizing army

praises Wilkes for capturing Mason and Slidell

communicates Lincoln's approval to McClellan

loses head during Jackson's raid

bitter letter of McClellan to

becomes McClellan's merciless enemy

tries to prevent reappointment of McClellan

wishes to take troops from Meade for Rosecrans

repudiates Sherman's terms with Johnston

insults Sherman

his relations with Grant

at time of Early's attack on Washington

on bad terms with Blair

persuades Lincoln to use an escort

plan to assassinate

## Stephens, Alexander H

in Congress with Lincoln

on reasons for Georgia's secession

opposes secession

elected Vice-President of Confederate States

denies plot to seize Washington

letter of Lincoln to

wishes to treat for peace with Lincoln

his attempt foiled by Lincoln

admits desire to place Lincoln in false position

nominated by Davis on peace commission

## Stevens, Thaddeus

leader of House in 1861

denounces Lincoln's emancipation scheme

considers Constitution destroyed

on admission of West Virginia

on unpopularity of Lincoln in Congress

accomplice of Booth, tried and executed

## Swinton, William

on McClellan's self-sufficiency
on campaign of 1862
on extraordinary powers given Meade

## Tanet, Roger B

his opinion in Dred Scott case discussed
administers inaugural oath to Lincoln
attempts to liberate Merryman by habeas corpus
denounces Lincoln's action as unconstitutional
succeeded by Chase

## Tatnall, Captain Josiah

destroys Merrimac

## Taylor, Dick

amusingly tricked by Lincoln

## Taylor, General Zachary

his victories in Mexican war
supported by Lincoln for President
urges New Mexico to apply for admission as a State

## Tennessee

refuses to furnish Lincoln with troops
at first opposed to secession
eastern counties of, Unionist
forced to secede
desire of Lincoln to save eastern counties of
prevented from Northern interference by Kentucky's "neutrality,"
seized by South
plan of Halleck to invade
eastern counties freed from Confederates

defeated

forces peace plank into National Democratic platform

## Vicksburg

siege of-

## Virginia

at first opposed to secession

carried by Secessionists

makes military league with Confederate States

becomes member of Confederacy

northwestern counties of, secede from

comment of Lincoln on

nominal State government of

## Voorhees, Daniel W

in House in 1861

## Wade, Benjamin F

in Senate in 1861

thinks country ruined in 1862

issues address denouncing Lincoln for veto of reconstruction bill

obliged to support Lincoln rather than McClellan

## Wadsworth, General James S

commands forces to protect Washington

considers troops insufficient

## Walker, L.P

in Confederate cabinet

## Walworth, Chancellor R.H

denounces coercion

## War of Rebellion

first call for volunteers

protection of Washington

elect Lincoln to Congress

oppose Mexican war

elect Taylor

defeated in 1852

join Know-Nothings in 1856

**White, Hugh L**

supported by Lincoln in 1836

**Whiteside, General Samuel**

in Black Hawk war

**Wigfall, Lewis T**

jeers at North in 1860

**Wilderness**

battle of

**Wilkes, Captain Charles**

seizes Mason and Slidell

applauded in North

condemned by Lincoln

**Wilmot, David**

in Congress with Lincoln

in Senate in 1861

**Wilson, Henry**

hopes that Douglas will become Republican in 1858

in Senate in 1861

introduces bill to emancipate slaves in District

on negro troops

admits small number of radical emancipationists

denounces Blair to Lincoln

**Winthrop, Robert C**

chosen speaker of House